DREAMS AND NIGHTMARES

The publisher gratefully acknowledges the generous support of the General Endowment Fund of the University of California Press Foundation.

DREAMS AND

NIGHTMARES

IMMIGRATION POLICY,
YOUTH, AND FAMILIES

Marjorie S. Zatz and Nancy Rodriguez

UNIVERSITY OF CALIFORNIA PRESS

University of California Press, one of the most distinguished
university presses in the United States, enriches lives around
the world by advancing scholarship in the humanities, social
sciences, and natural sciences. Its activities are supported by
the UC Press Foundation and by philanthropic contributions
from individuals and institutions. For more information, visit
www.ucpress.edu.

University of California Press
Oakland, California

Library of Congress Cataloging-in-Publication Data
Zatz, Marjorie Sue, 1955- author.
    Dreams and nightmares : immigration policy, youth, and
families / Marjorie S. Zatz and Nancy Rodriguez. — First
edition.
        pages   cm
    Includes bibliographical references and index.
    ISBN 978-0-520-28305-3 (cloth : alk. paper)—ISBN 0-520-
28305-8 (cloth : alk. paper)—ISBN 978-0-520-28306-0 (pbk. :
alk. paper)—ISBN 0-520-28306-6 (pbk. : alk. paper)—
ISBN 978-0-520-95889-0 (ebook) —ISBN 0-520-95889-6
(ebook)
    1. Immigrant youth—United States—Social conditions.
2. Unaccompanied immigrant children—United States—
Social conditions.   3. Emigration and immigration law—
United States.   4. Immigrant families—Law and legislation—United States.   I. Rodriguez, Nancy, author.   II.
Title.
    JV6600.Z38 2015
    325.73—dc23   2014039239

24   23   22   21   20   19   18   17   16   15
10   9   8   7   6   5   4   3   2   1

In keeping with a commitment to support environmentally
responsible and sustainable printing practices, UC Press has
printed this book on Natures Natural, a fiber that contains
30% post-consumer waste and meets the minimum requirements of ANSI/NISO Z39.48–1992 (R 1997) (*Permanence of
Paper*).

We dedicate this book to the children and families affected by immigration policies and practices. We hope our book contributes to a national dialogue and legislation that prioritizes the best interests of all children.

CONTENTS

Acknowledgments ix

1. Introduction and Historical Context 1
2. Prosecutorial Discretion: A Mechanism for Balancing
    Competing Goals 15
3. Legislative Inaction and Executive Action: Mixed Status
    Families, the Dreamer Movement, and DACA 49
4. Families Torn Apart: Parental Detention and Deportation 77
5. No Good Options: Unaccompanied Minors in the
    US Immigration System 113
6. Conclusions and Recommendations 157

Notes 167
References 173
Index 195

ACKNOWLEDGMENTS

We owe a tremendous debt of gratitude to our key informants Francisco Alatorre, Roxana Bacon, Michelle Brané, Emily Butera, Randy Capps, Evelyn Cruz, Dorien Ediger-Seto, Ashley Feasley, Mary Giovagnoli, Kimberly Haynes, Yali Lincroft, Victoria López, Lindsay Marshall, David Martin, Margie McHugh, Doris Meissner, Anne Marie Mulcahy, Christina Ortecho, Kristyn Peck, Jennifer Podkul, Allison Posner, Lorella Praeli, Nina Rabin, Jennifer Riddle, Beth Rosenberg, Cindy Schlosser, Aryah Somers, Matthew Wilch, Maria Woltjen, Wendy Young, and to those government officials whom we cannot name. Thank you for giving so generously of your time and your expertise. Our key informants were valuable guides as we sought to make sense of the contradictions and complexities in immigration policy and its intersection with the child welfare and criminal justice systems. In many cases, these experts were interviewed multiple times, and they reviewed sections of the book in which they were quoted and gave thoughtful feedback.

Special thanks are due to Roxana Bacon, Michelle Brané, David Thronson, and an anonymous reviewer for comments on an earlier draft. As we are social scientists and not immigration attorneys, we are especially appreciative of their careful review of the legal history and implications of laws. Thank you also to Veronica Lerma for her sharp eye in reviewing the final manuscript. Of course, any errors that remain are our own doing.

For comments, suggestions, and help along the way we also thank Madelaine Adelman, Kitty Calavita, Gray Cavender, Lauren Heidbrink, Nancy Jurik, Stephen Legomsky, Jamie Longazel, Cecilia Menjívar, Michael Musheno,

Marie Provine, Lisa Raffonelli, Susan Sterett, David R. Schaefer, Susan Terrio, and Maartja van der Woude.

An earlier version of chapter 2 was published in *Law and Social Inquiry* in 2014 as "The Limits of Discretion: Challenges and Dilemmas of Prosecutorial Discretion in Immigration Enforcement" (39(3):666–89). Earlier versions of this research were presented at New York University, the University of Delaware, and Monash University. We appreciate the thoughtful comments of colleagues at those institutions.

Thank you to our editor at the University of California Press, Maura Roessner, and to Francisco Reinking, Jack Young, and Pam Suwinsky for their help in the production process. Maura kept urging us on, as what we first called our "octopus" (that ungainly mass that is immigration policy and practice) gained a backbone (prosecutorial discretion) and finally took shape in this book. Maura, thank you for your good eye and ear and for your continual support and encouragement. We also are very grateful to Calvin Fleming, who graciously allowed us to use his stunning photograph as our cover image.

And finally, thank you to our children. To Marjorie's sons Richie, Patrick, and Cameron, and Nancy's sons Ethan and Isaac, we hope the world you inherit will be kinder to children seeking a safe haven and an opportunity to reunite with their families.

CHAPTER I

Introduction and Historical Context

For the president, I think his legacy is at stake here. . . . We consider him the deportation president, or the deporter-in-chief.

—Janet Murguía, president and chief executive officer of the National
   Council of La Raza (Epstein 2014)

I think politicians, in particular, have envisioned the immigration system as something that simply can be contained by building a high enough wall or keeping enough people out. What they rarely think about is all of the fallout and all of the unintended consequences. It's ultimately the kids who are suffering because we can't get our act together up front to devise an immigration process that really works for America today.

—Mary Giovagnoli, director of the Immigration Policy Center (interview
   October 10, 2012)

The lives of undocumented immigrants are filled with dreams and nightmares. Parents dream of better futures for themselves and their children. Young adults who were brought to the United States as children dream of finally becoming US citizens. Alongside these dreams, though, are nightmares. Children awaken from nightmares of immigration raids in which their undocumented parents or siblings are suddenly taken from them. And teenagers who always thought they were American find themselves "awakening to a nightmare" (Gonzales and Chavez 2012) when they discover they are undocumented, cannot get driver's licenses, obtain college loans, or legally work, and live under the threat of deportation.

Undocumented immigrant José Ángel N. (2014, 77) writes in his memoir of another immigrant who "left his hometown in search of the American Dream. Smuggling himself across the desert, he had walked right into a nightmare." The journey north is itself a nightmare for children who risk death, rape, and serious injury as they travel alone from Central America to the United States, hoping to escape violence and poverty and to reunite with parents they have not seen in years. Yet the number of children traveling to the United States by themselves, mostly from Guatemala, Honduras, and El Salvador, increases exponentially each year, reaching what in 2014 was called a "humanitarian crisis" by some and "an influx on top of the influx" by others.

An estimated 11.3 million unauthorized immigrants resided in the United States in March 2013 (Passel et al. 2014). Nearly two-thirds of these immigrants have lived in the United States for more than a decade, and almost half are parents of US-citizen children (Taylor et al. 2011; Passel et al. 2014). The law affects the lives and legal consciousness of undocumented immigrants and their families in multiple ways that are structured and nuanced by gender, age, race, ethnicity, and social position (Abrego 2011; Abrego and Gonzales 2010; Gonzales 2011; Gonzales and Chavez 2012; Kubrin, Zatz, and Martínez 2012; Menjívar and Kanstroom 2013). More than one-fifth of all children in the United States today have at least one parent who is an immigrant. A large subset of these children—4.5 million as of 2012—are US citizens who have at least one parent who is undocumented (Passel and Cohn 2011; Passel et al. 2014).

These families inhabit what Cecilia Menjívar (2006, 2011, 2012) has described as a state of liminal legality in which they are acknowledged but are legally nonexistent (Coutin 2000, 2003, 2007; DeGenova 2002). This liminality requires a hyper-awareness of the law, as their legal status may be uncertain and shifting.

CONTEMPORARY US IMMIGRATION POLICY AND PRACTICE IN HISTORICAL CONTEXT

Throughout its history, the United States has wrestled with its immigration policy and practice. Like law making more generally, immigration policy is characterized by temporary fixes aimed at resolving, at least for a time, conflicts and dilemmas resulting from larger social, political, and economic contradictions (Chambliss 1979; Chambliss and Zatz 1993). Since the country's founding, the politics of race, ethnicity, gender, and religion have been central to decisions about who should be included in the national fabric and who should be shut out (Calavita 1984, 2007; FitzGerald and Cook-Martín 2014; Gardner 2005; Hing 2004; Johnson 2003; Kanstroom 2012; Kubrin et al. 2012;

Ngai 2004). The needs of agribusiness and other economic sectors for cheap labor have competed with nativist fears that the United States will be overrun by people who look and sound different (Calavita 1992; Chavez 2008; Newton 2008). These debates play out on national and local stages in the form of moral panics about immigration and crime, fear of loss of jobs and other economic woes due to immigration, and concerns about national security and public safety (Longazel 2013; Varsanyi 2010; Zatz and Smith 2012).

The most recent attempt to comprehensively address the political, social, and economic dilemmas underlying US immigration policy was in 1986, with passage of the Immigration Reform and Control Act (IRCA). Though IRCA resolved some immediate problems, legalizing the status of large numbers of immigrants while simultaneously creating an enforcement mechanism that was supposed to deter employers from hiring undocumented workers, it was not a fundamental rethinking of immigration policy, and as a result the underlying contradictions remained (Calavita 1989). At least in part as a backlash against the legalization elements in IRCA, a decade later the Illegal Immigration Reform and Immigrant Responsibility Act (IIRIRA) and the Antiterrorism and Effective Death Penalty Act (AEDPA) were passed. As a set, these two 1996 laws provided local and state police with unprecedented authority to enforce civil immigration laws, expanded the number of offenses for which immigration detention is mandatory, and severely restricted the discretion of immigration judges.

Following the terrorist attacks of September 11, 2001, the Homeland Security Act of 2002 created the Department of Homeland Security (DHS). The Immigration and Naturalization Services, which had previously been situated in the Department of Justice, was disbanded, and immigration enforcement and integration were separated into three distinct agencies within DHS: US Immigration and Customs Enforcement (ICE), US Customs and Border Patrol (CBP), and US Citizenship and Immigration Services (CIS, or more typically USCIS). Each agency director reports to the secretary of DHS, which was created as a cabinet position.

The move from DOJ to DHS marked a conceptual shift in immigration policy and practice. The Department of Justice was always very aware of due process and equal protection requirements. As a result, immigration enforcement and immigrant integration took place within a context of checks and balances framed by constitutional law protections. In contrast, DHS's mandate is national security and law enforcement is its primary mission. Placing all immigration services under that umbrella legitimizes a focus on enforcement over all other aspects of immigration policy and risks a collapse of constitutional concerns. In combination with the 1996 laws and massive congressional appropriations for border enforcement, this restructuring has led to increasingly restrictive policies and practices, and to a dramatic increase in deportations.

Efforts by the George W. Bush administration to pass comprehensive immigration legislation in 2006 and 2007 failed. A wave of state and local anti-immigrant bills, ordinances, and ballot initiatives followed, beginning about 2005 and peaking in 2011 with introduction of 1,607 bills and resolutions, 306 of which were enacted into law (National Conference of State Legislatures 2012).

Tens of thousands of immigrants were picked up and deported in immigration raids on meatpacking factories and other worksites across the country, yet these raids also brought attention to the plight of immigrants' children and families. Churches, schools, and other local institutions were forced to confront the sudden arrest, detention, and deportation of parents of young children, many of whom were US citizens (Capps et al. 2007; Chaudry et al. 2010; Human Rights Watch 2007). In some communities the sentiment began to shift, as sympathetic media depicted nursing mothers separated from their babies and families unable to locate loved ones who had disappeared into the detention and deportation apparatus. The vulnerability of young people who came to the United States as children and grew up calling America home also became more visible, and demands to regularize the status of these "Dreamers," as they came to be called, grew more insistent.

Immigration Policy under the Obama Administration

President Barack Obama swept into office in 2008 with the support of 67 percent of the Latino voters and 66 percent of voters under age thirty. The nation's immigration policy was a key election issue, and the newly formed Obama administration anticipated passage of comprehensive immigration reform early in its first term. Once in office, however, the administration determined that the dire economic situation had to be its primary focus. All other domestic policies, with the exception of health care reform, were placed on hold for the first two years of Obama's presidency. As the recession bottomed out and the country slowly started to recover, congressional gridlock set in, with increasingly chilly relations between the White House and House Republicans making passage of any major domestic legislation unlikely. By 2010, it was clear that comprehensive immigration reform would not be enacted anytime soon, and the Latino and immigrant advocate communities became increasingly frustrated and disappointed by President Obama's unwillingness to follow through with what they saw as a key campaign promise.

Within this highly polarized context, the Obama administration needed to identify some options that could ease the plight of unauthorized immigrants living in the shadows while simultaneously addressing fears of uncontrolled immigration. Prosecutorial discretion emerged as a central mechanism in this balancing act and was initially understood by many as a down payment to Latino voters. Prosecutorial discretion offered a means of prioritizing who should be placed in removal hearings and deported and who should be given at least a temporary reprieve. Cases were prioritized based on assessments of a set of positive factors, such as strong family ties in the United States, including US-citizen children, and negative factors, such as criminal history or security threat.

Very quickly, however, the administration faced serious criticism from all sides. Political opponents calling for stronger immigration enforcement argued that ICE officials were not allowed to do their job, and that prosecutorial discretion amounted to an unofficial form of amnesty. The administration responded to this criticism by consistently filling immigration detention beds at the level appropriated by Congress. This had the effect of increasing the number of deportations, ultimately capping at just over four hundred thousand removals per year in fiscal year 2012. Immigrant communities and advocacy groups were angered by the unprecedented number of deportations. Rather than reducing the number of deportations, prosecutorial discretion just reshaped the population of deportees, and it did little to lessen the devastating effects on families. Parental detentions and deportations continued at high rates through 2012, though they decreased somewhat in 2013. In 2011 alone, more than five thousand children were placed in foster care when their parents were detained or deported (Wessler 2011b). In the face of this rising tide of detained and deported parents and fragmented families, many immigrants and their allies came to see prosecutorial discretion as an increasingly empty promise.

As the 2012 election approached, it became clear to Democrats that some major action was needed to convince Latino communities that they should bother to vote, and to vote for Obama. In this context, Deferred Action for Childhood

Arrivals, or DACA, was announced and quickly implemented in the summer of 2012. DACA is a form of prosecutorial discretion that offers eligible Dreamers relief from deportation and permission to legally work in the United States.

In return, the Latino community came out strongly in support for President Obama and other Democrats in the 2012 elections. Though they were still disappointed by his failure to enact comprehensive immigration reform and by the unprecedented numbers of deportations, they saw DACA as a significant step forward, and Barack Obama as a better bet than Mitt Romney, who had proposed "self-deportation" of Latinos living in the United States.

Following these elections, Senate Republicans realized they needed to act quickly to appease Latinos, and they joined with Senate Democrats to pass a comprehensive immigration reform bill on June 27, 2013, with a strong bipartisan vote of 68–32.

Throughout, the Obama administration took a hard line on immigration enforcement, hoping that this would push open a window of opportunity to make comprehensive immigration reform possible. House Republicans and other opponents were not placated, however, saying that DACA was a de facto amnesty program in violation of the law, and President Obama could not be trusted. House Speaker John Boehner made the decision not to allow a vote on the full Senate bill, though for a while he left a door cracked slightly open to the possibility of piecemeal legislation.

Immigration advocates and the Latino community despaired. More than a thousand immigrants were still being deported each day, ripping families apart. Mainstream media outlets such as the *New York Times* and the *Washington Post* regularly chastised the administration. For instance, the *New York Times* editorial board opined, "This enormously costly effort was meant to win Republican support for broader reform. But all it has done is add to the burden of fear, family disruption and lack of opportunity faced by 11 million people who cannot get right with the law" (*New York Times* Editorial Board 2014).

The Latino community called for President Obama to use his executive authority to take additional steps, expanding upon DACA. Yet immigration continues to be an area in which, to borrow from *Washington Post* reporters Phillip Rucker and Peter Wallsten, President Obama "has been skittish," first saying he did not have authority to halt deportations, then granting relief to those Dreamers qualifying for DACA but saying he could do nothing further (Rucker and Wallsten 2013). Former Principal Deputy General Counsel for the Department of Homeland Security David Martin concluded, "It would have been better for the administration to state its enforcement intentions clearly and stand by them, rather than being willing to lean whichever way seemed politically expedient at any given moment. . . . It was a pipe dream to think they could make everyone happy" (Thompson and Cohen 2014).

Unaccompanied Minors

By 2011, another dilemma was unfolding in Central America that would propel thousands, and then tens of thousands, of children to undertake the perilous journey to the United States by themselves. Poverty and lack of economic opportunity have historically been important push factors, sending young men, and sometimes women, to the United States in search of jobs that would allow them to remit funds home to their families (Abrego 2014; Boehm 2012; Dreby 2010; Menjívar 2012; Menjívar and Abrego 2009). Two other factors, though, have altered this dynamic in recent years.

First, and of primary importance, violence and accompanying corruption have become widespread in Central America's northern triangle, and the governments appear incapable of ensuring the safety of their citizenry. Honduras had the highest murder rate in the world in 2012, with 90.4 homicides per 100,000 population (United Nations Office on Drugs and Crime 2014, 24). The history of US military interventions in the region, support for corrupt domestic governments, the drug wars, and trade agreements such as the Central America Free Trade Agreement (CAFTA) that favor the United States at the expense of Central Americans have resulted in widespread poverty, structural inequality, and powerful drug cartels throughout Mexico and northern Central America. Rather than protecting the populace, state actors are complicitous with the cartels, and those who are unwilling to pay homage to the gangs risk not only economic devastation but also their very lives. In many communities, children are no longer able to attend school, and they fear that if they stay at home, they will die. These are the structural causes of the migration.

Second, with parents leaving to find employment in the United States, children also confront more generalized violence, including abuse by caregivers. When the southern border to the United States was more porous and the repercussions of getting caught less dire, young adults typically migrated back and forth, working in the United States but going home to visit with their children and other family members. Enhanced border enforcement makes this untenable, though, as smugglers raised their prices in response to the greater difficulty in bringing migrants across the border and it became too risky to try to cross alone. Consequently, children are separated from their parents for years, creating a strong pull factor as they seek to reunite with their parents.

These children and adolescents face incredible dangers on their way to the United States. Yet they are willing to risk death, dismemberment, and rape on their journeys, knowing they are at far greater risk if they stay at home. This stark reality was made clear to us when members of a United States Conference of Catholic Bishops delegation reported that mothers and grandmothers, who were waiting with them for the return of children caught by immigration authorities in Mexico, acknowledged that they brought their daughters and granddaughters to the local clinic to obtain birth control injections. These women knew the girls (and some boys) would likely be raped on their journey, but saw no other choice but to send them on their way, protecting them only against becoming pregnant by their rapists. For Catholic mothers and grandmothers to acknowledge this reality to a church delegation, the situation must be horrific.

The number of unaccompanied minors entering the United States has reached crisis levels, growing from a few thousand each year to 13,625 in fiscal year 2012 to 24,668 in fiscal year 2013 to 57,496 in fiscal year 2014. These numbers do not include Mexican youth who are turned around at the border.[1] The "surge," as it has been called, in unaccompanied youth and young mothers with babies and toddlers entering the United States has drawn extensive media coverage. It must be remembered, though, that the overall number of border crossers is still far lower than it was five or ten years ago, and unaccompanied minors represent only about 5 percent of the total population of children living in the United States without authorization.

Most unaccompanied minors are denied asylum and ultimately repatriated, returning to the very conditions they fled. As Jacqueline Bhabha, a leading authority on human rights and child refugees, asserts, these youth are "returned to the danger they fled. Some die; many live in hiding. This state-induced return migration prompts fundamental questions about state complicity in serious human rights violations against children" (2014, 204).

PROSECUTORIAL DISCRETION AND
THE BEST INTERESTS OF THE CHILD

The experiences of children and youth provide a prism through which the interwoven dynamics and consequences of immigration policy become especially apparent, as many of the policies and practices that are not explicitly directed at children nevertheless reverberate upon them. At the same time, the ramifications for vulnerable children may draw attention to aspects of policy and practice that the administration has the power to change, even in the absence of legislation. We are particularly interested in the mechanisms through which immigration policies and practices affect youth and families. Which mechanisms, we ask, mitigate their vulnerabilities, and which exacerbate harm?

One mechanism stands apart from the others given its overarching nature and potential reach, and it serves as a unifying theme throughout this book. Prosecutorial discretion, we suggest, has potential to help balance such competing goals as public safety and rule of law, on the one hand, and family unity and the best interests of the child on the other. Yet as we shall see, the flexibility of discretion also makes it controversial, and vulnerable to structural impediments and broader political challenges. These limitations are exacerbated by the ability of middle management and rank-and-file officers to disregard the policies, assuming they can wait out a change in administration, and by the fact that ICE attorneys are subject to review, promotion, and discipline by ICE's non-lawyer management.

International conventions and US domestic laws place the best interests of children at the forefront of decision making in most legal arenas. Yet in policy and practice, US immigration law ignores consideration of children's best interests. The prosecutorial discretion policies of the Obama administration clearly state that discretion should be considered in detention cases involving parents of US citizen or legal permanent resident children. But this ideal is not met in practice, as evidenced by the deportations of unprecedented numbers of parents since 2010, when the prosecutorial guidelines were issued (Wessler 2012a).

Prosecutorial discretion could also benefit children and adolescents who came to the United States alone. However, the number of cases of prosecutorial discretion involving unaccompanied minors is minimal. Legal representation might help to make the case for prosecutorial discretion, but, again, contrary to the principle of best interests of the child, few unaccompanied minors are represented by counsel. Efforts are being made by nongovernmental organizations and increasingly by the federal government to provide legal representation for the youth, but unlike in family court or even criminal court, representation is not mandated.

The DREAM Act expresses a clear concern for the best interests of young people who were brought to the US as small children, and thus cannot be held responsible for their violations of immigration law. It focuses on immigrant integration, addressing the problem of how young people who know no other country and identify as American can best participate in and contribute to American society. Although there is substantial public sympathy for Dreamers, the DREAM Act has still not been enacted into law. In its absence, the Obama administration offered Deferred Action for Childhood Arrivals. This form of prosecutorial discretion frees eligible teenagers and young adults from the fear of deportation and allows them to legally work in the United States. However, it is only a two-year reprieve. Youth are stuck in a sort of second- or third-class citizenship and, though their status is renewable, a new president could end the program at any time.

ORGANIZATION OF THE BOOK

Dreams and Nightmares: Immigration Policy, Youth, and Families takes a critical look at the challenges and dilemmas of immigration policy and practice in the absence of comprehensive immigration reform. Others have addressed the nuances of immigration law and the lived experiences of immigrants, and we draw upon their findings as appropriate. Our primary focus, however, is at the systemic level. Based on original interview data and government archives, we examine the bureaucratic processes of implementing these policies, and the interplay and tensions among policymakers, agency heads, street-level bureaucrats, immigration attorneys, community advocates, and grassroots activists. Looking across the multiple institutions that interact with immigrant families, we consider the specific structural mechanisms available to the administration, examine which of these have the potential to alleviate or exacerbate harm to youth and their families, and whether they are meeting their objectives.

Data and Methods

Our analysis is based on interview, observational, and archival data. During the period from February 2012 to May 2014, we conducted formal interviews with thirty-four immigration attorneys and advocates, child welfare advocates, and former government officials. Informants were selected based on their expertise, established through their publications, presentations on conference and plenary panels, and recommendations from others working in the field. Interviews were semi-structured and ranged from forty minutes to six hours, averaging one-and-one-half to two hours in length. Almost everyone was re-interviewed a second and often a third or fourth time, sometimes in a formal taped interview and sometimes more informally at meetings or over the phone, and in many cases we engaged in lengthy email dialogues. With their permission, these key respondents are named when we believe doing so will be useful to readers. In other places, when naming our sources does not seem necessary or where it might create difficulties for them, we do not identify our informants. Most interviews were conducted one on one, but in a few instances two or more representatives from the same office were interviewed together.

In addition to these formal interviews, we held lengthy informal conversations with five senior government officials, all of whom were attorneys in positions of authority and insider knowledge within their agencies, and with a representative of a Central American embassy, for a total of forty key informants. We do not identify these individuals by name or position, and though we took copious notes during our conversations, which sometimes took place in their offices and sometimes in coffee shops or restaurants, they were not taped. In most cases, we held second and third long, detailed conversations with these officials, and we also clarified points with them via email. Both our formal and informal respondents were provided opportunities to review those sections of the book in which we explicitly draw on their interviews to ensure accuracy and that we did not take their statements out of context. Thirty-nine of the forty key informants reviewed and provided comments on those sections of the manuscript.

Supplementing these interviews and conversations, spokespersons from two government agencies also provided emailed responses to queries, including statistical data not otherwise available. The first author also participated in five meetings of the Interagency Working Group on Unaccompanied Minors. These two-hour meetings were held in September 2012, January, May, and December 2013, and May 2014. They included representatives of the Departments of Homeland Security (ICE, USCIS, CBP, and the Policy Office), Justice, State, and Health and Human Services, the major nongovernmental organizations and immigration law clinics working with unaccompanied minors, and sometimes a few researchers. These meetings all took place in Washington, DC. We also observed fifteen panels, conferences, network meetings, and report launches involving government officials, policy analysts, and nongovernmental organizations, either in person in Washington, DC or, in a few cases, via webinars or conference calls. These ranged in length from one hour to a full day. In addition, we reviewed hundreds of archival documents including reports by nongovernmental organizations working directly with immigrant youth and families, government memorandums in the public domain or provided to the authors, published government statistics, and published reports by investigative journalists.

Following transcription of the interviews, the transcripts and notes from meetings and conversations with government officials were reviewed multiple times and thematically coded. When questions or inconsistencies arose, informants were contacted for clarification.

Chapter Summaries

Congress has the sole authority to enact federal legislation, but the executive branch has authority to set priorities as to how those laws should be enforced. The Obama administration identified its broad powers of prosecutorial discretion as a means of prioritizing immigration enforcement in ways that it hoped would keep the citizenry safe while mitigating harm to families. The "Morton Memos," as the guidelines promulgated by ICE Director John Morton have come to be known, serve as the backbone to prosecutorial discretion under the Obama administration.

In chapter 2, we review the legal history leading up to the Morton Memos and consider the extent to which Morton's directives diverged from earlier memos. What we call the limits of discretion quickly became apparent, as the administration's prosecutorial discretion policies were met with challenges from ICE officers and some legislators who saw the guidelines as going too far, and from members of the immigrant and advocacy communities who were disappointed that they did not go far enough. We conclude chapter 2 with an examination of prosecutorial discretion in practice, as we explore who is being deported and why.

In chapter 3 we focus on one form of prosecutorial discretion, deferred action. We discuss the development and implementation of the Deferred Action for Childhood Arrivals program in the context of legislative inaction, including both the failure of Congress to enact comprehensive immigration reform and the more limited and popular Development, Relief, and Education for Alien Minors (DREAM) Act. We analyze the important role of Dreamer social movement activists in development of DACA, and their efforts to expand DACA into a broader program of administrative relief when it was renewed in 2014.

Dreamers' families typically hold a variety of legal statuses. Often, some family members are undocumented, others are legal permanent residents or US citizens, and in recent years some may be "dacamented" young adults with deferred status. We examine these mixed status families, exploring family dynamics and the effects of growing up in mixed status households on child development and early education. We then look at the teenage years, when many youth learn that they are undocumented and at risk of deportation, and assess the constraints their legal status places on their educational and employment opportunities. We conclude the chapter with explicit attention to the structural mechanisms that help and hinder undocumented youth and youth in mixed status families.

In chapter 4, we explore the ramifications of immigration detention and deportation for families, and particularly families in which some or all of the children are US citizens but a parent is undocumented. If prosecutorial discretion was supposed to help keep families intact, we ask, why are so many parents of US-citizen children still being deported? We review the recent history of parental detention and deportation and assess the extent to which detained and deported parents represent threats to public safety. We next compare parental detention for purposes of immigration enforcement with the growing literature on parental incarceration, identifying points of similarity and divergence in their effects on children and families. We also address the complicated intersections among the immigration enforcement, criminal justice, and child welfare systems. We end the chapter with an assessment of the structural mechanisms related specifically to parental detention and deportation that mitigate and exacerbate harm to youth and families.

Whereas chapter 4 examines the collateral consequences for children when their parents are detained or deported for violations of immigration law, chapter 5 focuses on youth who are themselves caught entering the country without permission. Except in cases when they have been identified as trafficking victims or victims of abuse or neglect, Mexican and Canadian youth who seek to enter the United States are turned around at the border, and are not included in this discussion. Youth from noncontiguous countries who arrive without their parents and who are defined as unaccompanied minors are to be transferred from Customs and Border Patrol to the Office of

Refugee Resettlement (ORR) in the Department of Health and Human Services within seventy-two hours of apprehension.

We examine the exponential increase in the number of unaccompanied minors entering the United States—an increase that has gone from being called a surge to a humanitarian crisis. We ask why so many youth are coming to the United States from Central America and review their horrific experiences along the way. Then, we turn to their placement in ORR shelters, their initial legal and health assessments, family reunification, and their likely repatriation back to their home countries. We explore the types of protective status for which these youth may be eligible, the extent to which legal representation is available to them, and the nature of their immigration court proceedings. Once again, we close the chapter by drawing together various threads to assess the structural mechanisms available to help these youth, and the mechanisms and system stressors that worsen their situation, leaving them even more vulnerable.

We conclude in chapter 6 with an overview of our key findings, highlighting the mechanisms that exacerbate and reduce harm to children and families. We suggest ways in which our work informs related literatures on crimmigration, race and mass incarceration, and transnational family formation, point to factors that will be critical in the application of future immigration policy and practice, and offer a series of recommendations for policymakers.

CHAPTER 2

Prosecutorial Discretion

A Mechanism for Balancing Competing Goals

Mr. President, please use your executive authority to halt [deportations]. We agree that we need to pass comprehensive immigration reform, but at the same time, you have the power to stop deportations.

—Ju Hong, immigration reform advocate, San Francisco, November 25
   (Foley 2013)

ICE is crumbling from within. Morale is at an all time low as criminal aliens are released to the streets and ICE instead takes disciplinary actions against its own officers for making lawful arrests.

—Chris Crane, president of the National Immigration and Customs
   Enforcement Council 118, testifying before the Senate Judiciary
   committee (Starr 2013)

With deportations under the Obama administration exceeding the two-million mark by spring 2014, demands by advocacy groups and some members of Congress that President Barack Obama use his executive authority to suspend deportations grew louder and more pointed. Congressional Republicans countered that if he did so, they would immediately begin impeachment proceedings. And still others argued that taking executive action was not worth the political price and could jeopardize comprehensive legislation. Immigration scholars Karthik Ramakrishnan and Pratheepan Gulasekaram suggest that the political price would be steep, and "an executive order would be far more limited than congressional legislation, because future presidents could reverse the decision and unauthorized immigrants would still not qualify for a pathway to citizenship absent congressional approval" (Ramakrishnan and Gulasekaram 2013).

Not surprisingly given this ambiguity and risk, President Obama has been hesitant to use his executive authority to grant various forms of administrative relief.

One key mechanism that the Obama administration has employed, however, is prosecutorial discretion. This chapter seeks to untangle the tensions leading to, and at times undermining, the use of prosecutorial discretion in immigration enforcement[1]. We explore how prosecutorial discretion became a defining feature of immigration policy, if not practice, under the Obama administration. We then consider recent legal and political challenges to the use of prosecutorial discretion, including deferred action. As we demonstrate, the flexibility of prosecutorial discretion makes it a versatile tool, but also renders it controversial and vulnerable to political challenges. Finally, we examine whether prosecutorial discretion has changed deportation practices, particularly toward parents of US-citizen children. Although prosecutorial discretion may arise at many points within the immigration enforcement system (Motomura 2012), our focus is primarily on decision making by Immigration and Customs Enforcement (ICE) agents and prosecutors as they decide whether to arrest, process, detain, and deport individuals.[2]

THE NEED FOR DISCRETION

Modern bureaucracies would grind to a halt if they could not exercise discretion. Regulatory agencies, criminal courts, schools, and even the local corner convenience store all rely on the appropriate use of discretion to resolve situations in which goals collide. Yet although discretion is apparent in everyday life, how far it should reach, who should be able to wield it, and under what conditions—that is, the limits of discretion—are often less clear. The saga of prosecutorial discretion in immigration enforcement is an important but understudied story for sociolegal scholars, perhaps because social science research on immigration does not generally address prosecutorial discretion, and research on prosecutorial discretion typically focuses on the criminal courts or other regulatory bodies and not on the immigration context.

Jon Gould and Scott Barclay remind us that law and society scholars have long recognized the role of administrative and judicial discretion in creating the gap between the law on the books and law in action (Gould and Barclay 2012). And, Lauren Edelman's work on the tensions between law as it is promulgated and as it actually operates in various contexts demonstrates that organizational compliance is often more symbolic than substantive, thereby mediating the impact of laws on society (Edelman 1992; Edelman et al. 2011).

Michael Lipsky (1980) coined the term "street-level bureaucrat" to describe the sorts of policy choices that police officers, social workers, and other professionals make while in the field. Lipsky contends that street-level bureaucrats are not simply implementing policies, but also using their discretion to interpret policy, often to the chagrin of those who are attempting to manage them.

Stephen Maynard-Moody and Michael Musheno (2003, 2012) expand upon Lipsky, demonstrating across a variety of professions the multiple ways in which street-level workers assess how best to respond to rules promulgated from above given the situations they encounter on the ground. Evelyn Brodkin's research on how street-level organizations adapt to policy and managerial reforms further illustrates some of these trade-offs. Building explicitly on Lipsky's foundation, Brodkin argues that discretion is "a problem of rational choice" (2011, 259), and if we are "to understand how governance provisions influence discretion, it is necessary to carefully consider the nature of choice and constraint in street-level practice" (2011, 258).

Edwin Harwood's study of immigration enforcement in the 1980s also draws upon Lipsky, suggesting that balancing arrests and resources requires a series of policy adjustments. Some of these adjustments are promulgated from the top, but "official policy directives are often inadequate to the task of accommodating many of the problems that street-level bureaucrats confront in their work" (1986, 178). He continues, "And, as Lipsky notes, some of the coping mechanisms developed by lower-echelon officials may be basic to the organization's survival, even though they are contrary to official policy" (1986, 178). Similarly, Toch (2012) reminds us that the perspectives held by mid-level police administrators may differ from those of the leadership and from rank-and-file officers, because each reinterprets both policy and concrete events playing out on the ground in light of their respective positions in the police hierarchy.

We are particularly interested in the bureaucratic discretion wielded by those charged with enforcing immigration law, and specifically with what has come to be known as *prosecutorial discretion*. Because prosecutorial discretion is better understood in the criminal law arena and there are a number of important parallels in the development and implementation of discretion in the two spheres, a brief discussion of their shared history may be useful.

SHARED HISTORIES: PROSECUTORIAL DISCRETION
IN CRIMINAL LAW AND IMMIGRATION LAW

In 1975, Senator Ted Kennedy introduced legislation to create a US Sentencing Commission. Like state-level determinate sentencing statutes enacted in the late 1970s and early 1980s, federal sentencing guidelines were initially advocated by reformers seeking to reduce racial disparities in sentencing and provide alternatives to lengthy prison terms. About the same time, in 1976, Sam Bernsen, then general counsel to the commissioner for Immigration and Naturalization Services, penned what has come to be known as the first key memorandum defining prosecutorial discretion in immigration enforcement.

By the time the federal sentencing guidelines were signed into law in 1984 as part of President Ronald Reagan's conservative law-and-order movement, however, the guidelines had become far more rigid and the presumptive sentences significantly harsher. As Kate Stith and Steve Koh (1993) detail in their landmark analysis of the complicated legislative history of the guidelines, the various bills moving forward through the House and Senate between 1975 and 1984 reflected an underlying tension between two quite disparate goals. On the one hand, liberal proponents of the guidelines saw them as a means of reducing reliance on incarceration and lessening racial disparities by wresting discretion away from biased judges and parole boards. On the other hand, conservative forces sought crime prevention and retribution through a guarantee of incarceration for a wide range of offenses. The final version of the bill, approved as part of an omnibus continuing resolutions appropriation, had all the hallmarks of a crime control bill, with the reform elements essentially gutted.

Two facets of this legislative history are especially important for our purposes. First, there was clear recognition among members of Congress that discretion is "an enduring component of any sentencing policy. [Restricting judicial discretion] will not eliminate discretion, but merely shift the discretion to an earlier stage" (H.R. Rep. No. 1017, 98th Congr., 2d Sess. 94 (1984) at 35–36, cited in Stith and Koh (1993, 263)). For this reason, the House bill "required the Department of Justice to issue guidelines for charging decisions and plea negotiations to limit prosecutorial discretion" (1993, 262). Not surprisingly, then, Stith and Koh conclude that sentencing disparity "is as great now as it was before the Federal Sentencing Guidelines, though perhaps more hidden from view" (1993, 287). Other scholars have similarly recognized that sentencing disparities remain. Similar to the Whack-a-Mole game played by children, where stomping on an imaginary mole in one place causes it to pop up in another spot, discretion has simply shifted from judges to prosecutors (see similarly Champion 1989; McCoy 1984; Meithe and Moore 1985, Savelsberg 1992; Ulmer and Kramer 1996; Zatz 1984, 1987).

Second, the Sentencing Guidelines Act of 1984 singled out federal drug offenders for sentence enhancements. Earlier versions of the legislation included provisions for lengthy incarceration of habitual offenders, racketeers, and those committing new offenses when released on bail, but the final version added drug offenses to the list and incorporated a subsection "that operates almost as a mandatory minimum statute, requiring 'a term of imprisonment at or near the maximum term authorized' for repeat violent offenders and drug offenders" (Stith and Koh 1993, 268).

These two features of sentencing reform—shifting the locus of discretion from judges to prosecutors and moving toward mandatory imprisonment for drug offenses—were in large part replicated in immigration law, with legislation passed in 1988 and 1990 expanding the number of offenses—including especially drug offenses—for which offenders are automatically deportable. With passage in 1996 of the Illegal Immigration Reform and Immigrant Responsibility Act and the Antiterrorism and Effective Death Penalty Act, drug offenses and many other crimes that did not warrant detention and deportation at the time they occurred were redefined retroactively as deportable offenses.

In criminal court, prosecutors have authority to dismiss cases, but their primary discretion lies in the determination of which charge(s) to file, especially under federal guidelines and determinate sentencing statutes, where the charge largely determines the sentence. Similarly, prosecutorial discretion in immigration law largely occurs at the end of the process, in determinations about who should be deported, rather than in decisions about who should be admitted into the country (Cox and Rodríguez 2009).

Mirroring the lack of attention on the part of social scientists, legal scholars have also largely ignored prosecutorial discretion in immigration enforcement. With a few recent exceptions (Wadhia 2010, 2013; see also Hing 2013; Motomura 2012; Olivas 2012a; Rabin 2014), they are far more apt to write about immigration policy—the law on the books—than about how prosecutorial discretion shapes the practice of immigration enforcement—the law in action. As Shoba Wadhia notes in her review of prosecutorial discretion, "While many scholars have written articles about undocumented immigration, restrictions on immigration, and immigrants' rights, there is a dearth of literature on the role of prosecutorial discretion in immigration law" (2010, 244). Wadhia suggests that "the cost and justice-related theories behind prosecutorial discretion" are similar in the criminal and immigration contexts. Both, she argues, "have witnessed an explosion of activities that qualify as infractions subject to penalties." Immigration enforcement agencies, she continues, have "historically relied on documents produced and utilized in the criminal context to create guidance for immigration officers" and "the surge in immigration-related criminal prosecution raises a number of questions about how prosecutorial discretion is exercised against noncitizens in both the criminal and civil contexts" (Wadhia 2010, 268; see also Legomsky 2007; Motomura 2012; Wishnie 2012).

Multiple competing factors shape the use of prosecutorial discretion in immigration, including the availability of resources for identifying, detaining, and deporting individuals; the humanitarian consequences of removing persons with strong family and community ties, and especially those with US-citizen spouses or children and those who came to the United States as young children; and assessments of what constitutes a proportional response to unauthorized immigration and to crimes committed by immigrants (Banks 2013; Hing 2013; Kanstroom 2012; Olivas 2012a; Wadhia 2010; Wishnie 2012).

Daniel Kanstroom calls discretion "the flexible shock absorber of the administrative state. It is a venerable and essential component of the rule of law that recognizes the inevitable complexities of enforcement of laws by government agencies" (2012, 215). And, legislative restrictions on judicial discretion and limits on judicial review imposed in 1996 "have simply consolidated this discretion in the agency officials responsible for charging decisions. Prosecutorial discretion has thus overtaken the exercise of discretion by immigration judges when it comes to questions of relief" (Cox and Rodríguez 2009, 518–19).

This discretion is severely limited, however, by ICE's organizational structure and overarching law enforcement mission. ICE is the only agency empowered to represent the government in deportation hearings, and ICE attorneys are subject to review, promotion, and discipline by managers who come from law enforcement backgrounds. Prior to their incorporation into the Department of Homeland Security (DHS), government immigration attorneys were supervised by other attorneys, and those attorney managers recognized the need for trial lawyers to be granted wide latitude in handling their cases. As we shall see later in this chapter, the law enforcement focus of ICE's middle management became a serious impediment to the exercise of prosecutorial discretion.

DISCRETION IN US IMMIGRATION ENFORCEMENT: THE EARLY DAYS

Kanstroom reminds us that discretion has historically been a key component of immigration policy and practice. The Alien and Sedition Acts of 1798 "gave the President unfettered discretion to deport any alien he deemed sufficiently dangerous to warrant the sanction" (2012, 62), and the 1918 Alien Law was used to deport alleged anarchists, Bolsheviks and other dissidents. Similarly, scholars have identified the multiple ways in which US immigration law, since at least the mid-1800s, has selectively permitted and excluded entry based on race, religion, gender, national origin, and other considerations thought relevant at the time (Abrams 2005; Calavita 1984; Gardner 2005; Ngai 2004). For example, by defining Chinese women immigrants as prostitutes and thus excludable, the Page Act of 1875 prevented the immigration of Chinese women, thus slowing the growth of Chinese American communities while appearing more inclusive (Abrams 2005).

Discretion in immigration law enforcement was also critical in meeting the needs of agriculture and other economic sectors that relied on cheap seasonal labor. Writing just prior to passage of the 1986 Immigration Reform and Control Act, Harwood argues that "a tough, no-holds-barred enforcement policy" would have been difficult because well-organized interest groups wanted weak immigration enforcement, there were not sufficient resources to deport all unauthorized immigrants, and political considerations required trade-offs (1986, 168). According to Harwood, "Whether consciously articulated or not, political factors are often clearly intertwined with considerations of optimal resource allocations in the agency's effort to achieve what it considers to be the most advantageous enforcement strategy" (1986, 172). As a result, the Immigration and Naturalization Services (INS) "must engage in selective enforcement, and even underenforcement, of the law" (1986, 175). Similarly, Calavita (1992) demonstrates how the INS used its discretion during the

Bracero Period of 1942–1964 to ignore those undocumented workers that agribusiness needed, while deporting those who were seen as troublemakers.

The recent literature on proportionality adds another dimension to this discussion. Proportionality is "the notion that the severity of a sanction should not be excessive in relation to the gravity of an offense" (Wishnie 2012, 416) and "provides a basis for balancing the government's interest in punishment and an individual's fundamental rights" (Banks 2013, 1267). Accordingly, deportation should only be used when it is a proportionate response to a criminal act, and the length of any bar to reentry must also be proportionate to the offense. Thus, Daniel Kanstroom concludes, "The key question is not whether the rule of law demands the elimination of discretion—that is simply impossible. Rather, the more serious question is: what is the proper relationship among enforcement duties, such as inevitable discretion, basic rights claims, and judicial oversight?" (2012, 214–15; see also Motomura 2014; Stumpf 2009).

LEGAL UNDERSTANDINGS OF PROSECUTORIAL DISCRETION IN IMMIGRATION POLICY AND PRACTICE

According to a senior official in the Department of Homeland Security, the starting point for the Obama administration's conceptualization of prosecutorial discretion was Sam Bernsen's 1976 memorandum. At the time, Bernsen was general counsel to the commissioner for Immigration and Naturalization Services. His memo defines prosecutorial discretion as "the power of a law enforcement official to decide whether or not to commence or proceed with action against a possible law violator. . . . The reasons for the exercise of prosecutorial discretion are both practical and humanitarian" (1976, 1). Bernsen further asserts that prosecutorial discretion "is inherent in the nature of [the INS's] enforcement function." He suggests a number of reasons why deportation proceedings may be cancelled, including proceedings that were "improvidently begun." In such cases, "the person is placed in the 'deferred action' . . . category, meaning that deportation proceedings will not be instituted or continued against the alien" for policy or humanitarian reasons (Bernsen 1976, 6). As we shall see, the concept of "deferred action" reappears over time, most notably in the Vanison et al. memo (n.d.) and in the Deferred Action for Childhood Arrivals policy (Napolitano 2012).

Between Bernsen's memorandum establishing the rationale for prosecutorial discretion in immigration enforcement and the contemporary context,

Congress adopted three key pieces of legislation: the 1986 Immigration Reform and Control Act (IRCA), the 1996 Illegal Immigration Reform and Immigrant Responsibility Act (IIRIRA), and the 1996 Antiterrorism and Effective Death Penalty Act (AEDPA). IRCA was a comprehensive immigration policy, combining a legalization program with employer sanctions for hiring undocumented workers. Although IRCA was generally seen as a major, even if time-limited, win for immigration advocates, the 1996 laws slammed the door on immigrants. They substantially broadened the category of deportable offenses and, reminiscent of federal sentencing guidelines, they significantly undermined, and in many cases essentially eradicated, judicial discretion.

The final version of the 1996 laws, according to then-INS General Counsel David Martin, was a "perfect storm" that expanded the grounds for deportation, was retroactive, and precluded most relief possibilities, even for legal permanent residents[3]. Similarly, Lindsay Marshall, then director of the Florence Immigrant and Refugee Rights Project told us:

> 1996 is sort of like the big year in immigration enforcement. . . . They massively expanded the number of crimes that can make people deportable. They started this mandatory detention provision that . . . by legislation, it sort of stripped away the discretion of ICE to decide whether to release someone. . . . That is used as a reason why they have to detain so many people, because the legislation has that mandatory detention provision. It also took a lot of discretion from immigration judges. It used to be that immigration judges could always, no matter what the case, before making a final decision about deportation, they could consider the impact on US-citizen children before making that decision. And now, unless somebody is eligible for a defense from deportation and there is an element of that defense that says, "you can consider the impact on US citizen family members," they can't consider it. A lot of their discretion was taken away in those situations. So that was a really pivotal year.[4]

Even when immigration judges want to take family ties into account, we were told, "their hands are tied" if immigrants, including legal permanent residents, have an aggravated felony conviction, regardless of how long ago the offense occurred, whether it was a deportable offense at the time, and even whether it was a felony. Looking back over the years leading up to 1996 and the changes in immigration enforcement that followed, the Supreme Court declared in March 2010, "The landscape of federal immigration law has changed dramatically over the last 90 years. While once there was only a narrow class of deportable offenses and judges wielded broad discretionary authority to prevent deportation, immigration reforms over time have expanded the class of deportable offenses and limited the authority of judges to alleviate the harsh consequences of deportation" (*Padilla v. Kentucky* 2010, 1478). . . . These changes to our immigration law," the Court concluded, "have dramatically raised the stakes of a noncitizen's criminal conviction" (2010, 1478).

Prosecutorial Discretion in Light of the 1996 Laws:
Commissioner Meissner's Memorandum

Given the harshness of the 1996 laws and the limitations they imposed on judges, some members of Congress and the Clinton administration were concerned that the 1996 laws might be interpreted as eliminating *all* forms of discretion in immigration enforcement. Bo Cooper, then general counsel for INS Commissioner Doris Meissner, wrote an influential memorandum dated October 4, 1999, in which he outlined the legal bases for prosecutorial discretion, proposed limits on discretion, and offered examples of its proper use. Cooper had considerable experience in immigration policy, having served as principal legal advisor to INS in two earlier administrations. His memorandum was explicitly "intended to be the first step in the INS' examination of its use of prosecutorial discretion" (Cooper 1999, 1). But the discretion itself, he argued, is not new. Rather, like other law enforcement agencies, INS "does not have the resources fully and completely to enforce the immigration laws against every violator [and so] it exercises prosecutorial discretion thousands of times every day" (1999, 3).

A month later, twenty-eight members of Congress sent a letter to Attorney General Janet Reno and INS Commissioner Doris Meissner, citing Cooper's memo and affirming their sense that the 1996 laws did not erase all elements of discretion.[5] The letter states, "There has been widespread agreement that some deportations were unfair and resulted in unjustifiable hardship" (Hyde et al. 1999, 1). Examples cited include removal proceedings against "legal permanent residents who came to the United States when they were very young, and many years ago committed a single crime at the lower end of the 'aggravated felony' spectrum, but have been law-abiding ever since, obtained and held jobs and remained self-sufficient, and started families in the United States" (1999, 1). The letter concludes with a request for guidelines for INS District Directors, "both to legitimate in their eyes the exercise of discretion and to ensure that their decisions . . . are not made in an inconsistent manner"

(1999, 2). Commissioner Meissner's November 17, 2000, directive established this guidance and an implementation process. The "Meissner Memo," as it has come to be known, has stood the test of time, becoming the standard upon which later prosecutorial discretion memos rely.

Explicitly referencing the similarities with prosecutorial discretion in the criminal law context, Meissner states, "There are significant differences, of course, between the role of the U.S. Attorneys' offices in the criminal justice system, and INS responsibilities to enforce the immigration laws, but the general approach to prosecutorial discretion stated in this memorandum reflects that taken by the Principles of Federal Prosecution" (Meissner 2000, 2, n. 2). Echoing the memo from her general counsel as well as the Supreme Court opinion in *Reno v. American-Arab Anti-Discrimination Committee* (1999), which recently had been decided, Meissner stresses that INS "officers are not only authorized by law but expected to exercise discretion in a judicious manner at all stages of the enforcement process" (2000, 1) and to do so "every day" (2000, 2).

Clearly identifying the dual bases for prosecutorial discretion—limited resources and humanitarian concerns—and anticipating potential criticism, Commissioner Meissner states that prosecutorial discretion "is not an invitation to violate or ignore the law. Rather, it is a means to use the resources we have in a way that best accomplishes our mission of administering and enforcing the immigration laws of the United States" (2000, 4). Meissner continues, "INS officers may decline to prosecute a legally sufficient immigration case if the Federal immigration enforcement interest that would be served by prosecution is not substantial" (2000, 5). This "individualized determination, based on the facts and the law," she asserts, holds even in cases in which an immigrant meets the criteria for mandatory detention under the 1996 laws (2000, 6).

Meissner outlines a set of factors to be weighed when deciding whether to exercise prosecutorial discretion. These factors should be considered in their totality, rather than piecemeal. They include the person's immigration status (with lawful permanent residents generally due greater consideration) and length of residence in the United States; history of prior immigration violations or criminal offenses; humanitarian concerns including family ties in the United States, whether the person is now or is likely to become eligible for admissibility, cooperation with law enforcement, honorable US military service, and community opinion; and the extent to which use of resources in this case meets national or regional priorities (2000, 7–8). Recognizing that the various regional offices "face different conditions and have different requirements" (2000, 10), Commissioner Meissner reiterates that INS personnel "at all levels should understand that prosecutorial discretion exists and that it is appropriate and expected that the INS will exercise this authority in appropriate cases" (2000, 10). This determination was affirmed a year later by the Supreme Court, which held in *INS v. St. Cyr* (2001) that certain discretionary waivers of deportations remain available to noncitizens.

Post-9/11 Organizational Shuffle

Eleven days after the terrorist attacks of September 11, 2001, President George W. Bush created an Office of Homeland Security within the executive branch and appointed Tom Ridge as its first director. With passage of the Homeland Security Act a year later, immigration authority was transferred to the newly formed Department of Homeland Security, with immigration enforcement concentrated in one agency, US Immigration and Customs Enforcement. Joining ICE in the newly formed DHS were Citizenship and Immigration Services, Customs and Border Patrol, Coast Guard, Federal Emergency Management Agency, Federal Law Enforcement Training Center, Transportation Security Administration, and the Secret Service. According to a former senior government official, the FBI, CIA, NSA, and other powerful agencies refused to move, resulting in this conglomeration of "second-tier" law enforcement and security agencies whose "constant struggle to be taken seriously by the real big boys is an undercurrent that drives a lot of DHS decisions."

Echoing the comments of several immigration attorneys and policy analysts we interviewed, immigration attorney Lindsay Marshall described creation of ICE as "kind of like a self-fulfilling prophecy. You create this agency that is supposed to go after people, and they've put a lot of resources there." The resulting "pressure on the agency to keep those numbers up and do that enforcement" and the "flood of resources" has "continued to ramp up the enforcement and the capacity in detention."[6] Similarly, another respondent depicted ICE as a "special agency that was focused on law enforcement. . . . That is their mandate and their mission."

Stepping Stones to the Morton Memos

A surge in border enforcement activity resulted in a tripling of caseloads in immigration courts between 2001 and 2005, stretching limited agency resources and making prosecutorial discretion an important tool for achieving agency goals. This led to the next major stepping stone toward today's exercise of prosecutorial discretion—a 2005 memo by William J. Howard, principal legal advisor for ICE. In addition to the value of prosecutorial discretion in times of scarce resources, Howard also reiterated that it "is a very significant tool that sometimes enables you to deal with the difficult, complex and contradictory provisions of the immigration laws and cases involving human suffering and hardship" (Howard 2005, 8).

Two years later, in the wake of a series of raids of meatpacking plants and other worksites hiring large numbers of undocumented immigrants, DHS Assistant Secretary and ICE Director Julie Myers issued a memorandum highlighting "the importance of exercising prosecutorial discretion when making administrative arrest and custody determinations for aliens who are nursing mothers" (Myers 2007, 1). Although her memo was limited in scope, Myers explicitly states that field agents and officers are "not only authorized by law to exercise discretion within the authority of the agency, but are expected to do so in a judicious manner at all stages of the enforcement process" (2007, 1). Absent threats to national security, public safety, or other investigative interests, she asserts, nursing mothers should not be detained. Myers references Meissner's memorandum as providing the appropriate process for reaching discretionary decisions and attaches that memo to her own, thus reaffirming its legal guidance.

With the 2008 elections, the Democrats again regained the White House, and President Barack Obama appointed former Arizona governor Janet Napolitano to head the Department of Homeland Security. President Obama had hoped to pick up where President George W. Bush left off and to enact comprehensive immigration reform early in his first term (Weiner 2013). Those efforts failed, and by 2010 the growing antipathy between House Republicans and the White House made passage of immigration legislation, and most any other initiative, unlikely in the near future. In this context, the Obama administration and Democratic members of Congress started looking for administrative means of achieving their goals. As a government official told us, "Nothing can replace comprehensive immigration reform, but in the absence of that, we'll enforce laws in the smartest possible way."

Roxana Bacon, then chief counsel for the US Immigration and Customs Service, recalled being asked during a social event sometime around March 2010, "What else can we do if we don't get comprehensive immigration reform?" She would not say who made the request, but when asked if it came from someone high up she affirmed, "Very high." She recounted, "So I went back and looked through a lot of notes and . . . I picked out five or six, or ten or twenty, I can't remember what I started with, I think there were about fifteen things you could do just through administrative fiat." Denise Vanison, another political appointee from USCIS's (US Citizenship and Immigration Services) Policy and Strategy Office, and two career staffers, Debra Rogers from Field Operations and Donald Neufeld from Service Center Operations, reviewed and commented on Bacon's initial draft.

The resulting memo, "Administrative Alternatives to Comprehensive Immigration Reform," reflected the perspectives of both political appointees and career civil servants. It identified a set of options that would promote family unity, foster economic growth, achieve improvements in process, and reduce the threat of removal for certain undocumented immigrants (Vanison et al. n.d.). Ultimately, the draft memo was leaked, some members of Congress were angered by the proposed actions, and the director of USCIS distanced himself from the document. "As a result," Bacon told us, "all of those ideas then couldn't resurface. It was really kind of over at that point."[7]

The Morton Memos

It is in this context that ICE Director John Morton wrote what have come to be called the Morton Memos. These memos drew upon what was by then a well-established policy of prosecutorial discretion to focus agency resources on a prioritized set of immigrants. Interestingly, we were told that Morton's first memo was also leaked. That may explain why, when it was initially issued to all ICE employees on June 30, 2010, it was missing the standard law enforcement disclaimer that the memo creates no enforceable rights or duties. This language was later added, and the memorandum was reissued on March 2, 2011.[8] The second and third Morton Memos were both issued on June 17, 2011. A fourth memo, providing guidance on the use of immigration detainers consistent with these earlier directives, was issued on December 21, 2012.

The first Morton Memo, "Civil Immigration Enforcement: Priorities for the Apprehension, Detention, and Removal of Aliens," identifies ICE's civil enforcement priorities, with highest priority given to those immigrants posing a danger to national security or a risk to public safety. Second priority goes to recent illegal immigrants, and persons who are fugitives or who otherwise obstruct immigration controls are assigned third priority. ICE detention resources are to be directed in support of these priorities but should not be expended upon "aliens who are known to be suffering from serious physical or mental illness, or who are disabled, elderly, pregnant, or nursing, or demonstrate that they are primary caretakers of children or an infirm person, or whose detention is otherwise not in the public interest," except under extraordinary circumstances or the requirements of mandatory detention, and then only with the approval of the field office director (Morton 2011a, 4–5). If a person falls within these categories and is subject to mandatory detention, field office directors are to request guidance from their local Office of Chief Counsel.

The memo continues, noting that particular care is needed "when dealing with lawful permanent residents, juveniles, and the immediate family members of citizens." Additional guidance on prosecutorial discretion, Director Morton states, will be forthcoming; meanwhile, ICE officers and attorneys should continue to be guided by the Meissner (2000), Howard (2005), and Myers (2007) memoranda.

Pushback from the ICE union and individual officers in the field was almost immediate. In response, Morton issued his second and third memos. These directives made the priorities even more explicit and restated in stronger language that he expected the guidelines to be followed. They also reflect a subtle humanizing shift in language—where immigrants were referred to primarily as "aliens" in the first memo, by the third memo the references are primarily to "persons" and "individuals" with whom positive or negative factors are associated.

Morton's second memo, "Prosecutorial Discretion: Certain Victims, Witnesses, and Plaintiffs" (Morton 2011b), focuses on removal cases involving victims and witnesses of domestic violence and other crimes, as well as immigrants engaged in nonfrivolous efforts to protect their civil rights and liberties. The third memo, "Exercising Prosecutorial Discretion Consistent with the Civil Immigration Enforcement Priorities of the Agency for the Apprehension, Detention, and Removal of Aliens" (Morton 2011c), is broader in scope. Again, Meissner's 2000 memo continues to be the guidepost, with Morton's directives differing in only minor ways. Like Meissner, Morton identifies multiple points at which prosecutorial discretion may be applied. He reminds ICE officers that "certain classes of individuals warrant particular care," both positive and negative (2011c, 5). Positive, humanitarian considerations were called for in cases involving "veterans and members of the U.S. armed forces; long-time lawful permanent residents; minors and elderly individuals;

individuals present in the United States since childhood; pregnant or nursing women; victims of domestic violence, trafficking, or other serious crimes; individuals who suffer from a serious mental or physical disability; and individuals with serious health concerns." Immigrants with the following negative characteristics also require special care and consideration: "individuals who pose a clear risk to national security; serious felons, repeat offenders, or individuals with a lengthy criminal record of any kind; known gang members or other individuals who pose a clear danger to public safety; and individuals with an egregious record of immigration violations" (2011c, 5).

On December 21, 2012, ICE announced year-end removal numbers for fiscal year (FY) 2012. A new record was set, with 409,849 immigrants removed, surpassing the record set the prior year by more than 10,000 persons. The same day that those all-time high deportation numbers were released, John Morton issued a memorandum on "Civil Immigration Enforcement: Guidance on the Use of Detainers in the Federal, State, Local, and Tribal Criminal Justice Systems" (Morton 2012). This memo stipulates that ICE's "finite enforcement resources" are to be deployed in accordance with the priorities stated in his June 2010 memo. He was, in effect, saying that they were deporting more people than ever before, and, in return, the new detention guidelines were to be followed.

Deferred Action for Childhood Arrivals

As President Obama approached the end of his first term without passage of comprehensive immigration reform, or even the more limited Development, Relief, and Education for Alien Minors (DREAM) Act, which would have legalized the status of persons who came to the United States as young children (Dreamers), he faced considerable pressure to reassess the options available to the executive branch (Gilbert 2013; Motomura et al. 2012; Motomura 2014; Olivas 2012a,b). There is strong public sympathy for Dreamers, yet from the perspective of immigrants' advocates, the Morton Memos fell short when it came to the needs of these teenagers and young adults. As immigration policy analyst and former associate general counsel for INS and associate chief counsel for USCIS Mary Giovagnoli summarized the situation: "[While the ICE leadership and the White House] made it very clear in the memos it was supposed to [apply to Dreamers], there was absolute consensus [among advocates] that no matter what the memo said, it was not clear, and there were a lot of DREAM Act eligible or potentially eligible people who were still facing deportation, who in some cases had been deported. . . . Especially if you look at it from that lens, of the group that was most likely to be helped, [prosecutorial discretion] really had not worked."[9]

In an effort to safeguard the Dreamers, ninety-five law professors sent President Barack Obama a letter in April 2012 identifying three forms of discretionary relief available to him: deferred action, parole-in-place, and deferred enforced departure (Motomura et al. 2012). Deferred action for Dreamers had also been proposed in the memo written by senior USCIS staffers in 2010 (Vanison et al. n.d.). This support from experts in immigration law may have helped to stiffen Obama's resolve, though as we discuss in the next chapter, the importance of the Latino vote in the upcoming 2012 elections is generally considered to be the primary force behind the Deferred Action for Childhood Arrivals (DACA) policy.

DHS Secretary Janet Napolitano announced DACA in June 2012. It was quickly implemented, becoming effective just two months later, on August 15 (Napolitano 2012). Napolitano's "Exercising Prosecutorial Discretion with Respect to Individuals Who Came to the United States as Children" memorandum clarifies that deferred action is a form of prosecutorial discretion, and outlines how this discretion is to be exercised in cases involving persons brought to the United States as children. Noting that most childhood arrivals lack the intent to violate the law, Secretary Napolitano states, "Our Nation's immigration laws . . . are not designed to be blindly enforced without consideration given to the individual circumstances of each case. Nor are they designed to remove productive young people to countries where they may not have lived or even speak the language. Indeed, many of these young people already contributed to our country in significant ways. Prosecutorial discretion, which is used in so many other areas, is especially justified here" (Napolitano 2012, 2).

Under this program, applicants may be considered for deferred action for a period of two years (renewable) if they are not older than thirty; were under the age of sixteen when they entered the United States; resided continuously in the United States for at least five years; were present in the United States on June 15, 2012 (the date the program was announced); are enrolled in school, graduated from high school, obtained a GED, or were honorably discharged from the US military; and have not been convicted of a felony, significant misdemeanor, multiple misdemeanors, or of otherwise posing a threat to national security or public safety. Over the course of the summer of 2012, the educational requirement was clarified to include otherwise eligible young people who lacked a high school diploma or GED but who had re-enrolled prior to applying for deferred action.[10] This clarification made an additional 350,000 young people potentially eligible for deferred action and encouraged them to return to school to earn their high school diplomas (Batalova and Mittelstadt 2012). Persons granted deferred action under DACA may apply for work authorization and, as we discuss in more detail in chapter 3, some states permit "dacamented" youth to obtain driver's licenses and to pay in-state tuition at public colleges and universities.

The administration took several steps designed to reduce potential applicants' fears of coming forward. First, DACA applications are reviewed by ICE's sister agency, the USCIS, and are not to be shared with ICE except under unusual circumstances involving serious crimes. This was seen by many as a key factor. As a prominent policy analyst told us, "I think one of the things that made kids feel safer was that they were being told that there was going to be this wall between CIS and ICE." Second, the USCIS website provides detailed information on eligibility criteria. And third, USCIS worked closely with the advocacy community to make sure those criteria and the forms of documentation required to demonstrate eligibility were widely distributed and understood, thereby reducing the numbers of potential applicants who would be denied under the program.

An estimated 1.76 million young people are eligible for temporary relief under this program (Migration Policy Institute 2012). Immediately after it went into effect, applications began pouring in at an initial rate of about 4,400 per day. By all accounts, the initial applicants had the strongest cases. These tended to be young people who were enrolled in school and had substantial documentation that they met the eligibility criteria. Application numbers decreased following the initial surge, hovering around 1,500 per day through March 2013, then dropping to 1,000 per day in spring and summer of 2013, and then to about 500 per day through June 2014. Overall, 712,064 new applications were received between August 15, 2012, when USCIS began accepting applications, and June 30, 2014. Just under 5 percent of the applications (30,732) were rejected at intake. Of the 675,576 new applications accepted, 580,859 (86 percent) were approved and 23,881 (3.5 percent) denied, with the remainder still pending (USCIS 2014).[11]

With the re-election of President Obama in 2012, there was hope that DACA would be both a down payment and a test case for legalization under comprehensive immigration reform. As several of our informants suggested, DACA demonstrated that it is possible to implement such a program quickly and efficiently while still ensuring careful review of a wide range of background and biometric data on each applicant. Promotion of USCIS director Alejandro Mayorkas to the post of deputy secretary of DHS in December 2013 further inspired hope that the administration was preparing for legislation authorizing an expanded legalization program. By the spring of 2014, though, such legislation appeared unlikely, and the administration ramped up meetings with immigration advocacy and policy groups to renew and possibly expand DACA through executive action.

The renewal process was relatively smooth, but to the chagrin of Dreamers and their supporters, it did not expand the pool of eligible applicants. DACA 2.0, as some called it, was not a new version but rather more of the same, as once again the House of Representatives signaled that perhaps it would act on immigration during the summer of 2014, and once again the White House backed away to give legislators room to maneuver.

THE LIMITS OF PROSECUTORIAL DISCRETION: CHALLENGES AND DILEMMAS

Although they are more concrete in their identification of positive and negative factors and more forceful in their direction, the Morton Memos did not differ very significantly from earlier prosecutorial discretion memorandums. Nevertheless, both the Morton Memos and DACA were met with vehement critiques from some members of Congress and ICE officers for going too far, and from other members of Congress, the Latino community, and immigrants' advocates for not going far enough. The larger social context was politically charged as well, with anti-immigrant moral panics depicting immigrants as dangerous criminals, economic burdens on their communities, and a threat to American jobs (Chavez 2008; Kubrin, Zatz, and Martínez 2012; Menjívar and Kanstroom 2013; Newton 2008; Varsanyi 2010; Zatz and Smith 2012). These images, in turn, were juxtaposed against demonstrations of support for Dreamers, mothers separated from their children, and other sympathetic figures.

Organizational tensions that have historically plagued law enforcement officers and other street-level bureaucrats factor into this mix, but in this case the greatest opposition came from the leadership of one of the ICE unions, the National Immigration and Customs Enforcement Council, and particularly its president, Chris Crane. A second ICE union, the Federal Law Enforcement Officers Association, was more supportive of Morton and the prosecutorial discretion policies. And, according to a senior DHS official, the extent to which rank-and-file officers supported or challenged the directives varied, depending in part upon the dynamics of the individual ICE office, how the policy was implemented in that jurisdiction, and regional politics.

In addition to criticisms that the Obama administration was using prosecutorial discretion as an unofficial form of amnesty and thus not upholding the rule of law, the administration also confronted challenges from immigrant advocacy groups. These criticisms focused on the record high number of deportations, and especially deportations of parents of US-citizen children, and more general concerns that prosecutorial discretion was not being implemented as quickly or as widely as they had anticipated. As one advocate told us, "Prosecutorial discretion was supposed to be a down payment on legalization by the administration and it has, frankly, been a joke."

Challenges from within ICE

Challenges from within ICE included very public complaints filed by the Houston regional office, a unanimous vote of no confidence in Director Morton by the ICE Council, and a lawsuit filed against Homeland Security Secretary Janet Napolitano and Directors Morton and Mayorkas in response to DACA (*Crane v. Napolitano* 2012).

In the late summer and fall of 2010, ICE officers in Houston contested Morton's prosecutorial discretion policy, arguing that it called for a "secretive review process" resulting in dismissals of hundreds of cases that did not fit the agency's top priorities (Carroll 2011). The Senate Judiciary Committee, led by Texas Senator John Cornyn and other Republican committee members, demanded an investigation. In October 2010, they asked Secretary Napolitano to provide a detailed listing of the number of cases dismissed since January 2010 and "exactly how much funding your Department would require to ensure that enforcement of the law occurs consistently for every illegal alien encountered and apprehended by ICE or U.S. Customs and Border Protection" (Cornyn et al. 2010).

This was followed on June 11, 2011, by a unanimous vote of no confidence in ICE Director John Morton and Assistant Director Phyllis Coven by the National Immigration and Customs Enforcement Council. The statement by

Union President Chris Crane asserts that Morton and Coven "have abandoned the Agency's core mission ... and have instead directed their attention to campaigning for programs and policies related to amnesty" (Crane 2011; see also Feere 2011).

Morton immediately countered, issuing his second and third memorandums a week later, on June 17. As one attorney we interviewed described this back-and-forth volley, "I think what you're seeing from the administration is, 'You're not doing what I said, let me say it again,' and now, 'Okay, you really don't get it so let me outline exactly what I mean.'"

The next round came two weeks later, on July 5, when Representatives Lamar Smith (who, ironically, was one of the members of Congress asking INS to exercise prosecutorial discretion in 1999) and Robert Aderholt wrote Secretary Napolitano, calling the Morton Memos "a grossly irresponsible expansion of the use of prosecutorial discretion for the apparent purpose of administrative amnesty" and a violation of the will of Congress (Smith and Aderholt 2011, 2). They requested that ICE "utilize the extensive resources available to rigorously enforce the immigration laws of the United States and that ICE's future budget requests include the funds necessary to effectively support the men and women of ICE in executing their critical mission" (2011, 4–5).

Given this ongoing antipathy, it is perhaps not surprising that on August 23, 2012, one week after DACA went into effect, ten ICE officers sued in federal court to block the program on the grounds that it violates immigration statutes and the constitutional separation of powers (*Crane v. Napolitano* 2012). The case was dismissed by the US District Court for the Northern District of Texas without prejudice in July 2013 for lack of subject-matter jurisdiction.

Although Crane's rhetoric makes it appear as though the ICE rank-and-file are all in agreement with his position, only 7,700 of ICE's 20,000 employees are members of his union. Another 9,000 ICE agents are represented by the Federal Law Enforcement Officers Association, which did not join in the no confidence vote against Morton or the lawsuits against Morton and Napolitano, and which is generally more amenable to working with the ICE leadership (Preston 2013). Nevertheless, Crane's union has been extremely vocal, reflects more than one-third of ICE agents, and has considerable support from some members of Congress.

The challenges to the Morton Memos and DACA rest in part on differing interpretations of the legal basis for prosecutorial discretion, but also on different understandings of the limits of discretion on the part of state and local law enforcement. Opinions by the Department of Justice's Office of Legal Counsel in 1989 and 1996 (Kmiec 1989; Roseborough 1996) made it clear that state and local law enforcement may only arrest immigrants for criminal violations, *not* civil violations. In contrast, a 2002 memorandum to Attorney General John Ashcroft from his assistant attorney general, Jay Bybee, concluded, "This Office's 1996 advice that federal law precludes state police from arresting aliens on the basis of civil deportability was mistaken" (Bybee 2002, 15). Two months later, Ashcroft referenced Bybee's opinion in his remarks announcing the National Security Entry-Exit Registration System (Ashcroft 2002).

A guiding force behind the challenges to prosecutorial discretion and DACA has been Kansas Secretary of State Kris Kobach. Kobach serves as counsel for the conservative Immigration Reform Law Institute and helped write Arizona's SB 1070 and anti-immigrant legislation for several other states and localities. His "quintessential force multiplier" argument (Kobach 2005) rests on the Bybee interpretation, that is, that local police have the power to make immigration arrests. Kobach's legal challenges to prosecutorial discretion and DACA argue similarly that ICE agents have a duty to place unauthorized immigrants whom they encounter into removal hearings, and their supervisors do not have a right to interfere with that responsibility by telling them to use prosecutorial discretion.

In contrast, immigration law professor David Martin argues that Kobach's statutory theory is incorrect. Martin was one of DHS Secretary Janet Napolitano's law professors at the University of Virginia. He served as general counsel for INS from 1995 to 1998, and as principal deputy general counsel for Secretary Napolitano from 2009 to 2010. According to Martin, Kobach's theory "takes out of context a provision Congress enacted in 1996, marries it up with a misunderstanding of two provisions that have been in place for decades, and ignores the actual practice under those provisions" (Martin 2012, 169).

Why did John Morton face such serious challenges from ICE officers when his memos drew so clearly from the policies of other ICE directors and INS commissioners, especially Doris Meissner? There are at least five possible explanations. First, although immigration has always been a politically sensitive issue, the surge of anti-immigrant legislation at the state and local levels between 2007 and 2011 meant any discussion of immigration policy and practice would be difficult. Second, the antagonistic relationship between the White House and the Republican congressional leadership made changes to immigration policy particularly thorny, with members of the GOP assuming that President Obama, DHS Secretary Napolitano, and ICE Director Morton were trying to usurp congressional authority. Third, the Obama administration's tendency to hold its cards close to its chest until it was ready to go public with a policy hurt its ability to garner support for policy changes from members of Congress and other relevant parties. Fourth, the organizational context had changed markedly since Doris Meissner issued her memorandum. At that time, the three immigration services were integrated within the Department of Justice, an agency known for its attention to due process and equal protection requirements. Former chief counsel for Citizenship and Immigration Services Roxana Bacon describes the move from Justice, where a system of checks and balances framed by constitutional law protections predominated, to Homeland Security, whose mandate is national security, as "a sea change of focus."[12] Fifth, the culture within ICE was very enforcement focused. This single-minded enforcement mission was further strengthened by separation of immigration services into three distinct agencies within DHS (see similarly Rabin 2014).

Realistically, discretion is inevitable—ICE officers could not detain and deport the 11.7 million unauthorized immigrants living in the United States. Discretion provides flexibility, allowing decision makers to respond to varying circumstances and resources. But precisely because it is ever present, discretion is always available as a convenient rationale for critiquing political opponents perceived to be going too far, or not far enough, in following the letter or the spirit of the law. Thus we see Kris Kobach and Chris Crane, among others, seeking to mobilize outrage about the use of prosecutorial discretion and deferred action because they disagree with the substance of the policy decisions and their anticipated effects.

Challenges from Immigrants' Advocates

Deportations reached an all-time high under the Obama administration, climbing from 291,060 in FY 2007 to 409,849 in FY 2012 (United States Immigration and Customs Enforcement [USICE] 2012a) before dipping to 368,644 in FY 2013 (USICE 2012d, 2013). According to immigration scholar Daniel Kanstroom, this level of deportation "has vastly exceeded any historical precedent in terms of its size, its ferocity, its disproportionality, its disregard for basic rights, and its substantial negative effects" (2012, 5). The Latino community, immigrants' advocates and attorneys, and child welfare advocates were initially dismayed, and then increasingly frustrated and angered, by the large number of removals. Of special concern was the continued high numbers of parents who were detained and deported, and the resulting family fragmentation and trauma (Phillips et al. 2013; Rabin 2011, 2013; Wessler 2011a,b, 2012a).

Three primary criticisms emerged from our interviews. First, Morton encountered great difficulty changing the enforcement culture within ICE, and as a consequence the implementation of his directives was slow, uneven, and insufficient. Second, it was extraordinarily difficult to make the case for prosecutorial discretion for immigrants already in detention. And third, prosecutorial discretion did not extend to those caught in the mandatory deportation net.

Considering the implementation process first, Mary Giovagnoli, director of the Immigration Policy Center, suggested, "The prosecutorial discretion memos that were issued in 2010 were important and ambitious in their own right, and yet I think the criticism of them is that they really didn't go far enough in terms of being able to translate from a memo and an idea into a total change in culture. . . . In the grand scheme of things, I think most people on the outside [of government] were, like, 'Yeah, this is a drop in the bucket.'"[13] Similarly, immigration attorney Nina Rabin praised the Morton Memos as a positive development because they outline "specific areas for prosecutorial discretion. One of them is primary caregivers, and there are also some related to DREAM Act kids. So I think that it's definitely good to have those areas specified in writing." But along with other attorneys and advocates, Rabin also noted the slow and, at best, uneven implementation of Morton's guidelines. She continued, "[But] . . . I haven't seen a lot of change yet as a result."[14] Along these same lines, Victoria López, an attorney with Arizona's ACLU, said "I have not seen a change" as a result of the Morton Memos, and Yali Lincroft, a White House Champion for Change awardee who, at the time, was a policy consultant for the children's advocacy organization First Focus, reported, "It's not happening. It's not happening fast enough. . . . The line staff is not moving that fast."[15]

Some observers went further, concluding that in some jurisdictions ICE officers were purposefully pushing back or waiting it out until there was a change in administration. Michelle Brané and Jennifer Podkul of the Women's

Refugee Commission recalled that ICE officers in a southern state told them, "Those memos don't mean anything."[16] More colorfully, former USCIS chief counsel Roxana Bacon told us that while she views the policies as an important step in the right direction, many rank-and-file field officers were dismissive of them, calling the memos "toilet paper."[17]

Having heard such reports from the advocacy community, the American Immigration Lawyers Association and the American Immigration Council surveyed attorneys nationwide, finding that "while practices have improved in a few ICE offices, in the majority of offices ICE agents, trial attorneys and supervisors admitted that they had not implemented the memoranda and there had been no changes in policy or practice" (American Immigration Lawyers Association and American Immigration Council 2011, 4). This had not changed by 2012, at least in some jurisdictions, as an immigration attorney in Arizona told us that the chief counsel for ICE in that state "took the approach that she was going to construe it narrowly. She was going to be very sparse with her discretion and, as such, I didn't even consider that as an option."

In conversations with senior DHS officials in the fall of 2012, it was clear that they were aware of this problem. They recognized that implementation of the Morton Memos was far from perfect. They acknowledged that the implementation process was uneven and nonlinear, and there was definitely room for improvement in ensuring that rank-and-file officers employed the new policies. However, they believe that the memos did have a very real effect on enforcement policies.

From the DHS perspective, a key challenge was the gap between the expectations of many of the advocacy groups and what they believed to be the actual, realistic function of the memos. The advocacy community had anticipated that the Morton Memos would result in a dramatic reduction in overall enforcement levels and so was disappointed; in contrast, DHS saw the memos as providing a means of better prioritizing how enforcement resources were to be used. As a senior DHS official explained, the administration had to use the funds appropriated by Congress for immigration enforcement in good faith, but they had authority to prioritize how those funds should be used. They could, for example, direct ICE officers and agents to prioritize serious criminals, even though identifying and apprehending serious criminals takes more time than identifying and apprehending individuals who merely overstayed their visas. But they could not, in good faith, fail to use the appropriated funds for purposes of immigration enforcement.

The second problem concerns immigrants who are in detention. The congressional appropriation to DHS includes funds to maintain 34,000 immigrants in detention each day. According to Victoria López of the Arizona ACLU, "If you are in immigration detention, your case is not being looked at for prosecutorial discretion. They are supposed to be reviewing all of the cases. Well, they are reviewing the non-detained cases, but they are not reviewing the others."[18]

This finding may reflect the much greater likelihood of having legal representation among immigrants who are not detained. Nationwide, 75 percent of those in immigration proceedings who are not detained are represented by counsel, compared with 26 percent of those who are detained. Ignoring detainees whose situations potentially warrant prosecutorial discretion is consistent with what one attorney called the "very aggressive enforcement mentality" within ICE. Whatever the reason, detention continues to be a barrier, even for those detainees who are represented by counsel. As Nina Rabin, co-director of the University of Arizona Immigration Law Clinic, told us, "I just haven't seen it. . . . I mean, in our clinic right now we are representing two people who have either no criminal history or very, very minor criminal history who are still in the middle of proceedings. . . . It just doesn't seem to me like it's actually resulting in that many actual changes in the way ICE handles cases . . . at least not those already pipelined."[19]

A third and related challenge highlighted by the advocacy community concerns the constraints created by the mandatory detention requirements in the 1996 laws. Mary Giovagnoli explained, "A lot of those people are only criminal aliens because you have defined them that way. The pushback has been that PD [prosecutorial discretion] itself isn't a solution if the people getting into the process are defined in a way that you've said they can't have access to that [discretion]."[20] Likewise, in discussing the large numbers of parents still being detained and deported, Emily Butera of the Women's Refugee Commission noted that many parents are subject to mandatory detention because they are re-entrants or because they came into the immigration system via the criminal justice system, so prosecutorial discretion never kicks in. As a result, "that policy does not really help them."[21]

PROSECUTORIAL DISCRETION IN ACTION—OR INACTION?

Critics claimed that Morton's prosecutorial discretion policies "grant amnesty to huge portions of the illegal alien population by executive fiat" (Federation for American Immigration Reform 2013). Why, then, didn't deportation numbers decrease significantly? A number of explanations are possible, including (1) it is too soon to see any systematic effect nationwide; (2) the number of unauthorized immigrants—11.7 million—is so large that ICE had to remove as many of them as was feasible each year if they were to make any progress in reducing the numbers; (3) Congress appropriated a specific dollar figure for immigration enforcement and, if those appropriations were not fully utilized, Congress might mandate even stronger steps; and (4) a tough stance was necessary to create a political climate in which comprehensive immigration reform would be possible.

Deportation numbers have stayed close to the 400,000 mark for several years. The FY 2013 numbers are lower than prior years, totaling 368,644 removals, but a more significant downward shift should have been visible if the intent was to decrease deportations, rather than reshape the population of deportees. And, Syracuse University's Transactional Records Access Clearinghouse (TRAC), which regularly reports on immigration court data obtained via Freedom of Information Act requests, found that immigration prosecutions reached an all-time high in FY 2013. According to TRAC, new cases were filed against 97,384 defendants, reflecting a 5.9 percent increase since FY 2012 and a 22.6 percent increase over the past five years (TRAC 2013a).

Even more telling, the number of court cases closed by prosecutorial discretion remains extremely low, totaling only 36,782 cases, or 6.9 percent of all immigration court cases closed between October 2012 and June 30, 2014. And, although there is substantial variation across jurisdictions, only five jurisdictions—Tucson, Seattle, Omaha, Los Angeles, and Charlotte—closed more than 20 percent of their caseload through prosecutorial discretion (TRAC 2014a). Closure rates via prosecutorial discretion did increase from FY 2012 to FY 2013, but they decreased again in the first quarter of FY 2014, with only 2,993 pending deportation cases closed via prosecutorial discretion between October 1 and December 31, 2013, nationwide (TRAC 2014b).

The second rationale is also unsatisfactory, because the number of unauthorized immigrants vastly surpasses the number of deportations. Rather, as the third possible explanation suggests, Congress appropriated funds to consistently fill 34,000 detention beds each day, and this translates into removal of 400,000 persons annually. As we were told, DHS understands this appropriation to mean that they must spend these funds on immigration enforcement, although they can determine priorities for which immigrants should fill those beds and, typically, be deported.

Along these same lines, the October 2010 letter to Secretary Napolitano from Senator Cornyn and his colleagues and the July 2011 letter from Representatives Smith and Aderholt make clear that at least some members of Congress are quite willing to provide more funds if DHS needs them in order to facilitate additional deportations (Cornyn et al. 2010; Smith and Aderholt 2011). This sentiment was reaffirmed in April 2013, when members of the House Appropriate Subcommittee on Homeland Security criticized Secretary Napolitano for asking for an appropriation of fewer than 34,000 beds. Secretary Napolitano suggested in this hearing that the bed appropriation is "arbitrary" and "artificial," and greater use of alternatives to detention would be more cost efficient. Nevertheless, committee members asserted that ICE was required to detain those "not clearly and beyond a doubt entitled to be admitted" and that she was "in violation of the law . . . by releasing these dangerous criminals" (US House Appropriations Subcommittee on Homeland Security 2013, 39).[22]

Fourth, while removal numbers had edged toward the 400,000 mark in 2010 and 2011, it was only upon release of the FY 2012 removal numbers, which for the first time exceeded 400,000 (at 409,849), that Morton issued a memorandum limiting the use of detention in federal, state, local, and tribal criminal justice systems to those meeting his enforcement priorities (Morton 2012). The total number of removals then fell about 9 percent in FY 2013, yet the Obama administration continues to speak regularly of enforcement priorities, of *who* is to be deported, rather than the total number of deportations. As policy analyst Randy Capps of the Migration Policy Institute told us, "The administration has stated that they have the capacity to remove 400,000 people per year, and that's their resource limitation. Within this limitation, they prioritize according to criminal history, length of stay in the United States, return following a prior removal, and other factors. The administration's policy has not been to reduce overall removals substantially, but rather to ensure that those removed fall into these priorities. Nonetheless, the total number of removals has fallen somewhat since the peak in 2012."[23]

Several of our informants commented that the Obama administration hoped these record-high deportations would demonstrate its commitment to border enforcement, thus creating a climate in which comprehensive immigration reform would be possible. If this was the administration's intent, however, the strategy backfired. The leadership in the House of Representatives remains intransigent in its refusal to bring comprehensive immigration reform to a vote, and the Latino community is frustrated and disappointed with President Obama's record on deportations.

WHO IS BEING DEPORTED?

Regardless of the rationale for maintaining high deportation numbers, has there been a change in who is being deported? Prosecutorial discretion is based on the premise that those who pose the greatest risk to public safety and security should be the priority for deportation, while persons with established ties to the United States and who make the greatest contributions to the well-being of US citizens should be least likely to be deported. Accordingly, we next ask, are persons with criminal records more likely to be deported? If so, for what sorts of offenses are they being deported? Conversely, are those with established ties to the United States, and especially parents of US-citizen children, now at lower risk of deportation?

Crime-Related Deportations: How Serious Are the Offenses?

The number of crime-related removals has varied historically. It rarely exceeded 7 percent of total annual deportations between 1908, when deportation statistics were first compiled, and 1986, when the Immigration Reform and Control Act was passed (Legomsky 2007). The numbers rose rapidly between 1986 and 1999, comprising the majority of all deportations for three consecutive years in the early 1990s (1993, 1994, and 1995) (Legomsky 2007). Crime-related removals fell once again, and then increased during President Obama's first term from 33 percent of all deportations in FY 2008 to 55 percent in FY 2012 (ICE 2012a, 2012c) and 59 percent in FY 2013 (ICE 2013). Immigration and criminal law became increasingly intertwined during this era through 287(g) partnerships between ICE and state and local law enforcement agencies, the Secure Communities program that checks all those arrested or taken into custody for immigration violations, and explicit identification of deportation as a tool for crime control (Eagly 2013; Sklansky 2012).[24]

Yet the crimes for which immigrants are deported are not typically serious violent offenses; rather, approximately 35 percent of the crime-related removals in recent years are for drug or DUI offenses. In contrast, 0.5 percent of the deportation cases in FY 2012 involved homicide convictions, and 2.5 percent involved sex offenses (USICE 2012c).

Syracuse University's Transactional Records Access Clearinghouse reports that 52.3 percent of immigration detainees in FY 2012 and the first four months of FY 2013 had criminal convictions. Of these, 9.6 percent were for driving under the influence, 6.0 percent for other traffic offenses, 2.0 percent for marijuana possession, and 10.5 percent for all drug possession and sale offenses, including marijuana (TRAC 2013d). These data are not directly comparable to ICE data for the same time period, however, because TRAC generally considers detention orders, which may or may not result in deportation at some later date, while ICE reports on all removals during the period in question. In addition, the data published by ICE do not distinguish the type of drug offense, while the TRAC data separate out marijuana possession from other drug cases. Nevertheless, both sources demonstrate that large numbers of persons without criminal histories are included in the detention and deportation population, and many of those with criminal histories had relatively minor offenses. Moreover, the proportion of DUIs and drug offenders among those *deported* in FY 2012 is substantially greater than the proportion of persons with DUI and drug offenses in the *detainee* population in FY 2012 and the first part of 2013, suggesting the sparse use of prosecutorial discretion when it comes to DUI and drug cases.

Bill Ong Hing (1980) suggests that drug offenders have historically been disfavored by immigration law, with *Nicholas v. INS* (1979) and *Bowe v. INS* (1979) essentially closing the door on relief in deportation hearings for those convicted of drug-related crimes, even if they are longtime legal permanent residents. And as we discussed earlier, legislation in 1988, 1990, and 1996 expanded the number of drug offenses that are deportable, and the 1996 laws made drug offenses deportable retroactively.

Moncrieffe v. Holder (2013) became a test case for whether possession of a small amount of marijuana should constitute an aggravated felony, and thus be a deportable offense. Adrian Moncrieffe legally immigrated to the United States from Jamaica with his family when he was three years old. He was arrested in Georgia in 2008 for intent to distribute marijuana, although he was in possession of only 1.3 grams of the drug. Moncrieffe pled guilty and received a sentence of probation. Because this was defined as drug trafficking, though, ICE began removal proceedings against him in 2010, and this legal permanent resident and father of two US-citizen children was ultimately deported and faced a permanent bar against returning to the United States (Winograd 2012). In a 7–2 vote, the Supreme Court determined in April 2013 that, because the Controlled Substances Act contains provisions under which conviction for possession of marijuana could be a felony or a misdemeanor, it was unclear whether Moncrieffe's conviction under Georgia law constituted an aggravated felony. Accordingly, the Court opined that cases in which there was no remuneration and only a small amount of marijuana do not qualify as aggravated felonies, for which deportation is automatic, and Moncrieffe should be able to return to the United States to contest his deportation.[25]

In addition to drug offenses, officials with whom we spoke confirmed that very few immigrants with DUI convictions are exempted from deportation. Davenport (2006) reports that circuit courts across the country have differed in whether they defined DUI offenses as crimes of violence and thus subject to deportation under the 1996 laws. The Supreme Court sought to clarify this in *Leocal v. Ashcroft* (2004), holding that DUI is not a crime of violence. However, as Davenport argues, the Court construed the question before it quite narrowly. As a result, whether felony reckless driving, including reckless DUI, is a deportable offense remained a question even after *Leocal* was decided (Davenport 2006, 868). In recent years, cases involving DUI and other traffic violations have constituted a significant portion of deportation cases. Daniel Kanstroom reports that in FY 2010, "27,635 had been arrested for drunken driving, more than double the 10,851 deported after drunken driving arrests in the last full year of the Bush administration" (2012, 86, citing Gamboa 2011). In 2011, this number had increased to 35,927 (USICE 2011), and in 2012, 36,166 persons were deported with DUI convictions (ICE 2012c).

This strong stance reflects the general view that driving under the influence is a serious public safety concern. Media attention to traffic fatalities resulting from drunken driving by immigrants has further fueled this concern. In the immigration context, the "poster child" for DUI fatalities, as a former government official termed it, was a Benedictine nun who died in an accident involving an immigrant from Bolivia. Carlos Montinelly Montano, who had two prior DUIs and whose deportation had been deferred twice, was driving under the influence on August 10, 2010. Montinelly Montano swerved off the road, hit a guardrail, and then crossed into oncoming traffic. He hit another car head on, killing Sister Denise Mosier and injuring two other nuns. A reporter for the conservative *New American* stated, "If ever there were a case that deserved public airing about the federal government's adamant refusal to enforce immigration law, this one is it" (Kirkwood 2012). Policy analysts told us that there have been "enormous media campaigns" around this and a few other high-profile cases, resulting in "sort of a constant public pressure around it." Similarly, in discussing DUIs with another former DHS official, we were told that DHS simply could not ignore DUIs, as so doing would just be handing ammunition to congressional opponents of immigration reform.

Yet another factor that helps to explain the increase in DUI deportations is improved technology and data banks. In part, these improvements result from the Secure Communities program, which allows ICE and the FBI to share information. It is now far easier than in the past for local law enforcement officials to determine whether someone they have picked up is undocumented.

The exclusion of persons convicted of DUIs from consideration for prosecutorial discretion is made explicit in the Deferred Action for Childhood Arrivals policy. The USCIS website includes a page with Frequently Asked Questions about DACA. This website makes it very clear that immigrants with a felony, significant misdemeanor, or multiple misdemeanors are ineligible for DACA. Offenses involving domestic violence, sexual abuse or exploitation, burglary, unlawful possession or use of a firearm, drug distribution or trafficking, and driving under the influence are identified as felonies or significant misdemeanors, regardless of the sentence imposed (USCIS 2013b).

Deportations of Parents

Immigration advocates hoped prosecutorial discretion would result in fewer family separations. They have been sorely disappointed, with almost one-quarter of all deportations between July 1, 2010, and September 31, 2012, involving parents of US-citizen children (Wessler 2012a). This represents a 400 percent increase from the decade 1998 through 2007 (Wessler 2011b, 11; see also ICE 2012b; Wessler 2011a). Although prosecutorial discretion has succeeded in reducing these numbers from approximately 90,000 per year (23 percent of all removals) to 72,410 (19.6 percent of all removals) in 2013, the number of parents deported, and the consequences for families, are still enormous.[26]

A directive issued on August 23, 2013, by Morton's successor, Acting ICE Director John Sandweg, raised new hopes among advocates. This directive, entitled *Facilitating Parental Interests in the Course of Civil Immigration Enforcement Activities* (Sandweg 2013), includes many of the recommendations from the advocacy community. If fully implemented, it has potential to mitigate a number of the problems they have identified. We discuss this directive more fully in chapter 4.

CONCLUSIONS

Efforts to enact comprehensive immigration reform over the past decade have collapsed each time they have been proposed. Positions on immigration are highly polarized, perhaps especially within the US Congress. Yet there are close to 12 million unauthorized immigrants in the United States, many of whom have long-standing ties to their communities and children who are US citizens. This chapter focuses on the avenues available for managing these tensions. Prosecutorial discretion, we suggest, is one such mechanism, as it helps balance competing goals such as public safety and family unification. Yet as we have shown, the flexibility of discretion also makes it controversial, and vulnerable to political challenges.

With deportations since President Obama took office hitting the two-million mark by spring of 2014 and the House of Representatives refusing to consider the Senate's comprehensive immigration bill (S. 744), immigrant communities, advocates, and some members of Congress have called upon the Obama administration to use its executive authority to provide administrative relief (Congressional Hispanic Caucus, n.d.; Grijalva et al. 2013). Specifically, they ask that President Obama suspend deportations not only for those Dreamers eligible for DACA, but also for their parents and others who would be eligible for legalization under the Senate bill. As immigration advocate Ju Hong called out to President Obama during a speech in San Francisco in November 2011:

> "Mr. President, please use your executive authority to halt [deportations]. We agree that we need to pass comprehensive immigration reform, but at the same time, you have the power to stop deportations."
> "Actually, I don't," the president replied, "and that's why we're here." (Foley 2013)

The limits of discretion, thus, remain contested.

Our analysis suggests that the Obama administration's prosecutorial discretion policies have potential to make a real difference in the lives of immigrant communities by focusing detention and deportation resources on truly serious offenders. Yet in the eyes of the immigrant community and their allies this potential has not been met, and they are dismayed at the number of families still being separated because of immigration detention and deportation. One important exception is DACA—the Deferred Action for Childhood Arrivals program. Here, the administration went beyond prosecutorial discretion guidelines to adopt a formal process for safeguarding those who qualify. We turn next to the politics of DACA, efforts to enact the DREAM Act, and the lived realities of mixed status families.

CHAPTER 3

Legislative Inaction and Executive Action

Mixed Status Families, the Dreamer Movement, and DACA

Learning you are undocumented *"is the beginning of this process of the other, of otherness, and not having the same level of security as the people around you."*
—Lorella Praeli, advocacy and policy director, United We Dream
(interview, May 14, 2014)

It is like *"awakening to a nightmare."*
—Roberto Gonzales and Leo Chavez (2012)

DACA is life changing.
—Doris Meissner, former commissioner of the Immigration and
Naturalization Service (Interview with Doris Meissner, December 6, 2012)

From the perspective of the immigrant community and their advocates, Deferred Action for Childhood Arrivals (DACA) has been the high point of the administration of President Barack Obama. DACA responds to a clear need for safety from the threat of deportation and for work authorization for the 1.76 million young people who are potentially eligible. It was put into place quickly, and it lays out a fair and equitable policy with consistent procedures for eligible youth and young adults to apply to have their status "dacamented."

DACA provides recipients a temporary reprieve from the threat of deportation, but it is a far cry from comprehensive immigration reform. Like other forms of prosecutorial discretion, decisions are made on a case-by-case basis consistent with stated guidelines. Under DACA, the guidelines have been formalized into an orderly, efficient, and relatively transparent review process that occurs in a context outside of law enforcement. DACA also confers work authorization and paved the way for some states to permit dacamented youth to obtain driver's licenses and to pay in-state college tuition. Even more important, we suggest, DACA provides a model for broader systemic change designed to mitigate harm to youth that is squarely within the purview of the executive office.

We focus in this chapter on the policy process and political mobilizations leading up to DACA, preliminary data on who has benefited from the program and who has been left behind, and, for those receiving deferred action, we examine the transition from being undocumented to being "dacamented."

First, though, we address why DACA was so necessary. Drawing on our own interview data as well as findings of other researchers, we examine the challenges confronting families whose members have a mixture of legal statuses, their experiences of integration and marginalization in the United States, and the impact of a parent's undocumented status on child development, early education, and health outcomes.

We then consider the experiences of members of the "1.5 generation" as they enter adolescence and early adulthood. These youth, who came to the United States as young children, cannot easily be categorized as either first or second generation. They are themselves immigrants, and thus first generation, but they grew up attending US schools, speaking English, and knowing only the United States as home, like second-generation youth. In the past decade, these youth have boldly come out of the shadows to claim their place within American society. They have renamed themselves Dreamers, reminding themselves and others not only of the DREAM (Development, Relief, and Education for Alien Minors) Act, which would legally cement their status in the United States, but also of their dreams, their untapped potential, and the many contributions they can make to US society.

We conclude with an assessment of the reauthorization of DACA and efforts to expand the eligibility criteria to include those who would have been eligible for legalization under Senate Bill S.744 had it passed the House of Representatives in 2013. This discussion brings us back to our starting point: In the absence of legislative action, what structural mechanisms are available to mitigate harm to youth and families, and what structural mechanisms exacerbate harm?

GROWING UP IN MIXED STATUS FAMILIES

In 2010, 5.5 million children of undocumented parents resided in the United States. Eighty-two percent of them, or about 4.5 million youth, were born in the United States and are US citizens. The remaining one million children are themselves undocumented. Nearly half of these undocumented youth— about 400,000—have one or more siblings who were born in the United States. And if we count up everyone living in these "mixed status" families, the total reaches nine million (Taylor et al. 2011).

Strained Family Dynamics

When family members hold different legal statuses, tensions are inevitable. Parents who came to the United States to provide a better life for their children may be afraid to apply for the very social services that would benefit their children. Siblings see that a brother or sister has opportunities denied to them solely because of when and where they were born. These distinctions lead to complicated, and often strained, family dynamics and to what Cecilia Menjívar (2006) has called "liminal legality," a sense of being caught in between statuses (see also Menjívar and Abrego 2009; Menjívar and Kanstroom 2013).

An attorney told us of a situation in which a parent disclosed to the child that he was unlawfully present in the United States in the safety of her office. She said, "They had lied to him his entire life. I mean, those situations are heart wrenching, because then the child is resentful. 'Why did you do this to me and not my other siblings? Why do I have to be the one that's penalized while everybody else gets to live a real American life?' Yeah, it's definitely a serious problem." Similarly, a child advocate described the sometimes painful dynamics in mixed status families where (pointing in one direction) "Oh, you are the US citizen kid, you are the hope of our future" and (pointing in the other direction) "You're going to be the one that needs to go to work at a minimum wage job so there is money for your brother to go to college."

Regardless of their own immigration status, fear of a parent's deportation shapes early life experiences for children of undocumented parents. As Dreamer activist Lorella Praeli told us, when we tell our "story of self," people will talk of being young and of their mothers handing them a piece of paper and saying, "This is who you call if *la migra* comes for me." She continued,

"You're young, and you're supposed to feel like your mom is going to take care of you, and all of a sudden you are being told, 'I may not come back.' You don't quite understand why, but you are taught to understand that, it is the beginning of this process of the other, of otherness, and not having the same level of security as the people around you."[1] If a parent is deported, family dynamics may change again. For example, an immigration advocate we interviewed recounted a situation in which a boy's father had been picked up by Immigration and Customs Enforcement (ICE): "I mean, just going to school and coming back and knowing that your dad's been detained, or he's in Mexico now. Sometimes Mom's crying. I talked to one of the kids and his life changed completely. He says that he got older [snaps fingers] like that. Now he is in charge. His dad is out of the loop. These fears that Mom has, he can see that. . . . The only income they had was his dad, and now that's gone, so now he needs to start looking for a job."

Although members of one's family and community are important sources of information and resources, their efforts to be helpful can also create pressure. For instance, undocumented young adults in romantic relationships with US citizens may be pressured to marry before they feel ready, told it is their responsibility to marry and start the clock on applying for visas for parents or other family members at risk of deportation. Likewise, if the family is undocumented and the teenager needs a car to go to work or school, someone else must buy the car, and the family must go through this intermediary to arrange car loan payments and purchase insurance. We were told of a situation in which a car was rear-ended; when the family contacted the insurance company they learned that their monthly payment was actually covering the cost of their own car and three others. This is likely not an unusual occurrence, because undocumented immigrants may not know the typical rate for car insurance in the United States, and they are vulnerable to exploitation by others within their community as well as outsiders.

Regardless of the child's legal status, children suffer when their parents are undocumented. Children must often serve as language and cultural brokers for their parents, which can alter family dynamics in multiple ways. Their parents' status affects young children's development and early educational experiences, as well as their later educational and employment opportunities and their sense of belonging and political integration. We turn next to a discussion of these consequences and how they have shaped the Dreamer political movement and policy processes.

Child Development and Early Education

Child development experts refer to the paradox of immigrant risk and immigrant promise, noting that children of immigrants tend to outperform children of native-born parents, particularly in lower-income communities. This is most apparent during adolescence, when children of immigrants who have not dropped out of school tend to perform especially well. Very little, however, is known about how parents' *unauthorized status* affects the educational, health, and social development of children and youth.

Research by Carola Suárez-Orozco, Marcelo Suárez-Orozco, Hirokazu Yoshikawa, and others is starting to fill this gap (see, for example Suárez-Orozco, Suárez-Orozco, and Todorova 2008; Suárez-Orozco et al. 2011; Yoshikawa 2011; Yoshikawa and Kholoptseva 2012). They find that young children of undocumented immigrants show significantly lower levels of language and cognitive development compared with the children of legal immigrants and native-born parents, increasing their risk of lower school performance and an array of later problems, such as dropping out of high school, blocked mobility, and economic stagnation. Thus, at least some of the positive effects of being a child of immigrants wash out when the parents are undocumented.

Hirokazu Yoshikawa's three-year study of the lives of four hundred children born in public hospitals in New York City to Mexican, Dominican, and Chinese parents finds that US-citizen children's cognitive development and language skills are harmed by ages two and three if their parents lack a pathway to citizenship. These deleterious effects surface through multiple channels. Parents who are trying to avoid contact with government authorities are often afraid to enroll their children in preschool, child care subsidies, food stamps, and other programs that improve children's development. These programs may also require information about the parents' employment, and parents who do not have work authorization may be unable or unwilling to provide this information. Yoshikawa notes one element of the paradox experienced by undocumented parents: "The very same government that could deport them also offered resources to their citizen children, in the form of public supports for families in poverty. . . . But of course, children cannot walk into offices and enroll themselves in these programs. When parents are reluctant to do so, children cannot benefit. . . . Far too often, that paradox leads to citizen children of the undocumented being excluded from supports from which their peers with documented or citizen parents benefit" (2011, 53).

Immigrant families, and particularly families in which the parents are unauthorized, have high rates of living in poverty. This has repercussions for children's cognitive development, language skills, and early education. For example, many immigrant parents cannot afford preschool learning materials or stimulating childcare, and they may experience food and housing insecurities (Capps and Fix 2012; Chaudry et al. 2010; Yoshikawa 2011). Parents may also owe significant debts to smugglers, further reducing family finances. Although these costs tend to be highest for Chinese immigrants, they are common to everyone who employs a smuggler. Moreover, because undocumented workers typically receive minimal pay, they often must work long hours at multiple jobs. This leaves them with little time to spend with their children, and their absence has psychological and developmental consequences.

Parents without work authorization move frequently in search of work; as a result, their children may change schools several times. School mobility, in turn, has been linked to lowered school performance (Suárez-Orozco et al. 2011). Regardless of the child's citizenship status, having parents who are unauthorized immigrants limits the youths' and parents' engagement in school. Parents are less likely to interact with teachers or be active in school when they fear deportation (Suárez-Orozco et al. 2011). They may also be leery of allowing their children to participate in field trips or afterschool sports because this requires paperwork, including health forms, that parents fear could expose their status. As immigration attorney and scholar Nina Rabin reflected on findings of her study of the effects of Arizona's SB 1070 on youth:

> The level of stress that these immigrant families are under impacts children at school, and that's a real issue for the schools to contend with. A lot of teachers we spoke to, in the really small study that I did, talked about the fact that they saw an impact on kids' performance in school and their level of stress and anxiety as a result of all the stress about SB 1070, and what was going to happen with it. And . . . with the climate being so hostile, in general, I think it places a strain on schools to encourage participation from parents . . . to come to conferences or meetings, or just generally be involved with the kids' education.[2]

In contrast, another attorney who worked on immigration cases in an urban community center suggested that parents felt that schools were safe, but other institutions were not. She recounted:

> I think parents generally feel like schools are a safe zone. They can go to school. They can ask questions. They can be there. They feel a general safety. I don't think

that they think there's any raids going on at schools. . . . Outside of school, there's not many other venues. In fact, I've had a lot of parents who are scared to go to the hospital. A lot of parents are scared to take their kids to the hospital, they'll require somebody else to take their kids to the hospital because, if the child is documented, they're not going to the hospital because they're afraid that ICE or DHS [Department of Homeland Security] will be called to pick them up because they don't have proof of insurance for the child. Undocumented children, even more so.

Access to Health Care and Other Benefits

US-citizen children are eligible for state and federal health benefits. Their undocumented siblings, however, are not. As a result, some children within a family may receive very good health care, including regular preventative care, dental checkups, and access to mental health provisions if needed. Others in the family do not have access to this care. This means that if one child in a family has a serious medical condition, treatment is available at relatively low cost, while the same treatment is not available for the undocumented sibling because the family cannot afford the expense.

Yet often even those children entitled to benefits do not receive them because of their parents' fear of engagement with authorities. Immigration scholar David Thronson suggests, "Citizen children in mixed status families thus often take on the status of undocumented children" (2010, 247; see similarly Menjívar and Abrego 2012; Suárez-Orozco et al. 2011; Yoshikawa 2011). Immigrant and children's welfare advocates and attorneys recounted numerous such stories, noting that these fears were especially virulent during the period 2006 through 2011, when state and local governments across the country were enacting the most vehemently anti-immigrant laws.[3]

As one attorney suggested, "I think one of the issues that really bears following is the implication of all the state-level anti-immigration legislation on US-citizen kids' abilities to access benefits," noting that the climate of fear led to beliefs that medical and other social service providers would be required to report undocumented parents to authorities. Similarly, attorney Victoria López of the Arizona American Civil Liberties Union [ACLU] told us that such proposals, whether enacted into law or not, send ripples of fear throughout the community. Her agency conducted a series of information campaigns to make sure people knew

that first of all, US-citizen children still qualified for these specific benefits, and that even if you are undocumented, you can still access emergency medical services and certain other services under federal law, and that public benefit employees should still not be asking certain questions of you even if you are undocumented and you are trying to access services that you or your child are still eligible for. . . . Even the announcement of these kinds of bills, even if they don't become law, have such damaging impacts for families. . . . Because if the school can ask me about my kid's immigration status, well maybe the doctor can ask me about my kid's immigration status, and maybe all these other folks that you would go to to access public services also put me in a position where I could be, where I or my family member, could be arrested and deported.[4]

This comment from a local attorney is consistent with findings across the country and reflects parents' fears of exposing themselves to the risk of deportation and their concern that use of public resources, even for their citizen children, could make them ineligible for legalization under future legislation (Menjívar 2006, 2012; Thronson 2010; Van Hook, Landale, and Hillemeier 2013).

In addition, a growing number of researchers have documented the ongoing stress caused by children's fears that their parents, and in some cases the children themselves, could be deported at any time. This manifests in depression, anxiety, and separation disorders, and other mental health problems that affect children's development and educational success (see Boehm 2012; Brabeck and Xu 2010; Brotherton and Barrios 2011; Capps et al. 2007; Chaudry et al. 2010; Hagan, Eschbach, and Rodríguez 2008; Hagan, Rodríguez, and Castro 2011; Menjívar and Abrego 2012; Yoshikawa 2011).

UNDOCUMENTED TEENS AND YOUNG ADULTS

Throughout the K–12 years, schools provide a safe cocoon for undocumented students. In *Plyler v. Doe* (1982), the Supreme Court decreed that every child living in the United States has a right to attend public schools, regardless of his or her immigration status. The rationale for this decision was that the students were not responsible for their citizenship status because they had entered the country as young children. To deny these youth education, Justice Brennan argued, would create a lifetime of hardship and a permanent underclass, and would "not comport with fundamental conceptions of justice" (*Plyler v. Doe* 1982, 220; see also Gleeson and Gonzales 2012; Olivas 2012b; Shaina and Small 2013). As Justice Brennan recognized, the primary and secondary school years are formative to youths' later success. Shannon Gleeson and Roberto Gonzales take this a step further, arguing, "The result of the school socialization experience is to empower undocumented youth to dream big irrespective of their immigration status" (2012, 10).

By the end of high school, however, undocumented teenagers have come to realize tangible consequences of their immigration status. In most states they are unable to obtain driver's licenses. They do not have valid Social Security numbers and so cannot legally work. They are ineligible for federal financial aid for college, and in most states are not eligible for state-based aid. If they are also denied in-state tuition, the cost becomes exorbitant, making higher education, especially at four-year colleges and universities, an unattainable goal for many youth (Abrego 2011; Gonzales 2010).

Roberto Gonzales and Leo Chavez (2012) call this recognition "awakening to a nightmare." They draw upon Sarah Willen's (2007) concept of abjectivity to demonstrate how abjectivity and illegality combine to define and constrain daily life for members of the 1.5 generation. Based on interviews and surveys conducted in Orange County, California, they found that, as children, most undocumented youth "were not required to produce identification. It is only when they attempted to assert their position in the American mainstream that the importance of identification became essential. This was a defining moment, a challenge to their taken-for-granted identity and sense of belonging. This often came as a surprise to many who were unaware of their unauthorized immigration status or its significance" (2012, 262). Similarly, Abrego (2006, 2008, 2011), Coutin (2007), Gleeson and Gonzales (2012), and Menjívar and Abrego (2012) find that this awareness of not fully belonging, questioning of identity, and associated shame and stigma, typified the experiences of adolescents and young adults who came to the United States as young children. These feelings could materialize at any moment. For example, a Dream movement activist recalled going to the movies at age seventeen with a friend in her predominantly white neighborhood, only to be turned away because she did not have identification to get into the R-rated movie. In this way, everyday experiences can become defining moments, as youth "awaken to the nightmare" of what it means to be undocumented.

Following this awakening, Gonzales (2011) suggests that youth begin "learning to be illegal." With this change in their legal consciousness, youth come to recognize that they do not have all of the rights and privileges available to their friends, neighbors, and classmates. Their membership in American society is partial—what Susan Coutin (2000, 2003) calls the contradiction between one's physical and social presence in the country. These youth are not fully incorporated into American society, yet their sense of belonging is no greater anywhere else, as they grew up in the United States, speak English, attend US schools, and have always assumed that the United States was home.

Drawing on Cecilia Menjívar's (2006) work, Suárez-Orozco et al. assert that these youth are "in the untenable position of interminable liminality. These 'betwixt and between' residents of the United States attempt to perform symbolic and ritual claims of belonging without the corresponding reciprocal condition of acknowledgment" (2011, 444). Liminality theory, they suggest "becomes a particularly useful frame for understanding how their formal entry into adulthood is complicated—while, on the one hand, they are inevitably propelled into adulthood, on the other, they are denied participation in state-sanctioned rites of passage, like getting a driver's license or passport and facile entry into college or legally sanctioned passage into the work force" (2011, 454). Leisy Abrego (2011) adds that immigrants' understanding of this liminal legality, that is, their legal consciousness, is experienced differently depending upon their social position. Among the relevant factors contributing to undocumented immigrants' legal consciousness, Abrego assigns primary importance to the age at which they migrated and whether they are in the relatively protected confines of school or in the workforce. Even within the comfort of a college dormitory, the simple question, "Where are you from?," can raise anxieties and questions about what identity the undocumented college student can claim. As one respondent recounted to us, "I really struggled, I think it was the beginning of really owning what it means to be undocumented and not knowing how to deal with it."

Unauthorized teens and young adults must learn what they are not allowed to do, how to avoid drawing attention to themselves, and what to do if they are caught by immigration authorities. By paying attention to these changes in legal consciousness, we see "the effects laws have on migrants' day-to-day lives, revealing the ways in which undocumented persons experience inclusion and exclusion and how these experiences can change over time, in interactions with different persons, and across various spaces" (Gonzales 2011, 606; see also Menjívar and Kanstroom 2013). The ramifications can be huge. As Suárez-Orozco and her colleagues state, "Unauthorized young adults may find themselves tempted to secure false Social Security cards or driver's licenses in order to find work. . . . Once they dip their toes in the underground waters of false driver's licenses and Social Security numbers, they are at risk of getting caught in the undertow of a vast and unforgiving ocean of complex legal currents" (2011, 455).

Unlike their peers, for whom a minor delinquent act would likely result in probation or a diversion program, the results can be disastrous if undocumented teens get into trouble with school or legal authorities. Emily Butera of the Women's Refugee Commission told us this story of a boy she met in an Office of Refugee Resettlement (ORR) facility in Arizona:

> He told me that he was picking on a girl, but I think he was trying to flirt with her in that awkward way that adolescent boys do. In the process, he took her iPhone out of her hands. School security got involved and called the police. He was living in Maricopa County and the next thing you know, he has an ICE hold on him and he's placed into the ORR system. At the time I met him, he'd been away from his family for months. I can't even remember how long it was, but it was a significant period of time. This kid spoke perfect English. He'd been here since he was one. He didn't remember Mexico. He just wanted to go back to his school and back to his mom.[5]

For these youth, many of whom did not even know they were undocumented until their teenage years, the possibility of deportation is suddenly very real. They have no claim to relief, and in the blink of an eye they could be deported to a country they don't remember, where they don't speak the language or speak it poorly, and where they don't know anyone.

Going to College While Undocumented

One of the primary paths to success in US society is a college education. Yet for undocumented students to attend college requires that they "have squeezed their way through narrow openings along the educational pipeline" (Abrego and Gonzales 2010, 147). Not surprisingly, Passel and Cohn (2009) report that 40 percent of undocumented young adults ages 18–24 have not completed high school, compared to 8 percent of the general US population. Of those who did graduate from high school, only 49 percent went on to college, compared to 71 percent of the US population. These educational outcomes bifurcate, depending upon the age when the undocumented youth came to the United States. Three-quarters (72 percent) of the youth who came to the United States before age fourteen graduated high school, compared to 54 percent of their counterparts who arrived when they were age fourteen or older. And, 61 percent of those youth who came to the United States by age fourteen are in college or have attended college, compared to 42 percent of those who were fourteen or older when they arrived (Passel and Cohn 2009). Thus, youth who arrived in the United States as younger children have educational outcomes closer to the national norm.

Prior to about 2006, some states, such as Arizona, allowed their high school graduates to pay resident tuition, regardless of their immigration status. They were not eligible for financial aid, but at many public universities, the tuition was affordable. Then, in the wave of anti-immigrant legislative fervor sweeping the country, Arizona, Alabama, Colorado, Georgia, South Carolina, and Indiana passed legislation excluding previously eligible undocumented immigrants from paying resident tuition. This largely froze undocumented students out of a college education, especially because they could not obtain federal financial aid such as loans, grants-in-aid, or work study, or state-based aid in most of the country (Flores 2010; Gonzales 2010; Suárez-Orozco et al. 2011). Georgia went as far as to ban undocumented students from enrolling in selective state colleges and universities in 2010 if the institution "has not admitted all academically qualified applicants in the two most recent years" (National Conference of State Legislatures 2014a).

THE DREAM ACT, DACA, AND POLITICAL MOBILIZATION

Although some state and federal legislators have called for measures to curtail Fourteenth Amendment guarantees of citizenship for all those born within the United States (Preston 2011), there is also widespread sympathy for those youth who entered the country as young children and who have grown up calling the United States home. This sympathy has crystalized in the DREAM (Development, Relief, and Education for Alien Minors) Act, which would regularize the status of these young people and put them on a path to citizenship.

First introduced in April 2001 by Representative Luis Gutiérrez as H.R. 1582, the bill has been reintroduced almost annually. While it varies slightly from one iteration to another, the DREAM Act would make those youth within the ages specified (depending on the bill, this fluctuates between a minimum age of 12–15 and a maximum age of 30–35 at the time of the law's passage) eligible for conditional permanent residency status if they arrived in the United States before the age of sixteen, lived in the United States for at least five years prior to the date of the bill's enactment, graduated from a US high school or earned a GED or have been accepted to a US college or university, and have good moral character (that is, do not have a criminal record or pose a security risk, and are not inadmissible or removable on other grounds).

The DREAM Act has appeared in multiple formats. Some years, it has stood on its own; other years, it has been incorporated into comprehensive reform or attached to different bills, such as the 2007 Department of Defense authorization bill. It came very close to passing into law in 2007 and 2010. As Michael Olivas recounts:

> A little luck might have helped turn the corner: had Senator Kennedy been well, had Senator Specter not backed away, had the fires not broken out in California, had Senator Dodd not taken a walk, had there not been a presidential election looming, all for want of a nail. But all legislation, not just that affecting immigration, has to face the cards in play on the table at the time of its consideration. The 2010 efforts were also doomed, this time by extremely partisan politics and the crowded calendar of events in the 111th Congress, especially with voting just before and just after the midterm 2010 elections. (2012b, 81)

The Dreamer Political Movement

The youth who would have been eligible for regularized status under the DREAM Act have come to be known as "Dreamers." They have largely succeeded in their efforts "to capture the imagination of the American people and redefine what it means to 'be American'" (Aber and Small 2013, 88). They have developed a strong social movement and viable political presence and have "consciously and consistently established themselves and their movement as the heirs to the struggle for equality of Civil Rights era activists, staging provocative sit-ins and nonviolent protests, marches and acts of civil disobedience" (Aber and Small 2013, 89).

As occurs in every political movement, the various Dreamer organizations and their allies do not all agree on which tactics and strategies will be most effective in a specific context, or on the ideal end goals. These differences in perspectives manifest, for example, in disagreements as to whether and how far to align themselves with the Obama administration, whether pushing hard for executive action will derail possible legislation, and whether to publicly expose others who are undocumented.

Borrowing from the civil rights movement, Dreamers organized mass May Day marches in cities across the country in 2006, and in 2010 they enacted the Trail of Dreams—a 1,500-mile walk from Miami, Florida, to Washington, DC. They have also drawn from the experiences of the LGBT (lesbian, gay, bisexual, transgender) and Chicano movements. From the GLBT community, they learned the importance of putting a face and a human story to their experiences (Sharry 2013). They are coming out publicly so that neighbors, classmates, and coworkers are forced to recognize that they know many undocumented people, that they share similar values and goals, and they are not alien "others" to be ignored or condemned. Dreamers have staged events at border crossings and in schools, demonstrating the many ways in which they could, and in many cases already do, contribute to US society, and how their immigration status is a barrier to further contributions they might make. Some of the most visible examples include Jose Antonio Vargas, a Pulitzer Prize–winning journalist who came out as undocumented in 2011 in a *New York Times Magazine* story in an effort to advocate for passage of the DREAM Act, and groups of Dreamers dressed in graduation robes seeking entrée at border crossings in Arizona and Texas.

Lorella Praeli, director of advocacy and policy for the largest of the Dreamer organizations, United We Dream, told us that Dreamers learned five key lessons from earlier social movements. First, they came to recognize the importance of incremental change and small wins. Although comprehensive immigration reform is a primary goal, she said, if that does not seem likely at a given moment, then go for the narrower DREAM Act, and if that isn't possible, push for administrative relief, such as DACA. Second, they learned the power of personal narratives and oral histories. Third, as a youth-led movement, they quickly came to recognize the role that youth play in fighting for social change. Fourth, they realized that they have the agency to create change. Being young, she suggests, allows them to take risks. But they are also capable of taking charge, and they are not to be patronized or placated. And fifth, they have learned that when they come forward in public spheres as an organized group, they have the ability to confront power and demand action.[6]

Some immigrant rights advocates have at times been reluctant to push for a stand-alone DREAM Act out of concern that it would peel away the most popular element of comprehensive reform, making it even harder to enact the broader legislation they sought. When we asked Lorella Praeli how her organization chose between administrative and legislative strategies, she replied that she does not see them as exclusive strategies. Moreover, as a vibrant youth organization, she sees the movement as being in a good position to take the lead in making difficult, risky choices. As she recalled:

In 2010 the broad immigrant rights movement was focused on pursuing a CIR [comprehensive immigration reform] strategy. They wanted to push for comprehensive immigration reform. And we said no. Halfway through the year we realized it was actually not a winning strategy. We don't have the votes for CIR. We may not even have the votes for DREAM. But why don't we try to push for something narrow, and at that point compelling. Because this was a time . . . in 2010, Dreamers were just really beginning a lot of the forceful coming out. And I don't think before then people really knew or understood what it meant to be undocumented. Right? And so, we made the shift. We literally shifted the movement from CIR to DREAM. And then you had the lame duck vote. So then, DREAM fails December of 2010.

She continued, explaining the shift in the organization's focus from a legislative solution, which they determined was unlikely to succeed in the short term, to administrative relief:

And then we get together in Memphis Tennessee in March of 2011. And that is when we said . . . I mean in 2010 we had begun the conversations on administrative relief strategies, but we were still learning about it, we wanted to understand it. And in 2011 we said our primary target is going to be the administration. Based on our own political analysis, we don't believe that a permanent legislative solution is possible right now. And so, what is going to get us a win to build power, to give people temporary certainty and security, to resource our community so that they have the ability to work, and to feel safe from the threat of deportation? I mean, those were the things we were considering, and to continue to build, because if you are not making incremental wins, it is very hard. People need wins. And that is when we said we are going to shift, we are not going to focus on legislation, we are going to push the administration. That was early 2011.[7]

United We Dream and its allies decided on a multipronged strategy, highlighting thirty legal cases to educate others about undocumented youth. They developed the Education Not Deportation (END) campaign, and then in 2012 rebranded this as the "Right to Dream" campaign. As the 2012 elections approached, it was clear to movement activists that the Obama administration had failed to champion immigration reform. The Dreamers had helped to energize the Latino and youth electorates in 2008, and all they had seen from the Obama administration in return were more and more deportations. President Obama needed a strong Latino vote turnout in the 2012 elections, so movement activists asked themselves, How can we leverage this moment to get what we need? Although many on the left were concerned that the Dreamers were asking for too much, and this could risk the Obama presidency and result in a win for Republican candidate Mitt Romney, Dreamers used the opportunity to demand change and successfully pushed for administrative relief. As a former government official concluded, "The only reason there is DACA is because these kids stood up and they blocked and they chained and they put it in Obama's face and there wasn't any way he could win the election without doing something. Could he have done it the first time he promised to do it? Hell yes, he could have. He could have done a ton of different things."

On June 15, 2012, President Barack Obama, Secretary of Homeland Security Janet Napolitano, and Director of US Citizenship and Immigration Services (and since December 2013, Deputy Secretary of Homeland Security) Alejandro Majorkas announced the Deferred Action for Childhood Arrivals Program, with an effective date just two months later, on August 15, 2012.

DACA

Deferred action is not new, though prior to DACA it was best known as the mechanism that allowed late Beatle John Lennon to remain in the United States in the 1970s while Lennon and his wife, Yoko Ono, searched for Ono's daughter. Lennon had an earlier drug conviction in the United Kingdom, and this precluded his being granted residency (Olivas 2012a; see also Wadha 2010). Ironically, today a drug conviction is one of the key factors that would make an immigrant ineligible for DACA.

DACA is administered by the agency within DHS that is most supportive of immigrant integration, US Citizenship and Immigration Services (USCIS). The eligibility criteria have been well publicized, so those who are clearly not eligible do not need to risk coming out of the shadows and then being denied. DACA also has enormous symbolic value, providing a blueprint for how a legalization program might proceed under comprehensive immigration reform. For these reasons Tom Wong and his colleagues, among others, conclude, "The DACA announcement represented a victory for undocumented youth and their allies" (Wong et al. 2013, 1).

Yet as a policy analyst told us, because it is a form of prosecutorial discretion and does not have the force of law, "DACA can help, but it's the uncertainty, and PD continues that uncertainty" of whether a loved one can remain in the country indefinitely or whether the program will end and family members will once again be at risk for deportation.

Meeting the Eligibility Requirements

Approximately 1.76 million young people are potentially eligible for DACA (Batalova and Mittelstadt 2012). Of these, 72 percent, or 1.26 million, met the age requirement at the time DACA was announced, and another 28 percent were under age fifteen but could be eligible in the future. It is estimated that about 800,000 of the potential beneficiaries were enrolled in K–12 schools in 2012, another 390,000 had graduated from high school or had a GED, 80,000 had a college degree, and 140,000 were enrolled in college. The remaining 350,000 did not have a high school degree and were not enrolled in school, meaning they would need to re-enroll or complete their degrees or GEDs to qualify (Batalova and Mittelstadt 2012).

USCIS and community organizations have made substantial efforts to publicize eligibility criteria and resources. USCIS posted detailed Frequently Asked Questions on its website, and immigrant-serving community organizations and legal service providers have shared information and posted a host of resources online. The Immigration Advocates Network has collaborated with national partners to help advocates and applicants alike learn more about the program. In December 2013, they sent out emails to subscribers of relevant listservs announcing the availability of information through United We Dream's "Own the Dream" campaign website. These resources include an interactive online screening and application interview to help applicants learn about eligibility criteria and how to fill out the forms, a directory of free or low-cost nonprofit immigration legal services providers, another Frequently Asked Questions page that, when we visited it on May 12, 2014, included forty-seven questions, training materials, events, and news updates. The website also includes resources for advocates, such as guides for completing the application forms, strategies for proving that the education and residency requirements have been met, screening guides for other potential sources of relief (for example, Special Immigrant Juvenile Status), and tips for writing affidavits. The email from the Immigration Advocates Network also provided links to advocacy alerts, information regarding the availability of a driver's license in different states, and resources relevant to college attendance, including an interactive map showing which states provide some degree of tuition eligibility or financial aid for undocumented students.

Reflective of the technology-savvy generation to which DACA applicants belong, the Immigration Advocates Network, American Immigration

Council, and American Immigration Lawyers Association jointly created a free "Pocket DACA" app, available for Android and Apple smartphones and tablets, to help prospective applicants learn about DACA eligibility. Social media such as Facebook and Twitter supplement traditional media to provide information and to publicize success stories designed to inspire other eligible youth to apply (Wong et al. 2013). In addition, several universities and colleges, mostly in California, have opened Dreamers Resource Centers, which provide information about financial aid, internships, and other resources as well as academic and emotional support for undocumented college students. Finally, the Mexican consulate has been proactive in providing assistance to Mexican immigrants needing birth certificates, passports, and consular identification cards to establish their place and date of birth. Mexican consular offices across the United States have expanded their hours of operation, provided public outreach, and offered assistance to DACA clinics. Like the Pocket DACA app, the Mexican Consulate has also created a free micro-consular app, "MiConsulMex," for the Android and Apple platforms.

The availability of these resources has meant that very few individuals are applying for DACA unless they are clearly eligible. This may change if applicants with less clear-cut cases start coming forward in increasing numbers. With time, however, new sources of documentation are emerging. For example, in addition to school records, rent and utility receipts, vaccination records, and records confirming participation in a religious ceremony, we have heard stories of youth who have successfully used Facebook postings with GPS locators to show that they were in the United States on a given date.

DACA Implementation: Year 1 Applicant Demographics

Initial analyses of the first year of DACA's implementation have been conducted by Batalova et al. (2013), Singer and Svejlenka (2013), and Wong et al. (2013). Their analyses differ slightly in their estimates of the immediately eligible population because the true number of unauthorized immigrants living in the United States who were between the ages of fifteen and thirty-one on June 15, 2012, arrived in the United States before June 2007, were under age sixteen at arrival, and meet DACA's other requirements is unknown.[8]

Tom Wong and his colleagues estimate that 53.1 percent of the DACA population was immediately eligible to apply, and 61 percent of that population applied by August 15, 2013, the first anniversary of USCIS accepting DACA applications. Jeanne Batalova and her colleagues at Migration Policy Institute (2013) estimate that a slightly higher percentage, 57 percent of the potential applicants, were immediately eligible, and 49 percent of those currently eligible had applied by June 30, 2013. Their findings also vary a bit as a consequence of their differing sources. To supplement publicly available USCIS data, Singer and Svejlenka (2013) and Wong et al. (2013) obtained data on applicants from Freedom of Information Act (FOIA) requests to DHS. Their FOIA requests, and thus their findings, differ slightly, primarily in the time frame covered by the request.

Although the foreign-born noncitizen population in the United States is only 48.5 percent female, women are more likely to successfully apply for DACA. Wong et al. (2013) report that 51.2 percent of their FOIA sample was female, with men 1.4 times more likely than women to have their applications denied (see, similarly, Singer and Svejlenka 2013). The data also indicate substantial variation in application rates by national origin. Applicants in Wong et al.'s FOIA sample came from 205 countries, while Singer and Svejlenka's FOIA sample includes applicants from 192 countries. Both studies, however, report that more than 90 percent of the applicants were from Mexico, Central America, and South America, with the vast majority coming from Mexico. The far higher application rates from Latin Americans than from immigrants hailing from other parts of the world are generally attributed to the very effective outreach efforts by Spanish language media and immigrant-serving organizations in Latino, and especially Mexican, immigrant communities. There is also substantial intragroup variation within the Asian population, with the Korean ethnic media being far more proactive than the Chinese media (Wong et al. 2013, 31). This could explain the high application and approval rate for South Korean applicants. Immigrants from South Korean followed Mexicans, Salvadorans, Guatemalans, and Hondurans in the number of applications, and Batalova et al. report that 33 percent of the currently eligible Korean immigrants applied for DACA in its first year. The lowest application rates are from African immigrants, with only 1 percent of the applicants in Wong et al.'s FOIA sample migrating from Africa.

The average age of initial applicants in Wong et al.'s FOIA sample was twenty years old, and Singer and Svejlenka report that more than half (54 percent) were under the age of twenty-one. Advocacy organizations recognize that they did a better job of reaching young people than those at the older end of the eligible age range. As Allison Posner, advocacy director of Catholic Legal Immigration Network Inc. (CLINIC) told us, "The advocacy community did a great job reaching out to people in high schools and colleges. However, eligible applicants who are older and out of school, especially those with young families, did not receive as much outreach and thought that DACA did not apply to them. Some thought that because they had children of their own, they were ineligible. That's not true. Organizations are now trying to do a better job at reaching out to those who are eligible but have not applied and to dispel misconceptions about the program."9

Older applicants are more likely to be denied than younger applicants, probably because of the greater difficulty in establishing eligibility for people who have been out of school for a while and may have moved frequently. Although three-quarters of the applicants overall are from the western and southern parts of the United States (Wong et al. 2013), applicants over the age of twenty-one tend to live in states with long-established immigrant populations, such as California, Illinois, New York, and New Jersey (Singer and Svejlenka 2013). This may reflect the greater number of immigrant-serving community organizations, including churches and legal aid providers, in traditional destination sites.

Going from Undocumented to "Dacamented"

Gonzales, Terriquez, and Ruszczyk (2014) explore the initial implementation of DACA through analysis of a national Web survey of DACA recipients, the National Undacamented Research Project. This project surveyed young adults ages 18–32 who were eligible to receive DACA during the first sixteen months of its availability. They found that just over half of the survey respondents obtained driver's licenses, 59 percent obtained new jobs, 45 percent reported increased job earnings, and 21 percent obtained health care after receiving DACA. In addition, nearly half of the respondents opened their first bank accounts, and one-third obtained their first credit cards after becoming dacamented. As Gonzales and his colleagues conclude, "Although DACA does not address many of the problems these young people confront . . . its beneficiaries experienced greater access to U.S. institutions, enabling them to better achieve their potential" (2014, 1866).

One of the most important points of access is higher education. As of August 2014, sixteen states have classified at least some unauthorized immigrants as residents for tuition purposes if they graduated from state high schools, have two to three years residence in the state, and apply to a state college or university. Another two states permit undocumented students to pay in-state tuition through board of regents decisions, for a total of eighteen states providing residency status (National Conference of State Legislatures 2014a).

New resources are making a college education and even graduate school a reality for some Dreamers. In October 2013, Janet Napolitano, former DHS Secretary and now president of the University of California, pledged $5 million in university funds to assist the approximately 900 Dreamers attending University of California campuses (Rainey 2013). These funds will supplement state and campus-based financial aid made available to California's undocumented students under Assembly Bills 130 (2012) and 131 (2013). Soon after, former *Washington Post* owner Donald Graham created "TheDream.US," a $25 million fund to award full-tuition college scholarships to 1,000 students in the next year "who want to study nursing, teaching, computers, and business." With support from the Bill & Melinda Gates Foundation, Bloomberg Philanthropies, and the Inter-American Development Bank, among others, Graham created this fund because "I'm not wise enough to know what is the right immigration policy for the United States of America. . . . I know these students deserve a chance at higher education" (Layton 2014).

Washington Post journalist Pamela Constable has described DACA as "a legal ticket to self-respect." DACA recipients "are able to leave day-labor pools for steadier jobs in stores or trades and take part-time classes at community colleges. Their schedules are often grueling, but they are keenly aware that the clock is ticking. Every benefit DACA status confers—a Social Security card, a work permit, the right to drive—is valid for only two years." Again mirroring the complexities of mixed status families, however, she continues, "In the Washington region, immigration lawyers said that most of their DACA clients have parents who are in the country illegally. Some families have several children who received DACA; in other cases, one sibling was successful but another was too old or did not have enough documents to get approval" (Constable 2014).

What Is Next? Renewal of DACA

As DACA approached its second birthday, United We Dream and other advocacy groups called for substantial changes in "DACA 2.0," such as raising the maximum age of entry requirement from sixteen to eighteen, removing the age cap, including Dreamers in the labor force who do not meet DACA's education guidelines, making applying for DACA more affordable through a fee waiver for persons at or below 150 percent of the Federal Poverty Level, extending deferred action to five years rather than two, eliminating the "significant misdemeanor" bar and requiring that an individual must have served an aggregate of 365 days in order for their criminal record to bar them from the program, and granting DACA applicants parole-in-place if they are otherwise eligible for the program (Praeli 2014).

These requests were not met in the renewal of DACA, but Dreamers and other immigration advocates have continued to pressure the Obama administration to go beyond DACA, demanding that administrative relief be provided to all those who would have been eligible for legalization under S. 744, the comprehensive immigration reform bill passed by the Senate in 2013 (Praeli 2014; Preston 2014). As part of this strategy, Dreamers are actively engaging with key members of Congress whom they see as important allies in expanding administrative forms of relief.[10]

The Congressional Hispanic Caucus sent DHS Secretary Jeh Johnson a confidential draft memorandum, which was leaked to, and published by, the *Washington Post* on April 4, 2014. Reminiscent of the history of the leaked memorandum authored by Denise Vanison, Roxana Bacon, Debra Rogers, and Donald Neufeld suggesting the use of deferred action in 2010 (Vanison et al., n.d.), this memorandum begins by saying:

> The President shared with us in a recent meeting that he has asked you to do an inventory of the Department's current practices to see how it can conduct enforcement more humanely within the confines of the law. Below are several policy options that offer affirmative administrative relief within the purview of the law with the goal of family unity. In addition, we have also included recommendations on enforcement reforms that DHS can implement to better focus its resources on targeting those who pose a serious threat to our communities and reflect a more humane approach to immigration enforcement." (Congressional Hispanic Caucus, n.d., 1)

Among other recommendations, the Hispanic Caucus calls for DHS to protect parents and siblings of DACA recipients, as well as parents of US citizen or legal permanent resident children, against deportation, stating that this would help keep families intact and reduce the number of children in foster care. The caucus memo recommends that these family members be allowed to apply for a work permit, and for extension of humanitarian parole to immediate family members if they have been deported. The memo advocates for a review of ICE's civil enforcement priorities and of the use of prosecutorial discretion, termination of Secure Communities and the 287(g) programs, and limiting the use of detention to the highest-priority cases.

Yet consistent with the zigzag progress that has bedeviled immigration reform, in late May 2014, President Obama asked DHS Secretary Johnson not to make results of his review of administrative options public until Congress recessed in August, so as not to jeopardize last-ditch efforts to pass legislation in the House. Similarly, he asked the Department of Defense to delay a plan to allow persons granted relief under DACA, and who have specific language or medical skills, a path to citizenship by serving in the military (Kuhnhenn 2014). As the *Washington Post* reports, "The White House is concerned that Republicans would balk if the administration takes unilateral action to stem the deportation of undocumented immigrants, ending any slim remaining hopes of a legislative compromise" (Nakamura 2014). By late summer, House Republicans had made clear that a legislative compromise was not in the works. Rather, they promised impeachment proceedings if President Obama took unilateral action that they felt exceeded his authority.

Perhaps in an effort to strengthen President Obama's resolve, on September 3, 2014, more than 130 law professors sent a letter to the president reaffirming the constitutional basis for prosecutorial action, and for formalizing that policy decision through procedures such as deferred action and work authorization (Wadhia et al. 2014). Three days later, the president announced that he would delay taking executive action on immigration until after the midyear elections, as requested by fellow Democrats facing difficult contests. The delay did not achieve its objectives, as Democrats lost the Senate as well as the House. Finally, on November 20, 2014, President Obama announced his intent to pursue executive action to expand the deferred action program to shield five million unauthorized immigrants from deportation and provide them with work authorization, redefine priorities for ICE, and streamline the visa application process.

COMPLICATIONS AND CONTRADICTIONS

Focusing our lens on mixed status families, and especially the dreams and nightmares of the 1.5 generation, brings the complications and contradictions of contemporary immigration policy in the United States into sharp relief. We have seen multiple attempts to pass comprehensive immigration reform in the past decade. Whenever those attempts appeared at risk of failing, immigration advocates and their supporters in Congress and the White House tried for the more modest DREAM Act because there was more support for young people who came to the United States as young children than for their parents. Although some feared that the DREAM Act would peel off support from comprehensive legislation, others felt whatever might work should to be tried.

Early in the Obama administration, there was talk of what forms of administrative relief might be available to the executive branch. Deferred action was proposed, but instead the administration chose to demonstrate that it was taking a tough approach, hoping that so doing would make comprehensive reform more feasible. Instead, two million immigrants were deported under the Obama administration's watch, and the advocacy community began calling President Obama "deporter in chief." An organized coalition of Dreamers and their allies confronted the Obama administration with the necessity of offering administrative relief if they were to help get out the vote in the 2012 election. This strategy was successful, and half a million young people have been granted deferred action and permission to work in the United States. Yet close to eleven million undocumented immigrants still do not have such relief, and mixed status families are now further complicated, with some family members having US citizenship or legal permanent residency, others who are dacamented having a smaller set of privileges, and still others remaining undocumented. Within this shifting context, we next review the key structural mechanisms that have exacerbated harm for mixed status families and members of the Dreamer generation, and those that mitigate harm.

STRUCTURAL MECHANISMS THAT EXACERBATE HARM

The educational and developmental ramifications for children of their parents' undocumented status are becoming increasingly clear. In part, this is due to families living in poverty and to the long hours that most undocumented immigrants work, often at multiple jobs. Compounding the problems faced by immigrants with legal status, who may also struggle with finding work that pays well, undocumented parents often have debts they must pay to smugglers, and they are vulnerable to exploitation by unscrupulous employers who may not pay them for a job completed. This translates into children not having access to good preschools, resources that might further their development, or even to their parents' time and energy. The multiple barriers to health care and to educational and social services further deprive citizen children of undocumented parents from services to which they are entitled. When children cannot access these services, their development is stymied, avenues for success are systematically closed off to them, and they are not able to contribute to society to the extent they might if they had received these benefits.

The exclusion of undocumented students from federal financial aid and from state-based aid in the majority of states is another structural barrier to full integration of the 1.5 generation in American society. When students who grew up in the United States, attending local schools for most of their life, suddenly realize that they are not considered residents of the state where they live, this has profound consequences for their sense of belonging. It also has serious financial implications. Having to pay nonresident tuition and lacking access to financial aid in most states means that higher education becomes an unattainable dream for youth who must watch from the sidelines as their friends, neighbors, and, in many cases, younger siblings go on to college.

Finally, exclusion of "dacamented" youth from the Affordable Care Act, while perhaps politically expedient, means that Dreamers must continue to struggle to pay for basic medical and dental care and reminds them of the liminality of their status—that they are not seen as fully American.

STRUCTURAL MECHANISMS THAT MITIGATE HARM

In the absence of comprehensive immigration reform and even its more limited variant, the DREAM Act, Deferred Action for Childhood Arrivals has been the primary mechanism for reducing harm for members of the 1.5 generation. DACA represents a major victory for immigration advocates. Nevertheless, it has limitations. Chief among them is that DACA is a temporary status that must be renewed regularly. The program was probably limited in this fashion to make it harder for opponents to accuse the Obama administration of conducting an end run around congressional authority to legislate immigration law. As former INS Commissioner Doris Meissner told us, "That makes it uncertain and costly for beneficiaries because they must pay an application and fingerprint fee to obtain renewal of their status. Still, in the absence of immigration reform or any other avenue for legal status, DACA is life changing. It provides protection from deportation and the ability to work legally. Depending on state laws, it can also permit going to college and getting a driver's license. There are major pluses for young people."[11]

One of the key structural dilemmas when DACA was being developed in the summer of 2012 was how best to define its educational requirements.

Advocacy organizations and immigration policy centers worked closely with government officials to define these requirements so as to include youth who may have dropped out of school, but who could now return and gain their diplomas or GEDs. The revised definition of being enrolled in school on the date when you apply for DACA—regardless of whether you had previously quit and now were returning to school—brings an estimated 350,000 more students out of the shadows and into the DACA eligibility pool (Batalova and Mittelstadt 2012). In addition, it gives families a reason to keep older children in school rather than allowing, or encouraging, them to drop out of school to take care of younger siblings while the parents work, or to go to work themselves to help support the family.

In his analysis of *Plyler v. Doe* and the education of undocumented children in the United States, Michael Olivas (2012b) describes the DREAM Act as "Doe goes to college." As federal law, the DREAM Act would have facilitated college education for eligible undocumented students nationwide by enabling them to obtain federal loan, grant, and work-study funding. DACA is not able to go this far. Yet as we discussed in this chapter, as of spring 2014, eighteen states have extended in-state tuition, and in some cases state-based financial aid, to undocumented immigrants who meet eligibility criteria, either through state legislation or through board of regents decisions (National Conference on State Legislatures 2014a). Thus, to borrow from Michael Olivas, Doe can more readily go to college, at least in some states.

DACA's most obvious benefit, of course, is to keep youth safe from deportation. But the increased numbers of undocumented youth who will now graduate from high school because of how the educational requirements were written, and who will continue on to college because of DACA and the state laws enacted in support of this program, are also tremendously important means of mitigating harm to youth and families.

In DACA's wake, there has been substantial state-level legislation permitting dacamented youth to obtain driver's licenses. In places where public transportation is limited, DACA's work authorization is seriously constrained without permission to drive. As of May 2014, eleven states and the District of Columbia allow undocumented immigrants to obtain driver's licenses, and another three states issued driving privileges to certain immigrants (National Conference of State Legislatures 2014b).

The coordinated engagement among government officials, nonprofit advocacy groups, Dreamer networks, local community organizations, and the media has been critical to informing relevant communities about DACA, including who is eligible, how to demonstrate residency and the other requirements, and how to apply. The degree of support across agencies and the speed with which those resources were engaged has been impressive and is in large part responsible for the early success of the program.

The expansion of deferred action in President Obama's November 2014 executive action will potentially affect five million people. As Dreamers had hoped, it removes the age cap for DACA, includes youth brought to the United States before January 1, 2010, and extends relief for three years at a time rather than two. It will go far to reduce family separations, offering deferred action and work authorization for parents of US-citizen or legal permanent resident children who have lived in the United States for at least five years and meet other eligibility requirements. Although Dreamers were disappointed that the administrative relief will not extend to their parents unless they have siblings who are citizens or legal residents, this carefully crafted expansion of deferred action illustrates that DACA was a viable vehicle for administrative reform and could serve as a blueprint for future forms of relief (Cavendish et al. 2014).

CONCLUSIONS

This chapter focuses on the everyday experiences of undocumented youth and the children of undocumented parents. Millions of Americans live in mixed status families, with siblings encountering what may be vastly different opportunities depending upon where and when they were born. When parents are undocumented, the whole family lives in the shadows. The next generation suffers, because US-citizen children do not receive the educational, health, and other social benefits they are due. When teenagers realize they are undocumented, they see their options suddenly cut off. The implications for civic society are potentially huge, as large numbers of youth are made to feel that they do not really belong.

The Dreamer social movement has brought these teenagers and young adults out of the shadows and into the streets, where they are claiming the rights and privileges of membership in the society they have always called home. Fed up with congressional gridlock, they have pressured President Barack Obama to use the power of his pen and to enact administrative forms of relief so that their parents, siblings, and friends can live, work, and go to school without fear of deportation. On November 20, 2014, President Obama used his power and took such action.

We turn next to the ramifications of parental detention and deportation, and of life under the threat of deportation. As we discuss in chapter 4, the intersection of the immigration system, the child welfare system, and at times the criminal justice system, can have devastating effects on youth and their families.

Families Torn Apart

Parental Detention and Deportation

The immigration detention and deportation process can move really, really, quickly and the child welfare process, in a lot of cases, moves slowly. In addition to the systems not communicating with each other, parents are caught between working on these two timelines that are out of alignment.

—Emily Butera, Women's Refugee Commission (interview,
    February 13, 2012)

Where the parent's alienage trumps the rights of the citizen child to parental care and companionship at home, citizenship loses all effective meaning for children.

—Jacqueline Bhabha (2014, 8)

One of the central contradictions of US immigration law concerns the value placed on the family. Emblematic of this contradiction is Congress's continued reluctance to ratify the UN Convention on the Rights of Children, even though the United States played a central role in developing the Convention and Madeleine Albright signed it on behalf of the United States in 1995. Article 9 of the Convention states, "A child shall not be separated from his or her parents against their will, except when competent authorities subject to judicial review determine, in accordance with applicable law and procedures, that such separation is necessary for the best interests of the child." Moreover, Article 23 of the International Covenant on Civil and Political Rights, which the United States has ratified, provides that "the family is the natural and fundamental group unit of society and is entitled to protection by society and the state." Yet the best interests of the child and family unification are at best secondary considerations when decisions are made to detain and deport parents.

Legal scholar David Thronson describes the approach to children in immigration law in terms that are far from the language of the UN covenants. He states, "U.S. immigration law has a distinctive veneer of family friendliness that creates an appearance of advancing children's interests and general notions of family unity.... Upon closer inspection, however, immigration law's limited and often antagonistic approach to children is revealed. The failures of immigration law to advance, or in most instances even consider the interests of children, place it far from mainstream values and legal conceptions regarding children" (Thronson 2013, 53). Similarly, Wendy Young, director of Kids in Need of Defense (KIND) told us, "Immigration law wasn't written with kids in mind, or family unity in mind necessarily, with the exception of the family-based visa system."[1] Under this system, family members receive a significant proportion of the visas distributed each year, and children may obtain what are known as "derivative" visas when their parents meet certain qualifications, such as for asylum. The converse does not hold, however, as US-citizen minor children are not eligible to apply for visas for their parents.

This chapter continues our discussion of immigration policy and families. We are particularly interested here in understanding what happens when two competing goals—family reunification and best interests of the child on the one hand, and a law-and-order approach that prioritizes public safety and punishing law violators on the other—come into conflict, resulting in parental detention and deportation, and how this compounds difficulties for mixed status families.

As we discussed in chapter 2, deportation numbers have risen dramatically since the early 2000s, affecting unprecedented numbers of families. Immigrants and advocacy organizations hoped the election of President Barack Obama would result in fewer family separations, but they have been sorely disappointed. Although deportations of parents of US-citizen children started to decrease in 2013, parental deportations continue to wreak havoc on families across the country. When a parent is detained and, in many cases, deported, family members experience great fear and uncertainty. The most immediate concerns are, Is the parent all right? Where is the parent? Will he or she be deported? Where, and with whom, will the children live? Can they see or talk with their parent? The convergence of the *immigration, criminal justice,* and *child welfare* systems complicate answers to these questions, creating a rippling set of ramifications for children and families.

In the best-case scenario, the children continue to live with another parent, an older sibling, or a relative who takes good care of them, and they stay in contact with the detained or deported parent. Even this option is problematic, however, as children are separated from their parents with no hope of reunification in the near future. In other cases, the children may end up living with an abusive parent or in the foster care system. The parent(s) may ultimately have their parental rights severed and, depending largely on the child's age, he or she may be adopted, go from one foster care placement to another, or become homeless.

In other cases, children follow their parents, moving to the parent's country of origin. Just considering Mexico, about 300,000 US-born children moved to Mexico with their parents between 2005 and 2010 (Passel, Cohn, and Gonzalez-Barrera 2012). The child or teen may not know the language or customs of his or her parent's homeland and may not receive educational or other opportunities comparable to what is available in the United States. The youth may well return to the United States later, less prepared to succeed than would have been the case had the family been permitted to remain in the country. As a representative of a Central American embassy told us, "There are entire communities of US citizen kids in [country]. They have US passports, and we should expect that someday they'll come back to the US."

HOW DID WE GET TO THIS POINT?

In fiscal year (FY) 2012, spending for the US Customs and Border Patrol (CBP) and US Immigration and Customs Enforcement (ICE), including their enforcement technology initiatives, totaled more than $17.9 billion. This was nearly fifteen times the amount spent by their predecessor agency, the Immigration and Naturalization Service (INS), when the Immigration Reform and Control Act was enacted in 1986 (Meissner et al. 2013, 2). Funding for enforcement programs that target noncitizens arrested or convicted of criminal offenses, such as the Criminal Alien Program, 287(g), the National Fugitive Operations Program, and Secure Communities, grew from $23 million in FY 2004 to $690 million in FY 2011 (Meissner et al. 2013, 7). One consequence of this ramp-up of immigration enforcement, or what Meissner and her colleagues call "the rise of a formidable machinery," has been a massive increase in parental detention and deportation (see similarly Ewing 2014).

According to DHS, 108,434 parents of US-citizen children were removed from the United States between 1997 and 2007. Thirty-seven percent of these parents returned after their first removal and subsequently were deported on other occasions during the ten-year period, bringing the total number of removals of parents of US-citizen children to 180,466 (US Department of Homeland Security 2009, 4). This is likely an undercount, though, because data on family members were not systematically collected and some deportees may not have reported that they had children, fearing that they could be putting their children at risk.

In addition to undocumented immigrants, the 1996 laws also placed legal permanent residents (LPRs) at risk of deportation for current or past criminal offenses. A report issued jointly by the University of California, Berkeley and the University of California, Davis Law Schools, *In the Child's Best Interest?* estimates that 103,000 children, 86 percent of whom were US citizens, were affected by the deportation of a parent who had LPR status during the period from April 1997 to August 2007 (University of California 2010, 4).

Many of the removals occurred between 2005 and 2007, when large-scale workplace and home raids resulted in the sudden arrest, detention, and deportation of large numbers of parents. The raids had devastating effects on children and on the broader communities, as schools, churches, and neighbors were left to sort out who would care for the children, some of whom were nursing infants. Two key reports by the Urban Institute address that era. *Paying the Price: The Impact of Immigration Raids on America's Children* (Capps et al. 2007) and its follow-up, *Facing Our Future: Children in the Aftermath of Immigration Enforcement* (Chaudry et al. 2010) were based on interviews with arrested parents or their spouses and community members, including teachers, social workers, attorneys, consular officials, public officials, and staff at community organizations. The researchers sought to examine the immediate and short-term effects of parental arrest, detention, and deportation on 190 children in eighty-five families in six locations across the country. They report a wide range of effects, including family separation (in some cases, children went with one or both parents to the parents' countries of origin; in others, the children remained in the United States, separated from one of their parents), family economic hardship (including job loss, housing instability, and food scarcity), and behavioral changes in children (see also Golash-Boza 2012; Human Rights Watch 2007; Kanstroom 2012).

In response to the devastation they caused, one of the initial reforms the Obama administration put into place was to replace workplace raids with "paper raids" through which employers are audited and fines imposed if they are found to have hired unauthorized workers. The transition to paper raids was lauded as a positive step by those working with immigrant communities, because it reduced the trauma of children coming home from school to find that their parents had been arrested and taken to a detention center. However, the number of parents of US citizens deported continued to increase, even with cessation of large-scale workplace raids.

Many, if not most, deported parents attempt to reenter the United States, often being removed multiple times in an effort to reunite with their families. The most recent data on deportees' intentions to return to the United States were collected by the National Center for Border Security and Immigration at the University of Arizona. In the summer of 2012, they surveyed 1,000 Mexican nationals apprehended in the Tucson center (Grimes et al. 2013). Their data support what we heard from advocates and attorneys: that separated parents and children will seek to reunite as quickly as they can. Nine percent of the respondents reported having at least one child in the United States. Of these, 16 percent said they would attempt to reenter the United States within seven days, and 58 percent said they would try again at some point in the future. Another 5 percent of the sample had at least one parent in the United States; 14 percent of these respondents said they would attempt to reenter the United States in the next seven days, and 62 percent anticipate reentering in the future. More generally, 24 percent of the respondents cited family reunification as their reason for seeking to enter the country (2013, 9).

Similarly, Human Rights Watch reports that in districts such as Los Angeles and San Diego, where reentry cases predominate, defense attorneys estimate that 80 to 90 percent of their reentry clients have US citizen family members. When they asked a judge in Las Cruces, New Mexico, how often he sees illegal reentry defendants with US citizen family members, he replied that this occurs in 30 to 40 percent of his cases, adding, "It's an everyday occurrence" (Human Rights Watch 2013, 50).

Several defendants told Human Rights Watch they had reentered the country because their deportation had been so hard on their children, with impacts ranging from "depression and decreased performance in school to abusive conditions that could have led them to end up in the custody of the state" (2013, 54). Others felt they had to return because of "the pain their deportation had brought on their parents and siblings" (2013, 55). Human Rights Watch reports, for example, on situations in which a man's son died and he could not return to the United States for the funeral, a man whose wife was dying of cancer and he was trying to get back to help arrange for their oldest daughter to gain legal custody of her younger siblings, and parents who are seeking to regain custody of their children or who fear losing custody (2013, 54–56).

Immigration attorney and scholar Aryah Somers interviewed a number of parents who were deported to Guatemala, some of whom brought their children back with them, while others left the children in the United States. The parents who left their children behind, she said, were "very conflicted. If they knew the kids were okay, they might be all right, but if they don't know where the kids are, they plan to remigrate immediately." Unaccompanied youth left behind in the United States when their parents are deported are vulnerable to abuse and abandonment, and are "subject to systems of dependency they don't understand." Yet, as Somers points out, when deported parents bring their children back to their homeland with them, they confront the same situation that led them to leave in the first place, adding, "What to do then? Remigrate and leave the kids in Guatemala, so they can send money home? Or stay with them, and feel like they have failed?"[2]

PARENTAL DETENTION, PROSECUTORIAL DISCRETION, AND CRIMINAL HISTORY

If prosecutorial discretion was supposed to help keep families intact, why are so many parents of US-citizen children still being deported? One answer, as we saw in chapter 2, is that some ICE field officers ignore the policy, assuming they can outwait political appointees who come and go. A second possible answer is that all or most of these parents have committed serious crimes, and public safety requires that they be deported. Conversely, a third explanation is that the number of serious crimes did not increase, but rather the 1996 laws and ICE policy definitions expanded the net to include a much greater percentage of the noncitizen population.

The 1996 Illegal Immigration Reform and Immigrant Responsibility Act (IRIRA) and Antiterrorism and Effective Death Penalty Act (AEDPA) built upon the Anti-Drug Abuse Act of 1988 to significantly increase the number of offenses for which noncitizens are deportable. These laws redefined "aggravated felonies" to include fifty different crimes, some of which are quite serious; others are rather minor misdemeanors and not felonies at all.[3] Moreover, these provisions made all noncitizens—legal permanent residents as well as unauthorized residents—vulnerable to detention and deportation for violations of criminal law, and the provisions apply retroactively. This means, for example, that when a legal permanent resident is stopped for a minor driving violation and a criminal history check shows that he or she was convicted years earlier for an offense that was not considered an aggravated felony at the time, but is now, or has a warrant for nonappearance on a previous low-level charge, the person may be subject to deportation. In addition, Department of Homeland Security policy decisions to expansively define violations of public safety to include most DUI (driving under the influence) offenses enlarged the pool of persons at risk of deportation. Compounding this redefinition, the Secure Communities and 287(g) programs incorporated into the 1996 laws further widened the net by engaging local and state law enforcement in immigration control.

The official data on the rationales for parental deportations are very limited, and data definitions are inconsistent. ICE statistics released to Congress for the first six months of 2011 indicate that 74 percent of the 46,486 parents of US-citizen children deported during this period had been convicted of a crime. The *Arizona Republic* adds that another 17 percent had either been previously deported or had failed to comply with deportation orders and were now fugitives (González 2012). ICE returned to Congress to report on 2013 parental deportations, stating that in the first half of calendar year 2013, 91 percent of the parents of US citizens who were removed from the interior and 74 percent of the parents removed at the border had previous criminal convictions (United States Immigration and Customs Enforcement [USICE] 2014a). For the second half of 2013, ICE did not distinguish between interior and border arrests, stating only that 86 percent of the parents of US citizens who were removed during this period had a previous conviction (USICE 2014b). These reports do not specify the type of crime for which parents had been convicted. Yet as we showed in chapter 2, a substantial number of deportations resulted from relatively minor offenses which, had the person not been an immigrant, would have led to a short jail sentence, fine, or probation.

Considerable attention has focused on parents deported because of drug possession and driving under the influence. Referencing the media attention to Sister Denise Mosier, the Benedictine nun who died in an accident involving an undocumented drunk driver, an immigration attorney told us, "ICE got skewered on DUI, they are not taking that chance again." Indeed, a senior DHS official told us that they have to be concerned with public safety and "see DUI as a *serious* public safety offense," stressing the word *serious*. When asked how they would weigh a DUI against having US-citizen children in making deportation decisions, this official responded, "Things are weighted. The weight of a DUI is very negative; you would need a lot of positives to counter that." For instance, this official continued, if the DUI was twenty years ago and there was nothing more recent in the person's criminal history, then there would be good reason to let the person remain in the country if he or she was the parent of a US-citizen child.

PARENTAL INCARCERATION AND PARENTAL DETENTION: COMPARING IMMIGRATION DETENTION WITH WHAT WE KNOW ABOUT THE EFFECTS OF PARENTAL INCARCERATION ON CHILDREN AND FAMILIES

There is a growing literature on the effects of parental incarceration on children and families. This literature addresses mental health and behavioral issues, such as substance abuse, aggression, and delinquency (Hagan and Dinovitzer 1999; Murray and Farrington 2008; Rodriguez, Smith, and Zatz 2009; Tasca et al. 2014; Wakefield and Wildeman 2013; Wildeman 2010), as well as difficulties associated with the economic hardships, residential mobility, and family instability that often accompany parental incarceration (Arditti 2012; Tasca, Rodriguez, and Zatz 2011; Turanovic, Rodriguez, and Pratt 2012; Western and Muller 2013). The parental incarceration literature suggests further that trauma and sense of loss are exacerbated when the parent's arrest and incarceration are unanticipated, disruptive, and unexplained, and when visitation is difficult because parents are held in locations far from their children (Arditti 2012; Comfort 2008).

Many of these same problems are identified in the small but growing literature on immigration detention. Moreover, as Emily Butera of the Women's Refugee Commission told us, "there is no requirement that ICE allow a parent to make a phone call to make care arrangements for her children. Nobody ever says in any formalized way, 'Do you need to make a phone call to make arrangements for your child or for your dependent?' Occasionally, officers make ad hoc humanitarian decisions to do those sorts of things, but the agency doesn't require it."[4] The immigration literature further establishes that the fear that detention will result in deportation, and the uncertainty as to what a parent's deportation will mean for family members, adds to the trauma experienced by children. This uncertainty also exacerbates the structural difficulties that parents and other caregivers encounter as they attempt to keep the family intact.

Points of Similarity: Economic and Psychological Effects

According to Syracuse University's Transactional Records Access Clearing-house (TRAC 2013a), 95 percent of persons held in immigration detention are men. Many are the primary sources of economic support for their families. Lindsay Marshall, then-director of Arizona's Florence Immigrant and Refugee Rights Project told us, "There is a huge impact on children, communities, [and] schools when the dad is taken out of the picture and they are all of a sudden needing to be on food stamps and public assistance, and now mom needs to be in a shelter, where before she was in an apartment, they were fine, they could put food on the table. So the impact of just removing one person from a family [is huge]."[5] A colleague who joined our conversation added, "The ability to pay child support, that is a big one too."

In addition to the similar economic effects, the literature on parental detention in many ways mirrors what is known about the psychological effects of parental incarceration. Chaudry et al. (2010), for example, report considerable behavioral changes among children whose parents were detained or deported, including frequent crying, loss of appetite, sleeplessness, separation anxiety, and increased fear and anxiety generally. The most detrimental effects were found among children who saw their parents arrested at home. They experienced the greatest changes in sleeping and eating patterns, were more likely to exhibit multiple behavioral changes, and expressed much higher levels of fear and anxiety than did children whose parents were arrested outside the home.

Points of Difference: Fears That the Parent Will Be Deported

Although the literature on parental incarceration speaks primarily to the difficulties and challenges created by a parent's imprisonment, there is also recognition that in certain cases, particularly when parents are violent or have serious drug or alcohol problems, their incarceration can be a relief and reprieve for family members (Turanovic et al. 2012). This likely occurs in some instances involving immigration detention, but it appears to be much more unusual and is not an issue that is raised in the scholarly or advocacy literature.

On the contrary, organizations working with immigrants regularly report on situations in which an abusive partner who is a citizen or permanent resident uses the threat of calling ICE as part of his arsenal to control his partner. Then, if the mother is detained, the children may be left with the abusive parent because the mother never dared to report his abuse. And while some deportation cases result from crimes involving drugs, these are typically minor offenses not directly comparable to cases of serious, long-term substance abuse in the parental incarceration literature.

Prosecutorial discretion in immigration permits consideration of the effects of deportation on US-citizen children and cancellation of removal. Accordingly, children may become enmeshed in court hearings in a way that is not typical of criminal cases, appearing as witnesses and writing letters of support. As Lindsay Marshall of the Florence Project told us, "So a lot of our work is reading and submitting letters from kids, that are like, 'I want daddy home.' Or family members, sometimes kids, will testify in court. So just the impact of not just the separation, but the understanding of what is happening to your parents, and relying on family members and kids to be part of somebody's legal case in that way. I just think about that when I read some of those letters. Like, 'Dear Mr. Immigration Judge, please don't take my dad away.'"[6] Her colleague added, "And then to have your dad lose his case after you wrote that letter."

The negative effects on child development of parental detention and deportation, and of the fear that a parent could be picked up for deportation at any time, are becoming increasingly clear (see Brabeck and Xu 2010; Suárez-Orozco and Suárez-Orozco 2001; Yoshikawa 2011; Yoshikawa and Kholoptseva 2012). In addition, researchers report tremendous trauma as a result of family separation, whether because of the parents' deportation or their inability to cross back and forth between the United States and their home country to see children left behind (Abrego 2014; Bhabha 2014; Boehm 2012; Brotherton and Barrios 2011; Dreby 2010; Menjívar 2012; Menjívar and Abrego 2009; Pratt 2012; Suárez-Orozco, Todorova, and Louie 2002; Wessler 2013c; Women's Refugee Commission 2010).

Some of the most articulate voices speaking to the ramifications of parental deportation come from the Dreamers. As one Dreamer and DACA recipient blogged:

Those of us who are fortunate enough to still have our parents here live in fear every single day. If my parents are deported, I would either be left without a family, or I would be the sole caretaker of my 13-year-old and 11-month-old sisters. This could mean being separated from my family for years, or having to drop out of school just to be able to take care of my sisters. If I had to drop out, that would mean I would no longer be eligible for DACA, which would lead to my deportation as well. My parents have paid their taxes, they work, and they contribute every day, but my reality is that I have to be prepared for a day when they could be taken away. I am not alone. There are thousands who have had their parents or family members taken away, and thousands more who live in fear every day. (Navas 2013)

Fears of Loss of Parental Rights

Sometimes, the child welfare system becomes involved when a parent is incarcerated. This typically occurs when another parent is not able to care for the children, or when issues of neglect or abuse arise. In immigration cases, however, especially when the detained parent is a single mother, the child welfare system is far more likely to become involved, and the children may go into foster care and possibly adoption proceedings. In cases with very young children, the process can move extremely fast. In Arizona, for example, children under age three can be adopted after only six months in foster care (Wessler 2013c).

Joanna Dreby (2012, 2010) interviewed 91 Mexican immigrant parents and 110 children in New Jersey and Ohio between 2009 and 2012. She reports that one-quarter of the mothers she met were able to keep their families together following detention or deportation, but in another one-quarter of the cases, children were placed in foster care, the mother became a single parent, or the family tried to return to Mexico. As Dreby documents, parents feared losing custody of their US-born children, and children feared that a parent could be taken away at any time. The situation becomes even more complicated for abused women. Seth Wessler observes that abused women "were tormented by a dual fear: on the one hand, they worried that their children were unsafe living with men who abused them; on the other hand, they feared that if they called CPS to protect the children, they themselves might lose their parental rights if they remained in detention or were deported" (2011b, 35).

STRUCTURAL MECHANISMS THAT EXACERBATE HARM

One of our central objectives is to identify those structural mechanisms that exacerbate or mitigate harm to children and families. We turn next to those structural factors that exacerbate harm.

Lack of Judicial Discretion

The first mechanism we consider is lack of judicial discretion. A government official told us that immigration judges will take family ties into account to the extent permitted in cancellation of removal hearings. But, if the immigrant does not have legal permanent residency status, they must have been in the United States for at least ten years prior to going into removal proceedings and must meet a very high standard, demonstrating that removal will cause extreme and unusual harm to US-citizen family members, to have their orders of removal cancelled. Judges also have little discretion under the 1996 laws when legal permanent residents face removal due to a criminal conviction, even if they have US-citizen children. Moreover, any decision to exercise prosecutorial discretion rests with the ICE attorney, *not* the judge. Thus, while judges may remind ICE attorneys that they have the option to exercise discretion under the Morton Memos, the judges do not have the authority to do so themselves.

Lack of Coordination between ICE and CPS

The structural disconnect between the immigration and child welfare systems is a second source of harm for children and families. Immigration attorney Nina Rabin paints a poignant picture of parents "disappearing" into immigration detention, with family members unable to locate them. She identifies many of the broken links between the immigration system and the child welfare system, suggesting "the relationship between federal immigration enforcement and the state child welfare system cuts to the heart of fundamental tensions in U.S. immigration policy—between federal and state systems, enforcement and integration, and individual rights and immigration status distinctions" (Rabin 2011, 102)

Based on fifty-two surveys and twenty interviews with attorneys, judges, and case workers involved in the Pima County (Tucson) juvenile court system, Rabin concludes, "The government's failure to establish procedural mechanisms to allow detained immigrant parents to meaningfully participate in the dependency proceedings of their children violates their due process rights" (2011, 103). The disconnect between state child welfare and federal immigration agencies creates what she calls "Kafka-esque results in which immigrant parents are trapped between the two uncoordinated systems' processes" (2011, 103). Rabin notes, ironically, that parents have a much better chance of communicating with their children and case workers and of meeting the requirements of parenting plans if they are in jail rather than in immigration detention.[7]

The case of Felipe Montes serves as a primer for things that can go wrong. In December 2010, Felipe was deported after being picked up for traffic violations resulting from his driving without a license or registration (which he could not legally obtain because he was undocumented) in the North Carolina town where he and his wife, Marie, had lived for nine years. At the time of his detention, his older children were one and three years old, and his wife was pregnant with their youngest son. Two weeks after Felipe was deported, the county child welfare department took the children from their mother and placed them in foster care, citing Marie's economic, mental health, and drug addiction problems. Felipe had been the primary caregiver for his children and his wife prior to his deportation, and Marie stated that she wanted the children placed with their father. Instead, the three children were placed in two different foster homes pending adoption. The county child welfare office argued that the children would be better off being adopted and living in the United States than in Mexico with their father. The child protective services (CPS) officer expressed concern because Felipe's uncle's home, where the family would live, lacked running water and had a concrete roof and cement floor. Yet the home study conducted for the court indicated that conditions in the home were "good," and clean water was brought into the house daily.

Several nonprofit advocacy organizations became involved, helping to bring attention to Felipe's case and garnering more than 20,000 signatures on a national petition demanding that the family be reunited. Perhaps because of this publicity, Felipe was granted humanitarian parole to reenter the United States for his parental rights hearings. Two years after his deportation, he finally won the battle to regain his parental rights and was granted full custody of his children. He then sought prosecutorial discretion so that he could stay in the United States rather than moving the children to a country they did not know. Morton's prosecutorial discretion guidelines were promulgated six months after Felipe was deported, but he hoped they could be applied to his case retroactively. He was unsuccessful, and on March 22, 2013, Felipe and his three sons, now ages five, three, and two, returned to Mexico (Wessler 2012b, 2013a,b).

Felipe's situation was not unique. Many parents do not have paperwork in place stating who should serve as guardian for their children in case they are swept into the immigration system. As attorney Lindsay Marshall told us, when immigrants are caught up in a raid or pulled over by local law enforcement for a traffic violation "the kids could end up in the child welfare system, they could wind up with a relative, they can often, we see they can wind up with an abusive spouse. . . . And that deeply impacts the kids. . . . They might look at moving back where the parent is, and not necessarily knowing if they are a citizen, and knowing their rights to come back here or making the choice between staying here with the relative with citizenship, or going home with a parent. . . . You can just see the impact [on children] escalate."[8] Jacqueline Bhabha adds that the constant fear that a parent could be deported at any time raises questions for the child's sense of belonging, noting "where the parent's alienage trumps the right of the citizen child to parental care and companionship at home, citizenship loses all effective meaning for children" (2014, 89).

A government official also told us, "Mothers' worst fears are losing custody of their kids. Not even so much being deported as losing custody." This problem was also recognized by a DHS official with whom we spoke in 2012, who told us that DHS is trying to figure out a better way of working with child welfare agencies. As this official noted, DHS has no authority over state and local child welfare offices and policies, and there is tremendous variation across states in CPS policies and practices. As we discuss later in this chapter, the ICE parental interests directive announced in late summer of 2013 was a direct result of this understanding by DHS that a better mechanism was needed to communicate across jurisdictions and agencies.

Stresses and Strains for Child Welfare Systems

The inability of overburdened child welfare systems to properly handle cases involving detained and deported parents is another structural inadequacy. As Nina Rabin reminded us, immigration cases place "a huge strain on the child welfare system that it's not equipped to deal with." These cases are complicated, caseworkers often do not know what to expect regarding the parent's long-term prospects for staying in the United States, and they struggle with limited resources to arrange visitation for children, and to get out to the detention centers themselves. Rabin concludes, "What ends up happening is that the caseworkers don't have the resources available to work the case, and the parents don't get any meaningful services from the state, or the children get really compromised services as a result."[9]

The underlying problem, as Wendy Cervantes of First Focus explains, is that "these children are caught between three systems that do not always communicate well with each other: criminal justice, immigration and child welfare" (Cervantes 2013). She goes on to suggest:

> Often, the good intentions of actors within each of these systems result in unintended negative outcomes for children and families. For instance, the police officer who responds to a domestic violence call believes he or she is acting in the interest of public safety by taking both parties to the station for questioning. The ICE officer who investigates the arrested domestic violence victim after a fingerprint check revealing she is undocumented believes he is appropriately carrying out his responsibility to enforce immigration law. The child welfare worker who places the victim's children into foster care believes she is making the best decision for the children's safety and well-being. (Cervantes 2013)

A major concern noted by many immigration advocates is that child welfare caseworkers, attorneys, and family court judges lack knowledge about immigration, and thus do not understand the consequences of other legal decisions on immigration status. In response to this dilemma, in 2011 the Annie E. Casey Foundation published *When a Parent Is Incarcerated: A Primer for Social Workers*. This primer includes a chapter on immigrant parents in deportation proceedings, with information on how to locate, contact, and visit persons in immigration detention. The chapter provides an overview of detention transfer policies and the removal process for an incarcerated parent, including difficulties confronting parents' participation in dependency court hearings, how the transfer from jail or prison to immigration detention works, and options available to the family, such as returning the children to the parent's country of origin (Annie E. Casey Foundation 2011).

Along the same vein, Lindsay Marshall's *Families on the Front Lines: How Immigration Advocates Can Build a Bridge between the Immigration and Child Welfare Systems* (Marshall 2012) was written expressly to advise immigration and child welfare attorneys and advocates on lessons learned by the Florence Project as it navigated these two systems in Arizona. Rosie Hidalgo (2013) and Seth Wessler (2011b) add to this growing literature, describing the special difficulties that arise in cases of domestic violence when victims may be picked up in dual arrests and detained. In such cases, the victim is at risk of deportation and separation from her US-citizen children, who in turn may be placed with her abuser. Further complicating such cases, a parent who is unable to stop a partner who is violent or abusive toward the children may be charged with "failure to protect" and put into immigration detention and deportation, with the children placed in CPS care. These immigration advocates and attorneys call for better training for everyone in the system, from ICE officers through attorneys, judges, and child welfare caseworkers.

Seth Wessler's *Shattered Families* (2011b) analyzes the intersection of immigration enforcement and the child welfare system, drawing on interviews, focus groups, surveys, and ICE data. Wessler calculates that at least 5,100 children of detained or deported parents were in foster care in 2011. He extrapolates from this snapshot to estimate that another 15,000 children of detained or deported parents are likely to be in foster care over the next five years. Wessler also found that immigration detainees were held, on average, 370 miles from their homes, making visitation with their children very difficult (2011b, 12). Although ICE is now more attentive to the importance of locating detained parents closer to their children, the problem remains acute for women because the smaller number of women's detention centers means women may not be held within reasonable proximity to their families.

Routes to Engagement with Child Welfare Services

Wessler identifies three typical routes by which the children of detained immigrants enter the foster care system: the straight path, the parallel path, and the interrupted path. In the straight path, children enter foster care because the parents are detained and thus unable to care for their children. Wessler describes a case that fits this model: "A mother was picked up on charges that were entirely unrelated to the children. Considering the nature of the relatively minor allegations, had she been a citizen, there is no doubt that she would have bonded out in a day or two. We have here a good mom who had some issues. . . . But the fact that she was incarcerated with an ICE hold and then detained and deported means it's considered to be neglect now by our state's statutory regime. This case has been open two months and the kids are still in foster care" (Wessler 2011b, 26). Similarly, Nina Rabin told us that sometimes "parents are picked up for something that has nothing to do with child abuse or neglect allegations, but just because they're unavailable as a result of being placed in detention, the kids enter CPS."[10]

The parallel path in many ways mirrors the straight path. Here, the police response to a charge of child neglect or abuse brings a family to the attention of both ICE and child protective services. While some abuse and neglect cases are extremely serious, others normally would have resulted in a quick reunification. But when parents are undocumented immigrants, circumstances are no longer normal. For example, "a California man was arrested and his babies placed in foster care because a babysitter left the children alone for less than an hour and the police were called. When he arrived home, he was arrested for child endangerment, and when his information was run through the secure communities database, he was picked up and moved to detention" (Wessler 2011b, 26–27).

Nina Rabin reiterated the complications that arise in otherwise straight-forward cases when a parent is undocumented: "When CPS is involved with a family, and then immigration enforcement gets involved, the whole case gets much, much more complicated. . . . What might have started out as a fairly simple case where the kids would be reunified quickly becomes much more complicated once parents are in detention or deportation."[11]

Wessler's third model, the interrupted path, is typified by families who were already involved with child protective services when the parent was detained for immigration purposes. As Wessler notes, "In these cases, parental detention interrupts, sometimes irreparably, the process of family reunification." As an example of the interrupted route, Wessler cites the case of Magda, who was just weeks from being reunited with her US-citizen son. Magda and her son

> were spending the afternoon together on one of their biweekly supervised visits when Magda's son soiled his pants. With little money to spare, she decided to go to the dollar store across the street and steal the clothes he needed. She wanted to avoid taking her son back to the foster home without changing his clothes first. The security guard called the police, who arrested Magda for petty theft. The officers drove her son back to his foster home and Magda was placed in deportation proceedings. From detention, she could do little to maintain contact with her son, and their path to reunification was interrupted. (Wessler 2011b, 27)

The fear of formal loss of parental rights may be so great that families avoid interaction with the child welfare system if at all possible. Emily Butera of the Women's Refugee Commission told us, "There are a lot of children left behind in informal situations when their parents are detained and ultimately deported. The parent may have been given an opportunity to choose where the child would live before they were taken into custody, so they end up with a relative or a friend. But where there are older children, a parent may choose to leave the children on their own with other siblings acting as caregivers for younger siblings."[12]

Another attorney observed that a teenage sibling may take over the care of younger children following a parent's deportation in an effort to avoid involving CPS, particularly if the parent intends to try to reenter the United States soon: "It's not until a school counselor or someone else falls upon what's going on, or they don't have food and they show up at a social service agency, and someone's like, 'What do you mean you guys don't have food or you have no money? What's going on here?' They live in fear. The parents also sometimes are telling the kids to do that, to not tell anybody, and understandably so. You know, 'Let me send you some money, or have your *tía* come over and bring you tortillas and some food.'" Finally, sometimes teenagers are left behind when their parents are deported and they are not identified by the child welfare system. In such cases, they may simply be "bumped around between relatives."

Foster Care, Severance of Parental Rights, and Adoption

The process and speed with which parental rights may be severed in cases resulting from immigration enforcement is a third structural mechanism that creates substantial harm for children and families. The Adoption and Safe Families Act (ASFA) was designed to make it easier for children to be adopted so they would not languish in foster care. But in most cases involving immigration detention and deportation, the parents are perfectly fit, and the best interests of their child are to be reunited with their parents. The parent's immigration status creates a significant roadblock, however, particularly as it impedes their ability to comply with required parenting plans.

Sources of Confusion and Conflict

Although the actual numbers are unknown and probably relatively small, practically every attorney and advocate we interviewed recounted cases involving young children who were placed in foster care and then quickly adopted, with their parents' rights severed in absentia. According to one attorney, "The juvenile court shouldn't be terminating in those cases. The juvenile court should say, 'No, no, no, no, give actual notice to the parents. I want to hear from the parents. Have the parents paroled in, or I want them to be here telephonically or by video conference. I am not going to terminate someone's parental rights because they're in Mexico.' The nonchalant way that the juvenile court goes about their business is disgraceful." In one such case, an undocumented mother who had sole custody of her children because of domestic violence was being deported to her home country. According to the attorney, "The response I got from the judge was, and I quote, 'I will not return those US-citizen children to the squalor that is Mexico.'" Here, the family court judge's determination that it was better for the children to be raised in a wealthier country than to be with their mother meant the family would be torn apart.

We were continually reminded that the various systems do not communicate well. Attorneys describe a "real tension" because the timeline in the federal Adoption and Safe Families Act for terminating parental rights is not in sync with immigration case processing: "And so major decisions are being made by families and parents that are depending on a really confusing, messed up system. And the immigration court is completely oblivious that any of this is going on. . . . The adjudicator that is making a decision about the parent's right to stay in this country, like it doesn't even, like these child welfare issues just aren't relevant in most of the immigration cases, which is kind of amazing."[13]

Child protective services also may be reluctant to place citizen children in the care of undocumented relatives for fear that the relatives would not be able to financially support the children, would be unwilling to help the children apply for public benefits for which they are eligible, or might get picked up by ICE. Again we were told, "That runs right up against that foundational presumption in child welfare that family reunification ought to be the goal," and that a kinship placement is the next best thing for the child's well-being when a parental placement is not possible.[14] Advocates and attorneys were quick to tell us that such reluctance on the part of CPS varies from location to location, and depends at least in part on whether the locale is a traditional or new destination site. In states and cities with well-established immigrant populations, child welfare social workers generally understand the community better and are more comfortable with kinship placements.

When children are placed in foster care, they may be in homes where Spanish is not spoken or is not the predominant language. Monolingual Spanish-speaking children may not understand what is going on, making the situation even more distressing for them. If they stay in the foster home for a long time, young children may become more proficient in English than in Spanish. Staying in close communication with their parents becomes more difficult then, especially if they are not able to visit with their detained or deported parent easily or often. As child welfare advocate Beth Rosenberg told us, in such cases "it becomes harder and harder for the parent and child to stay connected, and the relationship becomes more tenuous, until ultimately the parental rights may be severed."[15]

Parenting Plans and Visitation

The inability of detained parents to be physically present for dependency cases, to comply with parenting plans, and to engage in visitation with their children is a theme that runs through most of the nongovernmental organization reports and our interviews. Parenting plans, also known as reunification plans, can call for psychological evaluations, substance abuse evaluations, parenting classes, and supervised visitation, among other requirements. As Emily Butera of the Women's Refugee Commission reflected, visitation

> can be impossible if the parent is detained in a different state than the child is living in, or the child is undocumented, or the child's caregiver is undocumented and it's not safe to bring the child to the facility. It might be too expensive. It might be that the reunification plan requires contact visitation but the detention center only allows visitation through glass. There are a lot of places where the visitation part can go wrong. Parents also struggle to participate in requirements like parenting classes, anger management classes, drug treatment classes and other programs that are a precondition to reunification but are not available in the detention system.[16]

Visitors to detention centers must be able to demonstrate that they have legal status in the United States, and children may not enter a detention center alone, requiring that they be accompanied by an adult who is a US citizen or has legal status. According to immigration scholar and attorney Evelyn Cruz:

> And so that is a problem. Minors normally don't have much identification themselves. A second problem, faced by a detained parent whose children are in foster care custody, is that it is difficult to set up a time for the parent to appear before the court that has the custody of the kid. If the detention facility won't honor that schedule, the parent is not able to contact the court at that point in time for a hearing. Also, the court-appointed attorney, if they have one, may be reluctant to

go and visit them because they are two hours away in the detention facility with difficult admittance requirements.[17]

Colliding Timelines

The timeline for termination of parental rights under the federal Adoption and Safe Families Act is very short. ASFA states that if a child is out of the parents' care for fifteen of twenty-two months, the state must move to terminate parental rights. This is a maximum time frame, and states may opt to sever parental rights even sooner. This timeline is even shorter for young children, decreasing to as little as six months in some cases. Yet with older children, the child welfare system may move much slower. Emily Butera eloquently summed up the problem of colliding timelines: "The immigration detention and deportation process can move really, really, quickly and the child welfare process, in a lot of cases, moves slowly. In addition to the systems not communicating with each other, parents are caught between these two timelines that are out of alignment."[18]

A similar point was made by Anne Marie Mulcahy of the Vera Institute of Justice, who said that once parents are detained and in removal proceedings, there can be significant problems with visitation, and with the parent's ability to participate in family court proceedings:

> Immigration can move detainees wherever they want, whenever they want, and so . . . when people are moved outside of the jurisdiction where their children are in foster care, they're no longer able to participate, unless the family court is great and allows them to appear telephonically, and the immigration service allows that to be arranged, which doesn't happen all that often. Those parents are really in a terrible situation; their rights are easily terminated because their failure to participate in the proceedings may be seen as a lack of interest and cooperation in getting their children out of foster care.[19]

Like Felipe Montes' case, Encarnación Bail Romero's situation offers a template for things that can go wrong (*In Re: Adoption of C.M.B.R.* 2011). As outlined by Michelle Brané in a Women's Refugee Commission blog (2011; see also Migration and Child Welfare National Network 2013), following an ICE raid of a poultry plant in Barry County, Missouri, in late May 2007, Encarnación and more than a hundred other immigrants without proper work authorization were taken into custody. Encarnación pled guilty to identity theft and was to be deported following a two-year sentence. For the first few days following arrest, Encarnación's brother and then sister cared for her baby, Carlos, who was six months old at the time of her arrest. But when Encarnación's sister could not care for Carlos full time, she sought child care services through the local clergy. After a few weeks, it seemed easier for the baby to stay with the caregivers during the week and with the child's aunt on the weekends. This continued until September, at which time Encarnación was asked whether she would permit adoption. She said no, and petitioned for a passport for her son so that he could go to live with her sister in Guatemala, where they could later be reunited. Nevertheless, a few weeks later, the potential adoptive family filed for adoption and termination of Encarnación's parental rights. The petition for transfer of custody, termination of parental rights, and adoption were served on the detained mother on October 15, only three days before the transfer of custody was to occur.

A number of violations of due process likely occurred. Among these, Encarnación was served papers in English, a language she did not speak, and her attorney was hired by the adoptive family, creating an immediate conflict of interest. Encarnación had asked the court to send her child to live with her sister in Guatemala. Nevertheless, the court determined that Encarnación abandoned her child when she went to prison without having made legal guardianship arrangements and allowed the adoption to proceed.

Encarnación contested that decision, and the ACLU and the Immigrant Child Advocacy Project at the University of Chicago's Young Center filed amicus curiae briefs in support of the appellant. In reversing the decision to terminate Encarnación's parental rights and permit her child's adoption, Judge Nancy Steffen Rahmeyer of the Missouri Southern District reviewed the initial determination by the trial court, which stated:

> Mother was unable to offer proof that she would be employable in Guatemala, had a home there, or had any way to care for Child, "leaving the court to believe that [Mother] would be unable to provide adequate food, clothing, or shelter to [Child] in her physical custody in the future." Moreover, the Court stated that '[Mother's] lifestyle, that of smuggling herself into a country illegally and committing crimes in this country is not a lifestyle that can provide any stability for a child. A child cannot be educated in this way, always in hiding or on the run." There was no investigative report about Mother's ability to parent, and there was no evidence to indicate that Mother was an unfit parent. The only evidence presented on behalf of Mother was a letter from her, indicating that she had someone on stand-by ready and willing to take responsibility for Child until Mother was released from prison and deported to Guatemala. (*In Re: Adoption of C.M.B.R., A Minor* 2010, 8; see also Thompson 2009)

In remanding the case, Judge Rahmeyer cited a related case, *In Re: Interest of Angelica L. and Daniel L.* (2009), in which the Nebraska Supreme Court opined, "Whether living in Guatemala or the United States is more comfortable for 'the children is not determinative of the children's best interests. . . . The 'best interests' of the child standard does not require simply that a determination be made that one environment or set of circumstances is superior to another."

Judge Rahmeyer reversed the decision and remanded the case back to trial court. The case went back and forth following additional appeals, until the Missouri Supreme Court again remanded the case back to the trial court in January 2011, and in July 2012 the court ruled against Encarnación, terminating her parental rights.

STRUCTURAL MECHANISMS THAT MITIGATE HARM

We turn next to those mechanisms and processes that may reduce harm to children and families. Immigration and child welfare advocates and attorneys have offered a number of recommendations that would improve conditions when parents are detained or deported. First and foremost is comprehensive immigration reform to legalize the status of these parents. Barring legalization, the second fundamental recommendation is for prosecutorial discretion to be fully invoked in cases of parental detention and deportation. Yet from the perspective of most immigration attorneys and advocates, prosecutorial discretion has largely failed when it comes to protecting families (see similarly Rabin 2013).

Beyond these overarching recommendations, advocates and attorneys have proposed specific suggestions that would ameliorate at least some harm to children and families. Most advocates report that the Department of Homeland Security and the Department of Justice are receptive to these concerns and willing to work with them. However, the pace of change within ICE, in particular, has been far slower than most advocates had hoped, and the agreement of top policymakers has not generally translated into systemic change in field offices. In this section, we discuss some of the key mechanisms that are being employed to reduce harm. These steps, which do not require congressional approval, are one way in which the Obama administration has sought to respond to pressure from immigrants' rights groups pressing for reforms in the face of record-high deportations and failure to enact comprehensive immigration legislation.[20]

Improving Access to Detained Parents: The Online Locator

One of the most common criticisms raised by attorneys and advocates was the difficulty in identifying where a parent is being held, especially when they are moved from jails to detention centers, and from one center to another across the country. In response, ICE launched an online detainee locator in July 2010. Family members, attorneys, and others can learn where someone is detained by entering the detainee's alien registration number, called an "A" number, and country of birth. This works if the person is a legal permanent resident and their registration number is known to family members, but if the person is undocumented they may not have an A number. In that case, the detainee's first and last names, date of birth, and country of birth may be entered instead, but these must be an exact match of the data in the system, which may or may not be correct.

Describing the difficulties with the online locator, child welfare advocate Yali Lincroft told us, "Good Lord, you have two spots for their name. Putting Omar Lopez from Mexico is nothing. There are five million Omar Lopezes from Mexico. You have to give me every middle name, you have to tell me the village, you have to be sure there is not an alias and did you put the accent in the right place. . . . It's garbage in, garbage out. Having the locator is the right first step—but implementation is spotty at best and there's no reliable third party agent to help families navigate this incredibly complex national system."[21]

Attorney Victoria López of the ACLU made a similar point: "I can access it. I have a computer, I can access the Internet. I can get that information in there if I have it. But there have even been times where I have been stumped, where I don't have all the pieces of information that the locator requires." She went on to clarify, "Sometimes people use aliases. Sometimes you don't know the A [alien] number. . . . It is really useless for a category of people who are just getting assigned an A number, and for the family members who are at home who don't know that number." López said that when she gives rights presentations, she tells people that if they have an alien registration number or some sort of status, they should be sure to write it on their emergency preparedness plan, along with dates of birth for everyone in the family.[22] It often takes three to four days before a detainee gets into the system, and it is during those first few days that family members are most fearful. Attorneys may call ICE and obtain information during that period, but only if they have a G-28, which is basically a Notice to Appear, on file that is signed by the detainee and states that the person is the attorney of record.

In addition to family members, child welfare caseworkers need to know how to reach detained parents. ICE's online detainee locator system can be very helpful, according to Emily Butera of the Women's Refugee Commission, but CPS caseworkers may not know the parent's A number or have other information needed to identify the parent's detention center via the online locator.[23] Anne Marie Mulcahy of the Vera Institute made a similar point, noting, "A lot of people don't know their own A number, much less their children, and service providers wouldn't know that."[24]

A senior DHS official with whom we spoke in fall 2012 recognized the problems with the online locator, but said his understanding was that it is now working better. And indeed, most attorneys and advocates working with detained immigrants say that although some problems continue, the tool has significantly improved their ability to locate detainees.

A related recommendation has been to allow detainees two phone calls upon arrest, so they can deal with childcare before being taken away. This has been incorporated into the 2013 ICE parental interests directive, discussed later in this chapter. Others advocated better use of technology to help families stay in touch. As a longtime immigration attorney suggested, "You can get free phones, you could have Skype, you could use technology to let the family communicate the way everybody else communicates with their far flung nuclear families. . . . Give people cell phones that are programmed with just the number for their kids. We could do that, there is no reason not to do that. You could get technology companies to probably give those away or give them at a reduced rate."

The Risk Classification Assessment Tool

In addition to the online detainee locator, a second technological advance offered by ICE was its computerized risk assessment tool. Announced in 2009 and long anticipated by immigration advocates, the risk classification assessment can help ICE officers determine whether alternatives to detention, including release, would suffice to ensure that the person will appear in court for their immigration proceedings and, if not, what type of detention placement is needed (Koulish and Noferi 2013). In February 2012, Emily Butera of the Women's Refugee Commission told us:

> We are waiting for the risk classification assessment to be rolled out. It's been pending now for a couple of years. I'm hoping that it will be rolled out by the end

of 2012. It goes hand in hand with the prosecutorial discretion but it will be a formalized process by which everybody who comes into ICE custody is evaluated in the same manner. Everyone will be assessed for certain vulnerabilities and balancing equities. Now the problem in terms of parent–child issues is that in the risk assessment context, it is primary caregivers of children who are going to be prioritized and not all parents. . . . The standards of the risk classification do not go as far as prosecutorial discretion.[25]

By July 2012, rollout of the risk classification assessment had begun, and it was deployed nationwide by March 2013. As we saw with prosecutorial discretion policies, policy directives from the national ICE office do not always play out as planned on the ground. The risk assessment tool is no different. Thus, although the tool has been welcomed by the advocacy community, some policy analysts and advocates anticipate that local-level ICE officers will claim, "Everyone says they've got kids" and ignore the assessments in making placement decisions. Accordingly, advocates are watching closely to see how this mechanism performs in practice.

Immigration researchers Robert Koulish and Mark Noferi are conducting an analysis of the risk assessment measure, based on data from ICE on initial risk classifications and resulting detention placements. The first installment of these data was obtained through the Freedom of Information Act (FOIA) in October 2013. These preliminary data are from one city and thus are limited in scope. Nevertheless, findings suggest that almost all detainees are assessed as being at medium or high risk of flight, including persons with long-term family and community ties and who are identified by the measure as posing low risks to public safety, leading to questions as to the tool's efficacy (Noferi and Koulish 2015; Koulish and Noferi 2015).

Location of Detention Centers

On January 4, 2012, ICE Director John Morton issued a Transfer Directive (Policy 11022.1) designed to minimize long-distance transfers of detainees. The directive establishes criteria for transfers and is intended to substantially reduce transfers of detainees who have immediate family members, attorneys of record, or cases pending or ongoing within that field office's area of responsibility. This "no transfer" policy is an important development, both because it facilitates family visitation and also because immigration attorneys, many of whom are working pro bono, are simply unable to drive for hours to meet with clients.

At the Point of Apprehension

The American Bar Association, in collaboration with a number of advocacy groups and attorneys, developed a "Know Your Rights" video designed to provide information for persons held in immigration detention on how to navigate the court system and what to expect before and during their trial. The video and self-help legal materials were distributed to all ICE detention centers across the country in June 2012.

In addition, the ACLU and other nonprofits conduct presentations in communities across the country. These forums include information on how to designate a power of attorney, whom to list on their children's emergency contacts at school, and other aspects of a backup plan. ACLU attorney Victoria López told us that the question "What about my kids?" comes up whenever she gives a rights presentation. Just two days prior to our conversation, five different women came up to her following her talk, asking what to do if there is a traffic stop and their children are with them in the car. She said:

> In some cases, police officers will allow you to call a family member or someone else to come pick up your children if they are going to arrest you, so be sure you have a phone number of somebody who you trust to come pick up your kids . . . or a couple of people that you can call that you can trust to take your kids in that kind of an emergency situation. Worst-case scenario, a police officer that is about to arrest you may not let you make a call to family, then your children will likely be taken by some kind of a CPS worker until they can identify a family member or someone to send the children to. And I think for many, many, many parents, that is the horror.[26]

Ironically, that worst-case scenario is the protocol ICE is supposed to follow when an individual is apprehended in a fugitive operation and their children are present. Jennifer Podkul and Michelle Brané from the Women's Refugee Commission told us:

> It is exactly the opposite of what you would want it to be. It actually says the first thing an ICE officer should do is call Child Protective Services and hand the child over. The second option is to call the police and have them take the child. And the third option, only to be used when the first two are not an option, is to ask the parent where they want the kid to go. But the funny thing is, we obtained that policy originally though a FOIA request. Nobody knew about it. ICE leadership didn't even know about it. We pointed the policy out to them, and noted that it was the exact opposite of what it should be. They were surprised to hear that it even existed.[27]

Along these same lines, Victoria López of the Arizona ACLU recounted having been on a panel earlier that week during which someone from another immigration advocacy organization showed a video clip of a home raid. In the video, Maricopa County Sheriff's deputies had teddy bears in their squad cars to give to children after their parents were taken away. Noting that on the one hand it is nice that the deputies were giving the kids teddy bears as a form of comfort, on the other hand, this signals that deputies knew they were about to separate families. "And that was part of the drill to get ready, you know, my flak jacket, my gun, my badge, let's put teddy bears in there because we are going to a home where there might be kids."[28]

ICE Parental Interests Directive and Point of Contact for Parents in Detention

In the spring and summer of 2012, there was talk within the advocacy community of having a CPS point of contact inside detention centers to help facilitate child welfare and custody cases. When we asked an immigration attorney what she thought of this possibility, she responded, "It seems like a good step. It is just going to be a matter of figuring out how this plays out practically for people who are in detention. You know, how often will they be able to access this liaison, will they be able to call this person, will that person come to the detention center and actually have in-person meetings with parents about their situation? How strongly is this person going to advocate for parents who are in detention, if at all? Or will this person simply be sort of a facilitator of, 'Here is the phone'"?

Others were less certain that parents would want to inform CPS officials that they had children. This reluctance was seen as potentially greatest among parents who thought their children were safely in the care of a relative or friend, and that involving CPS might make other family members, including older children who were not US citizens, vulnerable to deportation. Compounding these difficulties, CPS is a state rather than a federal agency, meaning that any policies and procedures would vary from state to state. If a parent is detained in one state and the child custody case is going forward in another state, some attorneys wondered, how much help could the local CPS point of contact actually provide?

At the federal level, a directive explicitly focused on parents who had been picked up for immigration violations seemed the next step to solidify Morton's prosecutorial discretion memos and better address the complicated nexus of immigration and child welfare law. On August 23, 2013, ICE Acting Director John Sandweg issued the parental rights directive, *Facilitating Parental Interests in the Course of Civil Immigration Enforcement Activities* (Sandweg 2013).

This directive incorporates many of the recommendations made by the advocacy community and has potential to mitigate some of the problems discussed in this chapter. It calls for designation of a trained point of contact at the supervisory level in each ICE field office and creation of processes to regularly identify and review cases involving parents. According to the directive, parents are to be detained close to the child(ren) and to the family court or location of other child welfare proceedings and not transferred outside of that area. Parents are to be provided transportation and escorted to family court hearings or proceedings if within reasonable driving distance so they may participate in those proceedings. If they are too far away to participate in person, or if an in-person appearance cannot be practically arranged, they are to be accommodated via video or teleconference from the detention center or field office. Parents are also to be permitted contact visits with their children; if these are not possible, they are to be provided visitation via video or teleconference, contingent upon the video alternative having been approved by the family court or child welfare authority.

Significantly, the directive goes on to assert that if a parent or legal guardian is to be removed from the country, ICE is to accommodate to the extent practical their efforts to provide for their minor children, including arranging guardianship if the child is to remain in the United States, or obtaining travel documents for the child to accompany the parent to the country of removal. This includes coordination with counsel, consulates and consular officials, and courts and/or family members in order to execute necessary documents, purchase airline tickets, and make other necessary preparations. And, addressing a major point of contention, ICE may provide sufficient notice of the removal itinerary to the detainee or his or her attorney so that coordinated travel arrangements may be made for the person's minor children. Once removed, the parent or guardian is to be granted parole, permitting reentry into the United States for hearings related to termination of parental rights if they must be physically present for that hearing. ICE may also parole previously deported persons into the United States for compelling humanitarian cases.

Perhaps anticipating pushback from opponents of immigration reform and to clarify how the directive fits into the history of prosecutorial discretion, a DHS official stated during an interagency working group meeting that it "does not increase the scope of prosecutorial discretion, it reiterates existing agency guidance. It is not DACA for parents."[29] The directive seems to have more teeth in it than some earlier prosecutorial discretion memos, in that it establishes a person in each field office with specific responsibility for carrying it out. But, as a policy advisor told us based on her analysis of the directive, "What struck me was just how limited it is in terms of its application to the volume of family situations that we are seeing." The directive includes multiple caveats, and like the prosecutorial discretion memos, it may be ignored in the field. Almost four months after it was issued, a DHS official told us that they have had a good response to the memo at the management level and half of the points of contact are supervisory detention officers. As for the response in the field, this official noted that they had only recently begun to have real conversations with field officers, some of whom see it as another piece of guidance they need to navigate around, though others are more engaged.

The timing is interesting, because this long-awaited directive was announced almost immediately after John Morton left ICE and John Sandweg was named acting director, and a month after DHS Secretary Janet Napolitano announced that she would be leaving DHS to become president of the University of California system. Perhaps the hope was that Chris Crane and other immigration hardliners within ICE would be less likely to undermine the directive if it did not come from Morton, or perhaps Secretary Napolitano was determined to make one more big push for vulnerable parents and children in case comprehensive immigration reform did not pass, especially as it got closer to the time when she was leaving office. From the perspective of advocacy organizations, they had been looking forward to such guidance being issued, and the immediate response on advocacy listservs suggests that the directive is viewed as a significant achievement.

Women's Refugee Commission Toolkit and Guide for Detained and Removed Parents

Three days after the parental interest directive was announced, Emily Butera posted Marta's story on the Women's Refugee Commission blog. Marta's experiences demonstrate the catastrophic results for families when the immigration and child welfare systems collide, and why detainees need help navigating the system. Marta was apprehended in her home with her four children, three of whom are US citizens, present. She was not given an opportunity to arrange for child care, and the children were placed into the child welfare system:

> During the two years she was in immigration custody, Marta . . . was not able to arrange for them to visit her, and she was only able to arrange for phone calls with them a handful of times. Marta struggled to navigate the complex child welfare system while in ICE detention, unable to meet in person with her own attorney, the child welfare caseworker, or anyone involved in her custody case. Ultimately, Marta was deported without her children. . . . Once in Mexico, she continued to struggle to meaningfully participate in the child welfare case, and eventually, her parental rights were terminated for all four of her children. (Butera 2013)

To assist parents such as Marta, Emily Butera and her colleagues in the Women's Refugee Commission developed a comprehensive toolkit for parents in detention. Published in January 2014 and available in English and Spanish, the toolkit is a ten-chapter compendium that systematically addresses each of the difficulties Marta and other parents encounter, from making care arrangements for their children, to what to expect when their children are in the child welfare system, to options if they or a child is the victim of domestic violence, to getting children back when released from detention, to what happens if they are deported. The first chapter concludes with a listing of "basic tips to protect parental rights." Later chapters provide step-by-step directions on options available, what to consider, questions to ask, and how to proceed. Sixteen appendices include contact information at relevant state and federal agencies and at migrant and child welfare assistance agencies in Mexico and Central America, state-specific child welfare handbooks and forms, sample letters and forms, and a host of other resources. The toolkit is intended to be consulted as needed, with each chapter guiding parents in different situations, rather than expecting someone in detention to read and process the entire volume in one sitting.[30]

As of August 2014, ICE had promised that the toolkit would be available online in all ICE detention centers and on library computers, but the Women's Refugee Commission had thus far been unable to confirm this in person. The commission also offered to provide paper copies of the toolkit in English and Spanish, but ICE has not yet taken them up on that proposal.[31]

Although the complete toolkit was not yet available when Sandweg's parental interests directive was issued, the Women's Refugee Commission published a precursor at that time—a two-page *Guide for Detained and Removed Parents with Child Custody Concerns*. The guide was to be quickly made available in all ICE facilities holding detainees for more than seventy-two hours and posted in the detention center's law library. However, according to Jennifer Podkul, it was nowhere to be seen at a detention center she visited in Los Angeles in late fall 2013.[32]

About the same time, the Florence Immigrant and Refugee Rights Project also developed a guide to protecting parents' rights, which should serve as an important supplement to the Women's Refugee Commission toolkit. It is specific to the needs of families in Arizona and provides local contact information, as well as broader information on legal rights and best practices, but can readily be modified to fit situations in other states.[33]

Although the toolkits and guide were developed by nongovernmental organizations, we include them in our discussion of structural mechanisms to ameliorate harm for two reasons. First, they address the operation of social structures and institutions, and the problems created when they intersect. And second, the Department of Homeland Security and the Department of Justice have promised that the complete Women's Refugee Commission toolkit and the two-page guide will be available, at least online, in all ICE detention centers, and Legal Orientation Program providers will be encouraged to distribute the toolkit.

Engaging Consular Officials

Engagement with consular officials from the parents' home country offers another structural avenue for reducing harm to children and families. In some cases, the consulate can assist detained and deported parents seeking to retain their parental rights, for example, by coordinating home visits and providing the family court with evidence that other requirements in a parenting plan have been met. They also can help coordinate travel plans when parents facing deportation want their children to return with them.

Many countries will permit children to hold dual citizenship if their parents are citizens of that country, even if the child was not born there. But, as immigration attorney Aryah Somers reminded us, if the child's birth was not registered with the consulate, the child does not have dual citizenship. Then, the consulate is unable to extend protections to the child because they do not have jurisdiction over US citizens. When children are in foster care, the situation becomes more difficult, and even if the child is registered and has citizenship in the parents' home country, the consulate may not be able to stop placement in an adoptive family.[34] Another attorney told us that sometimes in those cases, "CPS decides that it's better to internally place those children in the United States with adoptive families than return them to their biological parents in their home countries." She continued, "It's deeply troubling to me on a family law, on an immigration level, and on a personal level because, to me, you have two loving parents who are raising their children and, but for the fact that they were illegally in the country, they are now being torn from their children."

A representative from a Central American embassy recalled a case in which the CPS social worker said the parents never complied with instructions. According to the social worker, the parents were in the United States for months before their deportation but did not connect with their kids, who were in foster care. When asked, "Why didn't you go to see your kids?," the father said he was told he needed to arrange adequate housing for them, so he was working three jobs in order to make enough money. The mother was afraid that if she went to see her children, she would be deported, so she did not take that risk. The embassy representative said, "Some social workers think the parents are bad parents. It is just different ideas about parenting, not better or worse ... and some think the kids are better off in the US because the family lives in such extreme poverty." Seth Wessler echoes the concern that some judges and case workers are reluctant to reunite children with their deported parents, suggesting, "One of the central barriers to the reunification of children with parents who have been deported is a deep bias often articulated as a belief that children are better off in the U.S., regardless of who they live with" (2011b, 45). Wessler continues, "Because child welfare systems are tasked primarily with reunifying children with fit parents, the impact of this bias raises serious due process questions" (2011b, 46).

According to Michelle Brané, director of the Women's Refugee Commission Migrant Rights and Justice Program, they are hearing of fewer termination cases today than in the past, though she added that this does not mean that families are not still being separated. The reduction in court-ordered termination cases may indicate that public education is working, and parents are learning that they and their children have rights even when they are undocumented. It may also reflect recognition of parents' and children's rights on the part of ICE agents, and awareness by family court judges that the best interests of the child may be complicated in such cases.[35]

For example, the Migration and Child Welfare National Network reports on the case of temporary permanent resident, "John Doe," who twice appealed termination of his parental rights to a daughter born in the United States. John Doe worked with the Mexican consulate to conduct a home study and submit it to the court. This case, *In the Matter of the TPR of John Doe* (2012), was further complicated because the daughter had been living with foster parents for several years, one of whom worked for the child welfare agency and wanted to adopt her. Ultimately, the appellate court found that "there was no contention father had abused or neglected his daughter, nor that he was unfit to have custody, and that there was no evidence he had been given the ability to establish a relationship with her since he was legally barred from entering the U.S. It noted that the 'fact that a child may enjoy a higher standard of living in the United States than in the country where the child's parent resides is not a reason to terminate the parental rights of a foreign national'" (Migration and Child Welfare National Network 2013).

Although consulate officials were able to assist in these and other cases, detained and deported parents in child custody proceedings are unlikely to realize that their consulate *can* help them, or know how to contact them. In October 2013, the Mexican consulate unveiled an innovative application for smartphones and tablets called MiConsulMex (My Mexican Consulate). The app is part of the Mexican government's effort to connect with the 11.6 million Mexican nationals living in the United States and with Mexican Americans. Among its other features, the app offers a means for Mexican nationals in the United States to connect with consular officials in cases of emergency or immigration assistance (Migration Policy Institute 2013).[36]

Once a person has been repatriated, the home country may be able to provide more assistance than many immigrants recognize. As one of our sources suggested, the first question that should be asked when a deportee lands in their home country is, "Did you leave a child behind?" Many immigrants are fearful of telling US authorities that they have children because so doing might endanger undocumented family members, but they might be more willing to speak up when they reach their home country, and their consular officials may be able to assist them in maintaining their parental rights.

State Laws Such as California's SB 1062

While our focus has been on mechanisms operating at the federal level, or with the support of the federal government, some states have taken the lead in identifying means of mitigating harm to children and families. California's

The Reuniting Immigrant Families Act (SB 1064) is one such example. Drafted by Yali Lincroft and First Focus Campaign for Children and signed into law on September 30, 2012, this legislation is a response to family separation resulting from immigration enforcement. It "prioritizes keeping children with their families and out of the public child welfare system whenever possible, and helps separated families receive appropriate care and due process" (Lincroft 2013, 1). The law explicitly addresses the bias against placing a child with undocumented family members, requiring that social workers consider appropriate relatives for placement regardless of their immigration status and allowing counties to use the relative's consular identification card or passport as identification for purposes of background checks (Lincroft 2013, 3). Lincroft offered the following situation to exemplify the kinds of cases for which this bill was designed: "I remember I went a couple of months ago at the invitation of the Mexican Consulate in Fresno County to do an observation of a woman who was going to be deported after she had served her sentence, and she told me her story about how her child was in the foster care system. . . . She wanted her child to be with her mom or her sister. Neither of them was documented. They were both undocumented immigrants and this was before my bill passed. Right now, if my bill had passed, at least they would have had a fighting chance to have some resemblance of due process."[37]

At the federal level, the Help Separated Families Act, introduced by Representative Lucille Roybal-Allard (D-CA) on July 16, 2012, and again on June 28, 2013, includes a number of elements of the California law, and similar language was included in the 2013 Senate bill (S. 744). If enacted, the Help Separated Families Act would stipulate that parents, legal guardians, or relatives may not be disqualified as placement for a child solely because of their immigration status. In addition, it would require that states accept foreign identification documents, such as *matricula consulares* issued by consular offices, as sufficient identification for criminal background checks for purposes of child placement, and would express the sense of Congress that a minor legal infraction should not prevent placement of a child with a relative who would otherwise be considered appropriate. Finally, it would prohibit state or local government agencies from filing for termination of parental rights in foster care cases solely because the parent was removed from the United States or is involved in an immigration proceeding, unless reasonable efforts to notify the parent of the intent to file such a petition have been made or the person is determined to be unfit or unwilling to be a parent.

CONCLUSIONS

The dilemmas surrounding parental detention and deportation are complex, and they reverberate across multiple spheres. Although a growing body of social science research has examined the effects of parental incarceration on children, there has been far less research on the effects of parental immigration detention. We compare these two sets of findings, identifying a number of parallels and points of overlap, but also multiple ways in which parental immigration detention differs from parental incarceration. This is further complicated by the difficulties families encounter in locating and maintaining contact with detained and deported parents, and by wide variation from state to state in how the immigration and child welfare systems interact.

This chapter has addressed the dilemmas that parental detention and deportation policies and practices create for children, families, and the systems that work with them and identified a set of mechanisms that mitigate or aggravate harm to children. These mechanisms range in scope from the broad prosecutorial discretion policies discussed in chapter 2 to expansion of online detainee locators, to innovative state-level legislation designed to better connect the immigration and child welfare systems and consular offices so that parents may successfully complete required parenting plans and maintain custody of their children. The disconnect across the criminal justice system, the immigration system, and the child welfare system, we find, is extremely problematic, and the lack of coordination is exacerbated by their differing timelines.

A temporary reprieve expected to help five million undocumented immigrant parents was announced on November 20, 2014. As part of a set of immigration-related executive actions, eligibility for deferred action and work authorization was extended to parents of US citizens or lawful permanent residents who have been in the country at least five years, are not removal priorities, and are not otherwise ineligible for consideration (Johnson 2014). This action supplements and amends DACA. It is a significant protection for a large number of families, but it is limited in scope, and because it is not legislation, it may be terminated at any time by a future administration.

We turn next to the growing crisis as tens of thousands of unaccompanied minors are entering the United States. Most of these young immigrants are from Guatemala, El Salvador, and Honduras, and they come north seeking to escape the violence and strife, especially, as well as poverty and lack of opportunity in their homelands.

CHAPTER 5

No Good Options

Unaccompanied Minors in the US Immigration System

If you stay you will die, if you leave, you might; . . . either way it's better to try.
—A youth interviewed by the Women's Refugee Commission (2012, 9)

Immigration law wasn't written with kids in mind.
—Wendy Young, director of Kids in Need of Defense
   (interview, March 13, 2013)

Elián González's story galvanized public attention to the existence and complexities surrounding children entering the United States alone. Elián was five years old in 1999, when his mother and stepfather sought to bring him to the United States. Their raft capsized and they drowned, but Elián was rescued and brought to his uncle in Miami. The uncle wanted Elián to stay in the United States, but his father, still in Cuba, wanted the boy to come home to him. Ultimately, the child was returned to his father, but it created a media frenzy as the public sought to determine whether Elián's best interests were with his father in Cuba or with an unknown relative in the United States.

Attorneys and advocates working with unaccompanied minors told us that although Elián was unusual in terms of the attention he received, his story is emblematic of the inconsistencies in our response to unaccompanied minors. For example, whether a child is eligible for certain types of relief depends in large part upon the child's country of origin and our political ties—or lack thereof—with that government. And, as we have already seen, determinations of what is in the child's best interests may hinge on judges' perceptions of conditions in the parent's home country.

The conundrum of unaccompanied minors exemplifies the political, legal, and social contradictions and tensions inherent in US immigration law. Immigration attorney Aryah Somers, writing with unaccompanied minors Pedro Herrera and Lucia Rodriguez, states, "When children cross the border into the United States, they engage with this complex web of constructions of childhood, different realities of children's rights, laws that protect or punish, and systems that are sensitive to them, ignore them, abuse them or expel them" (Somers, Herrero, and Rodriguez 2010, 315). Similarly, Lauren Heidbrink reminds us, "Law provides an essential site for probing the tension between the unauthorized presence of migrant children and the social norms of children and the family embedded in legal discourses. The law is a potent force shaping the everyday lives of child migrants—where they circulate, how they engage with or evade the state, how and where they access resources and opportunities, with whom they construct social networks, and how they envision their futures" (2014, 85).

Susan Coutin (2000, 2007) suggests that immigrants have a special relationship with law because of its power over them. That is, legal rights and opportunities are attached to a legally defined status, or lack thereof. Although some children are eligible for protection because they have been identified as victims of trafficking or certain other crimes, or because a juvenile court has determined that reunification with one or both parents is not viable due to abuse, neglect, or abandonment, the majority of unaccompanied minors are subject to removal hearings and deportation.

This chapter seeks to further our understandings of unaccompanied child migrants, including their vulnerabilities, how they exercise agency, and the state's response to them. We explore the bureaucratic processes of implementing policies concerning unaccompanied children—that is, the law in action—and the interplay and tensions among policymakers, agency heads, street level bureaucrats, attorneys, and grassroots advocates as they seek to simultaneously uphold the law and meet the children's needs, typically under conditions of insufficient resources. We are especially attentive to the strains on a set of interrelated systems as a consequence of what has come to be called "the surge"—a massive increase in the number of unaccompanied minors entering the United States since about 2011—and the structural mechanisms available to the state that mitigate or exacerbate harm to these youth.

An unknown number of unaccompanied child migrants successfully evade immigration authorities and settle in the United States; given the total number of undocumented youth in the United States, the flow probably exceeds 50,000 per year. Mexican and Canadian youth caught at the border are screened by Customs and Border Patrol (CBP) to assess whether they have a credible fear of return or are victims of trafficking; if not, they are turned around at the border within seventy-two hours. Based on 2009 and 2010 data from CBP and the Mexican authorities, the Appleseed Foundation estimated that 15,500 unaccompanied Mexican children were apprehended annually, with most repatriated immediately (Cavendish and Cortazar 2011). Data for the first two-thirds of the fiscal year suggest that this estimate of about 16,000 Mexican youth is likely valid for 2014 as well, with 95 percent repatriated at the border (Gonzalez-Barrera, Krogstad, and Lopez 2014).

The remaining youth—those who are under age 18, have no lawful immigration status in the United States, and have no parent or legal guardian present and available to provide care and physical custody—are defined by the Homeland Security Act of 2002 as "unaccompanied alien children." Some, like Elián, set out with parents or other family members, becoming separated along the way. Most, though, come alone, or perhaps with a sibling, cousin, or neighbor. These youth are placed in the custody of the Division of Children's Services in the Office of Refugee Resettlement (ORR), which is an agency within the Department of Health and Human Services, for initial screening, temporary housing, and service provision.

The number of youth placed in ORR custody has grown exponentially in recent years. Using the period from fiscal year 2004 to 2011 as a baseline, about 6,775 unaccompanied minors typically entered ORR custody each year. This doubled in FY 2012 to 13,625 children, and doubled once again in FY 2013, reaching 24,668 children (ORR 2014). Government representatives at a meeting of the Interagency Working Group on Unaccompanied Minors in late May 2014 reported that they would certainly reach, and likely surpass, the anticipated level of 60,000 youth in FY 2014. This was a very close estimate; final numbers for FY 2014 indicate 68,541 unaccompanied minors were detained at the border, including some Mexican youth who were immediately turned back (USCBP 2014), and 57,496 youth were placed into ORR custody.[1] A representative from the Office of Refugee Resettlement described the number of unaccompanied minors arriving as "astounding" and "an influx on top of the influx," and a representative from DHS said the adjectives they are using to describe the situation have changed from "significant" to "dramatic" to "alarming."[2]

While in the past a large percentage of unaccompanied minors were from India or China, by 2012 their numbers had decreased drastically in comparison to the numbers of Central American youth entering the United States. Today the vast majority of these youth come from three countries: Guatemala, with 37 percent of the youth, Honduras with 30 percent, and El Salvador with 26 percent (ORR 2013b). These changed demographics reflect the deteriorating social, political, and economic situation within northern Central American, and also raise questions as to whether children from Asia are entering the United States in other ways, such as through trafficking and its associated domestic servitude and sexual slavery.[3]

Unaccompanied minors are younger than ever before, with 24 percent under the age of fourteen in FY 2013 compared to 17 percent in FY 2012. By FY 2014, the average age for youth from Honduras and El Salvador was fourteen, and fifteen for youth from Guatemala, according to the Office of Refugee Resettlement. A DHS official reported that they are seeing children as young as four years old coming into the country alone or with a sibling or cousin who is slightly older.[4] There has also been an upswing in the number of girls undertaking this arduous journey, with girls making up 27 percent of the youth entering ORR custody in FY 2013, compared to 23 percent in FY 2012. This trend continued into the first two-thirds of FY 2014, the latest date for which data are available, with girls making up 40 percent of all Honduran and Salvadoran youth and 24 percent of Guatemalan youth apprehended at the border (Krogstad, Gonzalez-Barrera, and Lopez 2014). Most alarming, the number of unaccompanied girls under age fourteen increased from 335 in FY 2011 (4.5 percent of all referrals to ORR) to 838 in FY 2012 (6.1 percent of all referrals) to 1,908 in FY 2013 (7.6 percent).[5] This accelerated rate of young girls making the journey alone was expected to continue into FY 2014.

Most of the youth have a clear destination in the United States. Many are joining parents or older siblings who migrated ahead of them, although others plan to stay with members of their extended family. Some of the youth will qualify for protective status, but most will ultimately face deportation proceedings and be repatriated to their home countries, where they will likely try again to reach the United States.

A number of recent studies have explored the underlying reasons for this surge in unaccompanied minors, the violence and trauma they experienced in their home countries and on their journey to the United States, their quality of care and service provisions while in custody and post-release, and their experiences upon repatriation. This chapter draws upon this research, but our specific focus is on the structural, systemic mechanisms that mitigate or exacerbate the vulnerability of these youth, as identified by attorneys, advocates, government officials, and service providers. In addition to interviews and data that are either publicly available or were provided to us, we draw on discussions at a series of interagency working group meetings on unaccompanied children attended by the first author between September 2012 and May 2014. These meetings include representatives of the Departments of Homeland Security (DHS), Justice, State, and Health and Human Services, service providers such as Lutheran Immigration and Refugee Service (LIRS) and the US Conference of Catholic Bishops (USCCB), nongovernmental organizations including the Women's Refugee Commission and Kids in Need of Defense (KIND), the Office of the United Nations High Commissioner for Refugees (UNHCR), and immigration law clinics.

THE DECISION TO MAKE THE JOURNEY

Several recent publications have addressed the root causes of the surge in unaccompanied minors making the treacherous journey from Central America, and specifically from Guatemala, El Salvador, and Honduras through Mexico to the United States (Bhabha 2014; Heidbrink 2014; Kids In Need of Defense [KIND] 2013, National Immigrant Justice Center 2014; Nazario 2006; Somers 2012a; Terrio 2015; United Nations High Commissioner for Refugees [UNHCR] 2014; United States Committee for Refugees and Immigrants 2013; United States Conference of Catholic Bishops [USCCB] 2014; Ward 2013; Women's Refugee Commission 2012). The National Immigrant Justice Center compiled data from hundreds of intake interviews with unaccompanied minors held in government custody in the Chicago area. They report that 52 percent of the youth experienced gang or other violence or domestic abuse, and 48 percent left because of poverty, natural disaster, because they no longer had anyone to care for them, or to reunite with parents. Altogether, 61 percent of the youth hoped to reunite with one or both parents living in the United States (National Immigrant Justice Center 2014, 2).

The inability of the home country to provide security for youth and their families was a major finding of the UN High Commissioner for Refugees' study on Salvadoran, Honduran, Guatemalan, and Mexican youth entering the United States since October 2011. The UNHCR found that 58 percent of the youth were forcibly displaced because they suffered or faced harm that rises to the level of potentially requiring international protection (2014, 6). Nearly half of the youth they interviewed (48 percent) had been personally affected by violence in the region involving drug cartels, gangs, state actors, or other organized armed criminal actors, and 22 percent had experienced abuse and violence by a parent or other caretaker in their homes (2014, 6).

The US Conference of Catholic Bishops conducted a fact-finding trip to the region in November 2013, concluding that a "perfect storm" of social, economic, and political problems "coalesced to create this phenomenon" (USCCB 2014, 2). Notwithstanding the importance of lack of jobs and of access to education, and a desire to reunify with family, they conclude, "one overriding factor has played a decisive and forceful role in recent years: generalized violence at the state and local levels and a corresponding breakdown of the rule of law have threatened citizen security and created a culture of fear and hopelessness" (2014, 2). Most notably, the Mexican-based Los Zetas cartel has contracted with local Mara Salvatrucha (MS-13) and Barrio 18 gangs to expand its influence in Central America. The growth of copycat and loosely affiliated gangs add to "the anonymous but increasing threat of violence affecting daily life" (USCCB 2014, 3). The gangs require protection money from families and small businesses, accost and rape girls and women, and viciously beat boys who are not willing to join the gang, making many youth and their families fear that they have no choice but to migrate.

A report by Kids In Need of Defense offers numerous examples of such cases from among the youth they have served. Alberto's case is typical of these youths' experiences. Alberto lived with his grandmother in El Salvador:

> When Alberto reached adolescence, he was scouted by gangs in his community and pressured to join. They followed him to school; Alberto would take different routes, but they would ultimately find him. On one occasion, they chased him with loaded guns and shot him. The gangs made a list of people who refused to join and posted it in the town; everyone on that list would be killed. Alberto's name was on the list. Fearing for his life, Alberto would only leave his home to go to school. . . . One of Alberto's cousins who had also refused to join the gang was killed by gang members. . . . Alberto's mother made arrangements for him to the come to the U.S. soon after. (KIND 2013, 19)

Similarly, the National Immigrant Justice Center reports on nine-year-old Beatrice: "After her sister was murdered in 2010, her family moved within El Salvador to escape the gang, but they never felt she was safe. Beatrice's mother, who lives in New York and sends money to the family, wanted Beatrice to join her because gangs were threatening to kill Beatrice unless the family paid 'protection' fees" (2014, 2).

Although gang violence is a major reason for the increased number of youth coming to the United States from Central America's northern triangle, gangs should be understood as a *part* of the larger context of structural violence, political instability, corruption, and economic uncertainty. It is this larger set of factors, which is often manifested through the immediate threat of gang violence, that weighs heavily in decisions by youth and their families that they should leave. These stressors may be aggravated when one or both parents have already migrated to the United States. For example, the remaining parent may become involved with a new partner who does not want the child or who is abusive. Grandmothers and aunts may no longer be able to care for a child left behind, and teenagers may feel, or be told, that it is time for them to head north, both for their own safety and to contribute to the family's finances through remittances.

The US government's history of military interventions and uneven development and trade policies were instrumental in creating the current crisis in the region, although these dynamics play out in slightly different ways, depending on the country. In Guatemala, repeated droughts and a coffee fungus have exacerbated the lack of economic opportunities and led to a food crisis, especially in rural areas where political violence and corruption have been rampant for decades (Women's Refugee Commission 2012; USCCB 2013). Three dominant themes emerged among Guatemalan children interviewed by the UN High Commissioner for Refugees: "deprivation, discussed by 29% of the children; abuse in the home, discussed by 23%; and violence in society, discussed by 20%" (2014, 9). Another 5 percent of the Guatemalan children reported having been victims of both abuse at home and more general societal violence. The UNHCR report adds that these problems are especially severe among members of the indigenous population, noting that the indigenous communities have been hard-hit by military and paramilitary conflicts (see similarly Menjívar 2011). Most of the Guatemalan children interviewed (84 percent) also cited family reunification, work, and educational opportunities as reasons for migrating to the United States (2014, 10).

Political instability in Honduras has led some to call it a failed state, unable to maintain the rule of law. According to the Women's Refugee Commission, "Over the past few years, Honduras has become one of the most dangerous countries in the world. In 2011, Honduras earned the dubious distinction of having the highest murder rate in the world, with 86 people killed for every 100,000, up from 82 in 2010" (2012, 9). The homicide rate rose to 90.4 in 2012, almost 1,900 percent higher than the US rate (United Nations Office on Drugs and Crime, 2014; Center for American Progress 2014). The Women's Refugee Commission continues, "In addition to the gang violence, women and girls face specific vulnerabilities to violence and lack meaningful access to justice. Violence against women and gender-based murders ('femicides') are on the rise in Honduras, with over 2,000 women murdered between 2006 and 2011" (2012, 10). Similarly, the UN High Commissioner for Refugees report found that 57 percent of the Honduran youth interviewed had potential claims for international protection: 44 percent were victims of, or threatened with, violence by organized armed criminal actors, 24 percent reported abuse at home, and 11 percent reported victimization both in the home and in society more generally. Deprivation, family reunification, and better opportunities for work or education were also cited, but these positive reasons were almost always linked to negative push factors (2014, 10).

El Salvador has been hard hit by the global recession and related reduction in remittances sent to support those left at home (USCCB 2014). Violence, especially gang violence, continues to be a primary factor, however, in young people's decisions to migrate to the United States. Again quoting the Women's Refugee Commission: "As in Honduras, the violence in El Salvador is largely the result of the rising influence of criminal gangs, which recruit children and teenagers to conduct illegal activities like drug trafficking and extortion. Gangs have increasingly begun targeting children at their schools, resulting in El Salvador having one of the lowest school attendance rates in Latin America" (2012, 10). The UN High Commissioner for Refugees study found that 72 percent of the Salvadoran children interviewed had potential international protection needs. Sixty-six percent of the youth cited violence by organized armed criminal actors, 21 percent cited abuse in the home, and 15 percent noted violence both in the home and in society more generally. In contrast, only 7 percent cited deprivation as a primary motivator for migrating (2014, 9).

Paradoxically, the militarization of the US border with Mexico has resulted in parents who are now living in the United States not daring to travel to their home countries to see their children or to bring their children back with them. Instead, the children are coming on their own. As an attorney told us, "Since it is so much more difficult to cross, a lot of families are staying in the United States and having the kids cross here on their own. A lot of families. So there are more women and there are more children."

As difficult as the journey is, the youth and the family members who help arrange for their journey report that they do not feel they have a choice, as conditions in their homeland are untenable. Lindsay Marshall, then director of the Florence Immigrant and Refugee Rights Project, summarized the situation for us: "And these kids, a lot of them are indigenous language speakers. A lot of them come from really abusive or neglectful families or just don't have anybody to take care of them. Victims of gang violence. They don't have a shot at a safe and productive life where they are. And so they are coming here."[6] Heidbrink (2014; see also Bhabha 2014 and Terrio 2015) reminds us that even when children do not make the decision to leave on their own, they are not just passively following determinations made by a parent, grandmother, or other family members. Rather, they are exercising agency as active participants in what is often a collective decision about whether they should migrate, and, if so, when, and where they should go.

THE DANGEROUS JOURNEY: PERILS ALONG THE WAY

The trip north has never been easy, but it has grown even more perilous in recent years. The trains through Mexico are extremely dangerous. Stories abound of migrants who have lost legs caught under wheels while climbing onto or jumping from *la bestia*, as the freight trains are called. Migrants are robbed, and may be thrown off the moving train if they are unable to pay the fees charged by gangs and corrupt police officers (Heidbrink 2014; Nazario 2006; USCCB 2013; Ward 2013). A low-hanging branch can leave deep gashes on faces and arms or knock a child who did not duck fast enough off the top of the train. Youth who do not tie themselves down tightly may roll off the train if they fall asleep. Despite these dangers, youth and their families often see migration as the only option available. As a youth in ORR custody told representatives of the Women's Refugee Commission, "If you stay you will die, if you leave, you might. . . . Either way it's better to try" (Women's Refugee Commission 2012, 9).

Children may leave home alone or as part of a small group of cousins, siblings, other relatives, or neighbors. Even when they embark on the journey together, they are often separated along the way while jumping trains, running from police or gangs, or circumventing immigration checkpoints in Mexico. They may travel much of the way unescorted or be handed off from *coyote* to *coyote*, depending on what they can afford. They may join up with other youth or adults, and perhaps those adults will watch out for them, but they may also rob the children or simply not help them if so doing increases the adult's own risk of getting caught.

Families that can scrape together the funds arrange for girls to travel by bus and to enter the country at border crossings with false papers, rather than risk the dangers of *la bestia*. For girls whose families cannot afford this, however, the trip is especially perilous. Girls are likely to be raped by gangs, traffickers, police, and even other migrants. Amnesty International reported in 2010, "It is a widely held view—shared by local and international NGOs and health professionals working with migrant women—that as many as six in 10 migrant women and girls are raped" (2010, 15). The US Committee for Refugees and Immigrants reports similarly that 57 percent of the sixty-seven female (child and adult) migrants they surveyed responded "all of the above" when asked what risks they would be willing to take—the risks identified included assault, rape, forced work, kidnapping, and death (2013, 38).

Rape has become so commonplace that women will arrange for their daughters and granddaughters to receive birth control injections, which last for three months, prior to embarking on the trip. A story told to us by members of the US Conference of Catholic Bishops delegation poignantly illuminates both the dangers and the sense of helplessness experienced by family members. Delegation members said that while they were waiting with grandmothers, mothers, and other family members for the bus bringing repatriated child migrants back to El Salvador, Salvadoran government officials warned the family members of what to expect, detailing the trauma that their children would likely experience. The mothers and grandmothers told members of the delegation that they knew their daughters and granddaughters might be beaten and raped, but they felt they had no choice, as they were certain the girls would be raped and might be killed if they remained in El Salvador.[7] As the mother of a sixteen-year-old girl told delegation members, "I know the journey is dangerous, but it's dangerous here" (USCCB 2013, 6).

Delegation member and associate director of children's services at the US Conference of Catholic Bishops Kristyn Peck recounted:

> These women were helpless. There is a desperation. There is a feeling that they had no ability to protect their children. This was in El Salvador, and they felt as

though they had no other option. They were describing this as an impossible decision. It was an impossible decision. We can't protect them here and we know they are not going to be safe on the journey, but we send them anyway with the possibility that there is hope at the end of the journey and that they will be protected when they arrive. This was a group of women who were ashamed. They felt like they had failed as parents. We heard again and again that they felt there was absolutely no other choice.[8]

The fact that these women, many of whom were devout Catholics, would tell church officials that they had arranged for their daughters to receive birth control signaled to members of the delegation, and to us, just how grave the dangers were for these girls if they stayed at home.

The same is true in Guatemala, where some women may bring their daughters to a clinic for a birth control shot before she sets out on her journey, knowing she may be raped along the way. Family members will tell their neighbors that they sent their daughters to Guatemala City rather than to the United States, so that if the girls are caught and repatriated, the girls will not be shamed by people assuming they are no longer virgins.[9] It does not matter that this loss of virginity was due to rape, involuntary prostitution required by traffickers, or the "payment" required for someone's help along the way.

We also heard stories of girls' creatively finding ways to protect themselves. Aryah Somers told us of a conversation she had with a Honduran girl: "I asked her, are you sure nothing happened to you on the journey, no one tried to touch you or abuse you or rape you or anything, and she said, 'No, I just told everyone I had AIDS.' And I was like, 'Oh my God, that is brilliant. You are so smart.' So, you know, I think that they try to prepare."[10]

The trip north has also become more expensive, costing $6,000–$7,000 per person from Honduras. For some, this is too expensive, especially given the risk that they will be caught. Susan Terrio recalls a sixteen-year-old boy pointing out that the *coyote*'s fee is only worthwhile if he is successful (2015). Otherwise, the family risks losing its home or land, if those were put forth as collateral, and still must pay the *coyote*'s fee. The interest charged on loans can be exorbitant, with families able to repay them only through remittances sent home from successful migrants.

In late 2013 and early 2014, stories were circulating widely about a three-for-one deal being offered by smugglers in Guatemala, at least some of whom were affiliated with the cartels. As reported by the US Conference of

Catholic Bishops delegation: "A new trend is for coyotes to promise three attempts for the price of one, with families taking a mortgage out on their home to cover the cost of the coyote and then the coyote failing in order to gain the deed for the family's land with the coyote taking ownership of the land himself personally, or as part of a criminal enterprise" (2013, 4). When this was reported at a meeting of the Interagency Working Group on Unaccompanied Minors, other participants stated that they also had heard about this "three-tries-for-the-price-of-one" deal, and of families losing their land as a result.

Along the way, youth may be held ransom by members of organized gangs or traffickers. Their families may be extorted for additional funds in return for their freedom, or the youth may be forced into involuntary servitude, including sex work, to pay off new debts incurred during the journey. Yet traveling alone is not a viable option for most youth. The build-up of the border through enhanced technology, personnel, and new fencing—what Meissner et al. (2013) call the "formidable machinery" of immigration enforcement—has forced immigrants to cross in increasingly dangerous sectors, and many die crossing the Rio Grande or from exposure and dehydration in the desert. As Susan Terrio tells us, "At a time when more children are migrating from Mexico and Central America, it is more dangerous than ever to enter the United States illegally. An immigrant attempting to cross the border in 2013 was eight times more likely to die than a decade ago" (2015, 38; see similarly Weber and Pickering 2011).

APPREHENSION AND TRANSFER TO ORR CUSTODY

The Homeland Security Act of 2002 transferred custody of unaccompanied minors from Immigration and Naturalization Services (INS) to the Office of Refugee Resettlement within the Department of Health and Human Services, effective 2003. This was re-emphasized in the Trafficking Victims Protection Reauthorization Act (TVPRA) of 2008, which requires Customs and Border Patrol (CBP) agents to transfer any minor determined to be unaccompanied, not from a contiguous country, or from a contiguous country but potentially eligible for protection from trafficking, abuse, or exploitation, to ORR within seventy-two hours of their apprehension.

A report by the DHS Office of the Inspector General determined that CBP policies regarding minors were in compliance with legal stipulations (United States Department of Homeland Security 2010). However, advocates continue to express concerns regarding the inappropriateness of CBP holding cells for children, the lack of basic legal advice while in CBP detention, abusive behaviors by CBP agents, and the lack of training among CBP agents who interview youth to determine whether they are victims of trafficking, abuse, or exploitation (Women's Refugee Commission 2012). In addition, the National Immigrant Justice Center reports that 1,366 immigrant children were detained for at least three days in adult detention facilities between 2008 and 2012. Of these, "nearly 1,000 children spent at least one week in adult custody" (2013, 1). This is likely an undercount, because they were only able to obtain data from thirty of the approximately two hundred adult detention facilities under contract with DHS at that time.

Responsibility for determining that a youth is in fact an unaccompanied minor and the appropriate placement level within ORR facilities falls to ICE. Immigration officers must determine that the person is under the age of eighteen, is not accompanied by a parent, and is not from a contiguous country. To identify appropriate placement within ORR, ICE considers whether the youth is a recent border crosser, has a history of prior border crossings or a delinquent or criminal history in the United States, or is suspected of gang or criminal involvement. Heidbrink (2014) argues that the DHS determination of whether a youth is unaccompanied is not always straightforward. In some cases, she suggests, it appears to depend on factors such as ICE and ORR bed capacity and other resources, and decisions to separately detain a family member with whom the youth was traveling or living (for example, because the adult had a prior criminal charge or mandatory order of deportation).

ORR PLACEMENT

Moving the custody and care of unaccompanied minors to ORR was lauded by immigration and child welfare advocates and attorneys, because many youth had previously been housed in secure juvenile detention centers where they could not access necessary legal and educational resources, including interpreters, and did not have adequate space for recreation (Bhabha and Schmidt 2006, 2011; Byrne 2008; Heidbrink 2014; Women's Refugee Commission 2009, 2012). In combination with the 1997 Flores Settlement Agreement, which set the minimum standards for care for immigrant youth under federal custody, this move has substantially improved conditions for unaccompanied minors.

Yet scholars and advocates raise ongoing concerns, including the length of detention within ORR facilities, children's uncertainty as to what will happen to them, placement of children in facilities that are more secure than is necessary, and the capacity of ORR to provide adequate and sufficient legal, educational, psychological, and other resources for the youth. Susan Terrio notes, "Detention centers are spaces of exception where the competing agendas of humanitarianism and security collide" (2015, 12). Lauren Heidbrink describes detention in even starker terms: "While migration is often framed as a disturbance, trauma, or rupture in the lives of children, detention becomes a traumatic experience marked by anxiety, uncertainty, and powerlessness in ways migration may not be for many youths" (2014, 111–12).

Most unaccompanied minors are caught by Customs and Border Patrol agents shortly after they have entered the country; typically within a week and often within hours (Byrne and Miller 2012). Because most youth enter the immigration system close to the southern border, the majority of ORR-contracted shelters are located in the southwestern United States. When the youth come into ORR shelters, or what Kimberly Haynes of Lutheran Immigration and Refugee Services prefers to call "transitional centers," they often show up "with burrs in their hair, and haven't had a shower yet. [Staff] are the first responders, assessing the circumstances and the kids' situations."[11] This assessment includes an evaluation of the youths' needs and determination of whether they will ultimately be released to a family member or to some other form of custodial care.

The number of youth in ORR facilities and where they are housed tends to be rather fluid, depending upon what is available that day. Options include large residential centers housing more than two hundred children each, staff-secure shelters, therapeutic shelters, residential treatment centers, group homes, community-based group foster care, and family foster care.

According to the Office of Refugee Resettlement, half of all youth were held in secure detention facilities when ORR took over responsibility for unaccompanied minors in 2003. As Table 5.1 demonstrates, this decreased to 7.5 percent in FY 2012 (5.3 percent in staff secure, 1.5 percent secure, and 0.7 percent in therapeutic secure placements), and to 2.4 percent in FY 2013 (1.4 percent in staff secure, 0.4 percent in secure, and 0.6 percent in therapeutic secure placements).[12] In contrast, the vast majority of youth are placed in shelters (84 percent in FY 2012 and 86 percent in FY 2013) or transitional foster care (6 percent in FY 2012 and almost 8 percent in FY 2013). Neverthe-

TABLE 5.1 ORR PLACEMENTS BY PROGRAM TYPE

Referred Placements for UAC	FY 12	FY 13
Long-term foster care	271 (1.8%)	288 (1.2%)
Residential treatment center	70 (0.5%)	6 (0.0%)
Secure	221 (1.5%)	107 (0.4%)
Shelter	12,369 (84.0%)	21,553 (86.1%)
Staff secure	779 (5.3%)	338 (1.4%)
Therapeutic staff secure	107 (0.7%)	154 (0.6%)
Transitional foster care	863 (5.9%)	1,938 (7.7%)
Group home	3 (0.0%)	130 (0.5%)
Blank	38 (0.3%)	527 (2.1%)
Total	14,721 (100.0%)	25,041 (100.0%)

SOURCE: Personal email communication from Office of Refugee Resettlement spokesperson Lisa Raffonelli to first author, March 26, 2014. ORR provided raw numbers; percentages calculated by authors.

less, several attorneys and advocates pointed out that even the shelters are highly restrictive places, and children are not allowed to leave the building, or even go from one part of the house or building to another, without staff escort. Although everyone acknowledged that some youth may require detention, overall most felt that this level of supervision was unnecessarily strict.

By 2012, the increased numbers of youth entering the United States had created enormous systemic strains. The most immediate pressure for CBP and ORR was finding emergency beds. They opened facilities along the southern border wherever they identified temporary space—including gymnasiums, Border Patrol stations, and a Texas Air Force base (Women's Refugee Commission 2012; Terrio 2015). These holding stations were in violation of the Flores Settlement Agreement, although the agreement included language permitting exceptions in cases of emergency, which ORR argued the surge constituted. In fairness, ORR was able to open additional facilities fairly quickly and closed the surge facilities.

Terrio reports that in 2012, ORR had 2,927 beds in sixty-nine facilities, and by 2013 they had 5,000 beds in eighty-three facilities (2015, 11). In May 2013, an ORR representative reported to members of the Interagency Working Group on Unaccompanied Youth that they had a 4,300-bed capacity and 3,800 children in their care, though they expected they would reach their maximum of 5,100 beds given the anticipated flow.[13] By May 2014, they had exceeded this capacity, and once again children were being held in CBP facilities for ten or more days, with some held in overflow emergency beds at the Lackland Air Force Base in Texas until sufficient ORR shelter space became available.[14] By June, youth were also being held at a naval base in Oxnard, California, and an emergency shelter in Nogales, Arizona.

For those youth who require foster care, ORR contracts with the United States Conference of Catholic Bishops (USCCB) and Lutheran Immigration and Refugee Service (LIRS). These voluntary agencies are accustomed to working with unaccompanied refugees, having done so for many years, and they have expanded their operations to include some minors who are not eligible for refugee/asylee status. They have developed a faith-based intervention that incorporates licensed safe haven shelters run by their local affiliates, screening, release practices, and post-release follow-up. Since late 2012, LIRS and USCCB have also operated transitional shelter care in small group homes where unaccompanied minors stay for 10–30 days.

While in ORR Custody: Legal, Medical, and Other Screenings

Once in ORR custody, youth receive a "Know Your Rights" legal orientation, typically offered in Spanish, and are screened by pro bono attorneys to assess whether they have a claim for refugee status or other forms of protection under the Trafficking Victims Protection Reauthorization Act.

Youth also receive medical, dental, and psychological screenings, and the staff begins the process of identifying and contacting a family member or other sponsor and certifying that this is an appropriate placement. If there is no family available, or if a home study suggests that the family placement is not safe, the youth may be placed in long-term foster care. Youth are still in federal custody while in long-term foster care, which may last for six months to a year or even longer while their eligibility for legal relief is sorted out.

In addition to ORR, the rapid and exponential increase in numbers has also stressed the network of pro bono attorneys, social service providers, and immigration judges. Most youth have their initial court appearance in removal proceedings scheduled while they are in ORR custody. Given the strains on the network of pro bono attorneys, they generally appear at this first hearing without benefit of legal counsel. Social services are also struggling to cope with the increased caseload. As Kimberly Haynes, director of Children's Services for Lutheran Immigration and Refugee Services told us, "It wasn't. ever anticipated that this model would need to be sustainable for this size of a population. Retrospectively, if we looked at the population we would need to sustain, I think we would have changed the model." The surge has "created a human service response they were never staffed for, or envisioned the magnitude of what occurred." In hindsight, she suggests, a more appropriate model would be to make many of the assessments after the youth is with family, in the community, and not while they are in ORR custody.[15]

In many ways, these providers resemble the street-level workers discussed by Lipsky (1980), Maynard-Moody and Musheno (2012), and others. They have to balance a huge caseload, exercise discretion in determining who needs or deserves which services based on what is often very limited information, and they must make these decisions quickly so they can move on to the next case. A former service provider told us that there is a push by ORR and the agency for which she had worked to process the youth as quickly as possible, and not to question them too much or encourage them to disclose situations in which they might be eligible for relief. The weight of these decisions is monumental for the youth, as it may mean they are sent back to a potentially deadly situation or placed with someone who will abuse or exploit them instead of caring for them, and the decisions must be made in a context of minimal interactions with highly traumatized youth.

The faster pace of processing as a consequence of the surge moves youth out the door quickly to make room for the next child who needs a bed. In FY 2011, the average length of stay in ORR was between sixty-nine and seventy-two days. By the winter and spring of 2013, ORR was reporting an average length of stay of fifty-three days, and by December 2013, it had dropped to thirty-five days (Office of Refugee Resettlement 2013a,b; Women's Refugee Commission 2012). As of early 2014, the average length of stay was down to thirty days.[16]

Attorneys, advocates, and service providers express mixed feelings about this faster process, reflecting the twin goals of quickly reuniting youth with family members and of ensuring that they are not at risk of abuse or exploitation. As Jennifer Podkul and Michelle Brané of the Women's Refugee Commission summarized, "This whole issue of ORR releasing kids so quickly creates a lot of tension within an advocacy community. Some people think it is good news. But it is not really good news in some cases, because of child safety concerns. It is difficult to advocate on behalf of these kids and take both sides. . . . We really need to think more about protections, protection not detention. So it is not so much a question of releasing versus not releasing, but of what is the most holistic best interest approach."[17]

Children and teenagers may not immediately open up to a stranger about any concerns they have regarding the placement. And although staff probably can spot a trafficker quickly, the faster processing means they may miss a sponsor who appears to be a loving uncle but who plans to keep the child out of school and force him or her to work to pay off the *coyote*'s fees or to provide care for family members, essentially as an indentured servant. Wendy Young, director of Kids in Need of Defense (KIND), told us:

> They do home studies for particularly vulnerable kids, and then they do follow-up services post release. But it is time limited. And I am not sure what percentage of kids they are able to reach. And I can tell you, there are horrific stories of what happens to these kids post release. . . . And I mean, just the stories of sexual abuse, not allowing the kids to go to school, forcing them to work. Sometimes in really inappropriate conditions. We have one girl who, her uncle told her, "I have to take care of you so you are going to make the money, you don't go to school." And she was like fifteen or sixteen and was cleaning a strip club. You know, just awful, awful stories. I am not a proponent of detaining kids, but I do think more needs to be done to make sure children are put in safe houses.[18]

For these reasons, service providers expressed concern that efficiency was preempting protection as a primary goal. Holding providers accountable for processing and releasing youth within thirty days did not always allow for a proper assessment of whether the placement was a safe haven.

Home Studies

Home studies play an important function for certain unaccompanied minors. The TVPRA of 2008 requires ORR to conduct home studies if the child is "a victim of a severe form of trafficking in persons, a special needs child with a disability, . . . a child who has been a victim of physical or sexual abuse under circumstances that indicate that the child's health or welfare has been significantly harmed or threatened, or a child whose proposed sponsor clearly presents a risk of abuse, maltreatment, exploitation, or trafficking to the child" (TVPRA 2008, Sec. 235c3(b)). Home studies may also be conducted in other cases, as needed. Like other services, though, the increased volume of children entering the system has reduced the number of youth receiving home studies. Data provided by ORR indicate that home studies were conducted for only about 5 percent of the unaccompanied minors in ORR custody in FY 2012 and 2013.[19]

The home study includes a review of the sponsor's financial status, criminal background check, verification of the relationship between the child and the sponsor through birth certificates or other documentation, and evaluation of the suitability of the care provider and the environment, including assessment of the home, child care arrangements, and perhaps local schools (Heidbrink 2014; Terrio 2015). Fingerprinting previously had been required, but is no longer necessary for biological parents.[20]

When we asked advocates and attorneys whether certain groups of youth were especially vulnerable, several mentioned the greater risk that Chinese and Indian youth were victims of trafficking or, if not explicitly trafficking, some form of indentured servitude to repay the costs of smuggling them into the United States. At the same time, they also worry that they may be too quick to assume that all Chinese youth are being exploited, and, conversely, that other youth are not trafficking victims. Lauren Heidbrink suggests that this screening may reflect institutional and personal biases that are

> woven into the institutional practices and procedures of ORR, ICE, immigration judges, and immigration law based on a child's illegality and country of origin. There was an institutional presumption that all Chinese and Indian children are trafficked and thus require a "suitability assessment" of potential sponsors or family members. . . . Such rigorous screening processes have not historically nor with such uniformity applied to Mexican and Central American youth, who are presumed to migrate for economic reasons or to reunify with family members already in the United States (2014, 96).

This tension between the need for careful home studies and the desire to reunite youth with family members and get them out of detention as swiftly as possible manifested in multiple ways. As an example, Maria Woltjen of the Young Center offered the case of a deaf child for whom a home study is required under the TVPRA:

> The government does a home study of the parent of a child who is deaf. The TVPRA[21] requires a home study, but it makes no sense, it's not logical. If the child were going to a relative, or a family friend, then yes, there should be a home study because that person may not know how to care for the child. If there's an allegation of abuse or neglect or abandonment by a parent then yes, do a home study, but if there's not, then I don't understand why a deaf child stays in custody with no appropriate education and no one who speaks his language, when his mother is here and she speaks sign language and he can't get reunified with her.[22]

FAMILY REUNIFICATION

Once the child has been screened and the placement determined to be appropriate, either through a brief assessment or a full-blown home study, the youth is reunited with his or her sponsor. Most of the experts we interviewed felt the family reunification process worked reasonably well. According to a study by the Vera Institute of Justice, between October 2008 and September 2010 more than 85 percent of unaccompanied minors were placed with family or other sponsors. Of these youth, 32 percent were released to parents, 19 percent to aunts or uncles, 9 percent to siblings, 3 percent to grandparents, 5 percent to cousins, 3 percent to step-parents or parent's partners, and 27 percent to family friends (Byrne and Miller 2012). The percentage of youth released to a sponsor increased slightly by December 2013, to 88–90 percent, about half of whom were released to parents.[23]

In the past, family members were required to claim the child at an ORR-contracted facility. Many were stopped by immigration authorities along the way, raising levels of fear and distrust within the immigrant community. As a government official told us, at that time "there were well-grounded fears that parents would be picked up by Border Patrol or ICE." Now, if the family provides the funds, the child and caseworker will fly to meet the parents, thus reducing the risk that parents or other family members without proper documentation will be picked up by immigration authorities at the bus station, or while passing through Border Patrol checkpoints along the way. The general approach of ORR to the parent or other family member's immigration status was described to us as, "sort of 'don't ask, don't tell.' And they don't. ORR doesn't share that information with ICE. They do share information about sponsors and their addresses. I don't think they give any information about their legal status, though." Similarly, a government official told us, "ORR has a single focus—the care and custody of kids. They do much better than INS ever did. The effect on the parent-child relationship has tremendously improved since ORR took over."

Post-release Services

The need for social and legal services upon release from ORR is, by all accounts, enormous, but current funding priorities allocate minimal resources for them. As a result, very few youth receive post-release services. As Terrio notes, "Huge resources go to electronic detection, risk assessments, psycho-social evaluations, preliminary legal screenings, detention bed space, staff recruitment, immigration adjudications, and deportations, whereas legal representation for minors in immigration court, comprehensive postrelease tracking, and long-term social services are not funded" (Terrio 2015, 12).

The TVPRA of 2008 requires that follow-up services be provided for children for whom a home study was conducted. Follow-up services may continue until the youth turns eighteen or the legal case terminates. Services may also be provided for a more limited time for youth released without a mandated home study if the screening while in ORR custody indicated that the youth could benefit from such assistance. Kimberly Haynes of LIRS explained:

> There are some key triggers in the shelter care that, once triggered, mean the kids automatically are required to be referred for post-follow-up services. Now they have gone back home, a case manager is getting linked up with them and support services are provided to the family as an entirety. . . . There is a whole prescription of what constitutes the key minimum service, and that includes linkages to school, mental health, legal and social support. They work around those kinds of issues to ensure that the families are linked up. But again, that's only for about 10 percent of the kids.[24]

ORR reports that 2,267 youth (16.6 percent) received follow-up services in FY 2012. About the same number of youth received services in FY 2013 (2,457), but given the greater volume of youth in shelter care, the percentage dropped to just 9.9 percent of the youth leaving ORR.[25] The percentage for FY 2014 is not yet available but is expected to reflect a further decrease, given the escalating numbers. Whether the decreased availability of follow-up services has negative effects on youth is unclear, as ORR stated in response to our query that they do not have data on how well children who received post-release services fare relative to those who do not receive services.

Post-release services are arranged through nongovernmental organizations (NGOs) contracted with ORR, principally Lutheran Immigrant and Refugee Services and the US Conference of Catholic Bishops. Wherever possible, they work with local providers who know how to navigate resources and services in the receiving community. For example, they know which medical providers will accept uninsured children and who to go to within the school system to enroll a child with special needs midyear. In these and other ways, these providers go beyond supplying services; they are building capacity in the community to accept and service these children and their families.

Follow-up services include mental health support for trauma, sexual violence, and generalized community violence. Service providers note that "trauma is huge," the percentage of girls who have been sexually assaulted is "way up," and "we have seen a steady increase in the sexual violence they have either experienced themselves, seen, or had exposed to them." Although ORR told us that they do not track data on pregnancies,[26] several different sources told us that approximately 6 percent of the girls are pregnant when they arrive in the United States. Others suggest the number of pregnant girls may be even higher; as one attorney told us, "We see quite a few girls that are pregnant." It is not clear whether they became pregnant in their home country or along the way, but as Kristyn Peck of USCCB told us, "Girls are at incredible risk for rape during the migration journey.... [The number] was really staggering."[27]

Follow-up services can also ensure that youth are being cared for properly and that they are reintegrated into their families. As one attorney noted, "These kids are coming up to join their parents or to work, but they haven't lived with their parents since they were two ... [and] most parents often have new children, new families." Kimberly Haynes adds, "It is really negotiating that re-immersion into the family construct that we see as a grave need. What we have been hearing through the attorney legal pro bono networks that we have relationships with is that they have a huge number of cases that are having homelessness, domestic violence, CPS involvement, family breakdowns, shuffling of kids around with different family members, because that support for integrating a child back into a family is not there."

Service providers may also help the youth obtain access to education. The Supreme Court ruled in 1982, in *Plyler v. Doe*, that all children are entitled to an education, regardless of their immigration status. Sometimes, though, schools do not wish to enroll the youth, especially midyear, and service providers must intervene. In spring 2014, the Obama administration issued new guidance reminding schools that every child must be allowed to enroll in public school.[28]

For the 90 percent of youth who do not receive federally funded post-release services, a few receive needed services from religious organizations or other nonprofits. For instance, USCCB has a small pilot program serving twenty-five released youth at any given time, funded through church funds, and KIND and Catholic Legal Immigration Network (CLINIC) provide services and legal representation through private donations.

Youth who age out of ORR custody at eighteen but who have not been reunited with family members are a particularly vulnerable group. Local agencies may be able to help support them while the youth tries to make a claim for legal protection, but because they are no longer in a federal program, they are not entitled to any services. More often, as Terrio describes, "aging out" signals "[t]he end of ORR jurisdiction, a transfer to ICE custody, and disappearance into the black hole of adult detention. Federal staff, attorneys, and advocates all related accounts of ICE officers arriving without prior warning to handcuff and remove youth from ORR facilities on their eighteenth birthday—often right after midnight" (2015, 153).

NAVIGATING IMMIGRATION COURT PROCEEDINGS

Removal proceedings are adversarial in nature and uneven in power. This power imbalance is especially visible in the case of childhood immigrants. Advocates and attorneys frequently tell stories of young children sitting in front of the immigration judge, their feet swinging in the air because they are too short to reach the floor, clutching a doll someone gave them. These proceedings are complicated under the best of circumstances, and for a child who may not speak English, or Spanish for that matter, and who is appearing alone before a judge, they are especially challenging. For this reason, KIND and the Center for Gender and Refugee Studies titled their 2014 report, *A Treacherous Journey: Child Migrants Navigating the U.S. Immigration System,* borrowing the common description of the trip north as treacherous to demonstrate that the trip through the immigration system is also fraught with peril.

Section 235 of the TVPRA calls for child-protection-based measures, including the appointment of child advocates, nonadversarial asylum interviews, permanent protection for certain at-risk children, and procedural and substantive considerations of the special needs of children (Somers 2011). Thus far, however, binding child-sensitive guidelines or regulations for immigration court proceedings are still lacking (KIND/Center for Gender and Refugee Studies 2014). According to immigration attorneys, children may be subject to hostile, insensitive, or inappropriate questioning by judges and ICE attorneys, and there is insufficient training for immigration judges regarding child development and best practices for interviewing children.

Unaccompanied children present a conundrum to the state. They are children, and as such are deserving of protection. Without adult guardians, the state becomes their protector. Yet this means the state must protect the youth against itself, in its enforcement capacity, and the state does not handle this contradiction well when it comes to immigration law. As Lauren Heidbrink states, "Youth encounter the state as both paternal protector and punishing regulator. The policies and practices of the state in response to the presence of unaccompanied children reveal how the state operates through an ideal of a unified entity yet splinters into a multipronged labyrinth with potentially conflicting objectives" (2014, 3).

A second, and related, contradiction that becomes apparent in immigration enforcement and adjudication of unaccompanied minors concerns the youths' vulnerability and agency. These young people have had to make life and death decisions for themselves while still in their home country and throughout their dangerous journey. Once in the immigration system, though, they are defined as lacking capacity to exercise that agency, and they are expected to accept having others make all decisions regarding their care, including whether and when they may rejoin family members. When they reach immigration court, however, unaccompanied minors are often left on their own, with no guarantee of legal representation or advocacy to help them maneuver through a system that Susan Terrio aptly describes as filled with "arcane rules, staff shortages, hearing backlogs, powerful government [ICE trial] attorneys, and disempowered judges" (2015, 162). As Somers et al. suggest:

> This creates an inherent tension in the system in that custodial and placement decisions for unaccompanied children are based upon an evolving and progressive child protection framework. At the same, however, the unaccompanied child can be deported in the removal system thereby thwarting the goals of this child protection oriented custodial system. This becomes even more complex when children . . . continue on in their removal proceedings, often without legal counsel. Unless there are broader legal protections for unaccompanied children, these two structural systems are at best, mismatched, and at worse, on a collision course (2010, 378–79).

In many jurisdictions, judges expect that the parent or sponsor will appear in court with the child. Yet family members may be afraid to come to court if they are undocumented. Anne Marie Mulcahy, director of the Unaccompanied Children Program at the Vera Institute of Justice, explained that in some jurisdictions, especially if there is a specialized juvenile docket, the judges

> have this unwritten, although not unspoken, policy that an undocumented parent or sponsor must come to court with the child but will not be asked about their immigration status, and ICE agrees with that for the most part. . . . In New York, because the judges don't allow inquiries into a sponsor's status, they are very upset if the sponsor is not there and sometimes will not move forward on the kid's case, to the kid's detriment. . . . Sometimes the ICE attorneys will threaten to re-detain the child because the sponsor hasn't shown up, so there are real negative conse-

quences to a child if his or her undocumented sponsor is afraid to appear in court in New York. In other cities, however, the courts make it clear that an undocumented sponsor who appears in court runs the risk of being detained and placed in removal proceedings, and therefore shouldn't be there, so they don't hold that against the child if the sponsor does not appear with him or her.

She continued:

> But the question then becomes, from the child's perspective, who appears with the child? Will an undocumented sponsor find someone else whom the child trusts who is documented to appear with the child in court, or will they send the child to court on his or her own to face the judge alone? If the child has an attorney, they're not at such a great disadvantage ... but for a kid who is twelve, thirteen, fourteen years old, fifteen years old, who doesn't have an attorney and has a court date and their parent won't go with them, I mean, how they even find the right courtroom is a huge question.[29]

Legal Representation (or Lack Thereof)

The TVPRA requires that youth in ORR custody receive a legal orientation, but there is no requirement or guarantee of legal counsel. Most of the funding for pro bono counsel flows through the Vera Institute of Justice, which supports a network of organizations that conduct trainings for pro bono attorneys and arrange legal screenings and legal orientations for youth in custody. These funds are supplemented by grants and private donations, but they are insufficient to meet the needs of unaccompanied minors. The sheer numbers of youth—sometimes four hundred children are screened in a day—and the small number of available pro bono attorneys means that screenings are hurried. Traumatized youth who just arrived in the country may be distrustful and so not divulge information that would make them eligible for relief. This reluctance to tell their stories to strangers is exacerbated for children whose first language is not English or Spanish, further complicating development of any real rapport with their attorneys during this quick screening.

When asked about the needs of unaccompanied minors, attorneys, advocates, immigration scholars, and even government officials immediately say "legal representation." Children, they argue, need more than a legal orientation and brief screening. They require representation by an attorney who understands the intricacies of immigration law and who can best present the child's legal case. According to everyone with whom we spoke, a patchwork of pro bono attorneys funded by grants and private donations, regardless of how committed they may be to the needs of these youth, is not adequate. Indeed, the Vera Institute reports that, in 2010, only 28 percent of detained children served by the ORR-funded Legal Access Project received in-house direct representation or pro bono representation (Byrne and Miller 2012, 24).

The likelihood of obtaining representation decreases rapidly once youth reunify with family members. When we asked Maria Woltjen, director of the Young Center for Immigrant Children's Rights at the University of Chicago, whether the problem was greatest when youth reunified with family members in receiving communities where there may be fewer immigration attorneys working, she responded:

> I think that's true, but I think it's true in New York City, too. There are hundreds of kids being reunified with family members in the New York and New Jersey area and the legal service providers are stretched to the max. At present, you can't use government funds to pay for legal representation so the legal services provider either has to use private funds to take the case in-house, or use pro bono attorneys. It's not an efficient system because often legal services providers don't have the resources to take the cases that can't be placed with a pro bono attorney. I think the national organizations like KIND have waiting lists of months. It's not that they don't want to represent all of the children, but they simply don't have the resources to take every case. There need to be resources. Given that there are not attorneys for every child, we expect kids to go to court, walk into a court building by themselves, walk into the courtroom and figure out what to do and say, and that's very, very difficult.[30]

Legal counsel for children has been described as a moral imperative. As Ashley Feasley of the United States Conference of Catholic Bishops told us:

> Children often times don't speak any English, many of them have no education or a limited education, and they are in a court proceeding where on the other side is a lawyer representing the government, and there they sit. For any person going through immigration processing, they have a similar situation, but for a kid it strikes at our conscience even more. . . . I know I have talked to any number of advocates, lawyers, and even a judge who would feel so much better if it were an even playing field, especially when a child is involved. Kids just are not competent to represent themselves.[31]

Given the dangers often awaiting immigrants if they are repatriated, immigration court has been described as the place where judges hear what are essentially capital cases with the equivalent of traffic court resources (Abbott 2013; Terrio 2015). Attorney Aryah Somers suggests that "zealous advocacy" is needed to protect children's due process rights and to argue for substantive legal relief: "Zealous advocacy for the right to be heard opens the path to prosecutorial discretion, alternative tools of humanitarian protection for children, and can, for the first time, ensure that the immigration system hears a more complete account of the lives of immigrant children. . . . Rather than being able to turn a blind eye, the immigration system may finally be forced to confront the harsh reality that deporting children implicates" (2012b, 198).

Many see the US District Court decision in *Franco-Gonzalez v. Holder* (2013), which guarantees counsel for immigrants with serious mental health disabilities who are in removal proceedings, as a step toward a similar guarantee for unaccompanied children. Immigration scholars and advocates note that the American Bar Association has developed standards for the treatment of unaccompanied minors that include appointment of an attorney, at public expense if they cannot afford one, to represent youth in formal proceedings or other matters that may affect their immigration status (King 2013, 376–77; see similarly Frankel 2011; KIND/Center for Gender and Refugee Studies 2014; Thompson 2008).

Provision of counsel increases the likelihood that youth will appear in court. An analysis by Syracuse University's Transactional Records Access Clearinghouse of more than 100,000 cases between 2005 and June 2014 found that among closed cases, 60.9 percent of juveniles who are not detained appear in immigration court, and when pending cases are included, this increases to 78.6 percent. Almost all youth represented by counsel appear in court—92.5 percent of youth in closed cases and 94.7 percent in closed and pending cases combined. In contrast, youth who are not represented by counsel have much lower appearance rates—27.5 percent for closed cases and 66.3 percent when pending cases are included (Immigration Policy Center 2014).

Government officials told us that providing counsel would be cost-effective, making overcrowded courts run more efficiently. This was confirmed in a May 2014 study conducted by the National Economic Research Council for the New York City Bar Association (Montgomery 2014). The guarantee of legal representation for unaccompanied minors was a key provision of the 2013 Senate immigration bill (S. 744), and in June 2014 the Obama administration announced that it was piloting "justice AmeriCorps" to fund one hundred attorneys and paralegals to provide legal representation to a subset of unaccompanied minors (Corporation for National and Community Service 2014).

The spike in the number of unaccompanied minors has exacerbated the shortage of counsel, with large numbers of youth appearing in fast-track hearings known as "rocket dockets" in immigration courts across the country. On July 8, 2014, the White House requested emergency supplemental appropriations, including $15 million for direct legal representation services to children and $2.5 million to expand the Executive Office for Immigration Review's Legal Orientation Program for parents and other custodians.[32] The next day, several major immigrants rights organizations jointly filed a nationwide class action lawsuit on behalf of undocumented children, challenging the government's failure to provide the children with legal counsel (*J.E.F.M. v. Holder*).

In addition to a guarantee of representation by an immigration attorney, many in the advocacy community call for a child advocate, similar to the guardian ad litem role in juvenile court, at least as a stopgap measure to help ensure that the child's best interests are considered. Immigration attorneys recognize that they are not always able to speak to the child's best interests. As Anne Marie Mulcahy of the Vera Institute stated, the child advocate "is a really important role in the process because the attorneys are not representing the best interests of the child. They're representing the legal interests of the child, which is not always the same." Government officials affirmed that while an immigration attorney would be sufficient for most youth, some, particularly younger children, also require an advocate.

Eligibility for Protective Status: T and U Visas, Asylum, Temporary Protective Status, and Special Immigrant Juvenile Status

The primary forms of relief for which youth are screened are T and U visas, asylum, and special immigrant juvenile status.

The T Visa

The T visa is for victims of severe forms of human trafficking. Adult applicants must have complied with any reasonable request for assistance from law enforcement officers investigating or prosecuting trafficking, and they must prove that they would suffer severe and unusual harm if removed from the United States. Significantly, children who were under the age of eighteen at the time of their victimization are exempt from this certification by law enforcement.

The definition of trafficking is strict. For example, Jennifer Podkul of the Women's Refugee Commission recounted the story of a client who was held hostage while trying to reach the United States, but who did not qualify for the T visa:

> I had a client who actually ended up being held hostage in Mexico but during the time she was held hostage, she was told that either her mother could send money or she could just have sex with all the men who worked in this smuggling house as a way to pay off her debt. That was work, right? She's doing something in exchange for financial gain. She was a child who I considered had been trafficked. Unfortunately under the trafficking definition in the US, you have to be trafficked in the US to be eligible for a T visa, so we ended up filing for asylum for her. Because there was some sort of exchange for financial gain that I felt like was some sort of labor, but just being held in a house where you're not able to do anything until your family pays money, it doesn't make you eligible for a visa for victims of human trafficking in the US.[33]

The U Visa

The U visa is for victims of rape, torture, trafficking, incest, domestic violence, sexual assault, prostitution, sexual exploitation, female genital mutilation, involuntary servitude, slave trade, kidnapping, and related offenses. Law enforcement must certify that the noncitizen victim has helped or is likely to be helpful in investigating or prosecuting the offense. Depending upon the jurisdiction, they may be more or less willing to provide this certification. The exemption from the requirement of law enforcement certification of victim assistance that exists for children under the T visa has not been extended to the U visa, although if the victim is a child under sixteen years of age, a parent, guardian or friend may fill this role. Child Protective Services may also certify the noncitizen's helpfulness if it has criminal investigative jurisdiction.

The difficulty in obtaining certification in some jurisdictions is exemplified in the following case, recounted to us by an attorney in Arizona. Although the story concerns a woman, not a child, it is nevertheless instructive. The case involved a woman who was raped and her throat slit during a carjacking. She was thrown into the trunk, managed to kick out a headlight, and the police shot the assailant in an ensuing gunfight. "The detective in charge did not want to sign the U visa for her because he said there was no investigation, there was no prosecution. She didn't have to aid them because he was dead. We fought a whole year to get that U visa signed." It was ultimately signed, "but the hoops we had to jump through on such an egregious crime. I mean, she almost died! It just goes to show you the mentality of our local law enforcement, some local law enforcement, in terms of immigrants. They just refused to sign it."

Asylum, Temporary Protective Status, and Special Immigrant Juvenile Status

Asylum is a form of relief for those fearing persecution in their home country because of their race, religion, nationality, political opinion, or membership in a particular social group. If a migrant applies for protection prior to entering the United States, the request is technically for refugee status, while those applying from within the United States petition for asylum status.

Some unaccompanied minors may be eligible for temporary protective status (TPS). This status is restricted to immigrants from a changing list of countries who were physically present in the United States when there was a designated, devastating natural disaster, civil war, or other unstable circumstance in their home country. As of July 2013, the countries on the TPS list included El Salvador, Haiti, Honduras, Nicaragua, Somalia, and Sudan (Immigrant Legal Resources Center 2013). However, few children receive TPS on their own, and parents with this status are not allowed to apply for their children to enter the United States as derivatives at a later date. Jennifer Podkul of the Women's Refugee Commission told us:

> I have a lot of clients whose parents knew that something bad was happening to them in their home country but they couldn't go to them or they would be risking any sort of status they had here, especially when they had TPS. I think not allowing TPS applicants to apply for their children is incredibly harmful because you have these people, especially from Central America, who've had TPS for years and years and years and it's become almost a permanent kind of status yet they're not allowed to apply for their children so they decide not to bring those children here and the children are left alone in their home countries, or they come here and they're out of status.[34]

The legal protection for which unaccompanied minors are most likely to be eligible is special immigrant juvenile status (SIJS). This status applies to "a child who is under the jurisdiction of a juvenile court or has been legally committed to the custody of a state agency, department, entity, or individual by such court, where the court has found (a) that the child cannot be reunified with one or both parents because of abuse, neglect, abandonment or a similar basis in state law, and (b) that it would not be in the child's best interest to be returned to the home country" (Immigrant Legal Resources Center 2013, 1).

As one attorney told us, "As a lawyer, it is easier to do the paperwork for an SIJS case than it is for a U or T, particularly because a U or T visa needs law enforcement certification." As a result, though, "some children are not availing themselves of the specialized benefits available to T and U visa holders even if they are technically eligible for these forms of relief" (KIND/ Center for Gender and Refugee Studies 2014, 52).

SIJ status requires coordinated action between the juvenile court and DHS. A juvenile or family court must first determine that the child is a dependent, and then USCIS must approve the request for legal permanent residency and halt any removal hearings against the youth. In a significant achievement for those advocating on behalf of unaccompanied minors, the TVPRA of 2008 expanded SIJ eligibility beyond youth in long-term foster care to include cases in which the youth is in detention or is living with one parent but cannot be reunified with the other parent because of abuse, neglect, or abandonment. This has come to be known as one-parent SIJ.

Immigration scholars Jacqueline Bhabha and Susan Schmidt describe SIJ as "a singularly positive intersection between child welfare and immigration procedures, but precisely because it implicates both of these statutory systems, it has been beset by complexities that have had a somewhat inhibitory effect on its protective potential" (2011, 7; see also Heidbrink 2014; Junck 2012; Terrio 2015).

Variation across jurisdictions in the willingness of juvenile court judges to certify a youth as a dependent of the state, and thus eligible for this form of relief, is one source of this complexity. According to Terrio, "Despite these reforms, detained youths continue to face obstacles. State judges and social service departments have denied their access to domestic courts for protective purposes, saying that they lack the jurisdiction over immigrant children" (2015, 175). Many judges are not familiar with SIJS or are confused by older regulations that are not as inclusive, and so they do not believe they have authority to grant the finding (KIND/Center for Gender and Refugee Studies 2014, 40). As one attorney told us, "It works well in some places and then in other places, not at all." As a result, youth in federal custody "either have to get released to a location where they would be eligible or they're out of luck." The juvenile court in Chicago, for example, is well known for being hostile to SIJ cases, with the result that youth in that jurisdiction are basically cut off from this potential source of relief. Thus this mechanism, which has great potential for mitigating harm to youth, is more readily available to some youth than to others, depending upon where they live.

One-parent SIJ claims are particularly difficult. In June 2010, the Immigrant Legal Resources Center surveyed immigrant children's advocates about their experiences with one-parent SIJ claims, finding substantial variation in how friendly the juvenile courts are to such claims (Immigrant Legal Resources Center 2010). As one attorney told us, SIJ claims would never work in her state because "the court won't take custody of a case in which there is a viable parent. Why would they?"

In an effort to provide more systematic information about this status, and because the formal regulations have not been updated since 1995, in May 2014 the USCIS published educational resources aimed specifically at juvenile court judges, child welfare workers, and others serving abused, abandoned, or neglected children. These brief resource memos provide basic information about SIJ and helpful tips for juvenile courts and child welfare workers.[35]

Finally, voluntary departure is technically a form of legal relief available under the TVPRA. Children who may have a legal means of returning to the United States at some future date might not want to risk the consequences of formal removal, which include bans on reentry for specified periods of time. For these youth, voluntary departure may be a viable form of relief, and if they are indigent they will be repatriated free of charge.

Complications for Gang-Affiliated Youth

In identifying eligibility for protection, attorneys must gauge not only which status seems most appropriate for a given youth's circumstances, but also which is most likely to be successful. This is especially problematic for youth trying to escape gang violence. Heidbrink reports that an attorney told her that in choosing between SIJ and political asylum claims, "In court, child abuse is more palatable than gangs" (2014, 57). There are very few cases in which a youth who has been identified as having any connection with a gang received refugee status (Frydman and Desai 2012). Reflecting this difficulty, the US Committee for Refugees and Immigrants hosts a webpage devoted to gang-related asylum resources.[36] Yet as Jacqueline Bhabha so cogently summarizes the current situation, "The prospects of refugee protection for children fleeing gang recruitment remain close to nil" (2014, 236).

Attorneys and advocates emphasized that many youth had no choice but to engage in at least low-level gang activity, such as patrolling a neighborhood or collecting protection money. Others may have engaged in much more serious offenses, but if they did so because gang leaders threatened harm to themselves or family members if they did not comply, then their gang involvement is the very reason why they need protection in the first place. The problem, we were told, is that the home governments are unable to control the gangs and may be complicitous with them, and yet any whiff of gang involvement is enough to make a youth ineligible for asylum.

NGOs with experience working with refugees suggest that youth who were forcibly recruited into gang activity most closely resemble child soldiers. As Kristyn Peck of USCC explained:

> I think a shift is really needed to see these children as being victims. If you take out what the activity was, but you look at the way they were recruited through force and/or coercion, and really their lack of ability to make the choice in these situations, they meet the definition of trafficking. . . . I don't see the child having a lot of help in that situation to make a decision, especially when they are asked to do these things at gunpoint. I think there is a real gap in protection for these youth because of the type of service they end up providing. . . . What models do we need to be looking at? I liken it somewhat to the child soldier situation, and maybe what we need to look at is what works with that population.[37]

Similarly, Kimberly Haynes of LIRS stated:

> The hard thing to decipher here is adolescent boys who come across with high levels of what the US would call gang involvement, but the humanitarian crisis world would call child recruitment issues. . . . It's basically back to the whole argument of child soldiers for the United States. . . . Our culture and media scenario isn't putting that picture on these kids. They are just putting the "gangbanger" kind of picture on these kids. When you look at those two histories and styles, of drug-infused youth who are given AK-47s to manage a border, it is very similar to what is happening in Honduras and Guatemala. So how we look at [these adolescent boys] adds to their vulnerability.[38]

Susan Terrio quotes an immigration judge as saying, "What do we do with children who have been abused or persecuted but are not eligible for asylum or any other relief? Do we terminate the case? Can we offer some kind of withholding of removal?" (2015, 191). Advocates have repeatedly argued that the best interests of the child should be considered before a youth who does not qualify for relief is repatriated (KIND/Center for Gender and Refugee Studies 2014; Thompson 2008). As attorney Lisa Frydman has noted, kids should not be left with the choice of living on the streets or in an abusive situation in their home country following removal.[39]

These are the very types of cases for which prosecutorial discretion might come into play. Under the Morton Memos, being a minor is a positive factor that "should prompt particular care and consideration" (Morton 2011c, 5), although recent entrance into the country would count against the youth. The reality is that very few cases involving unaccompanied minors are considered for prosecutorial discretion. According to KIND director Wendy Young, as of July 2012, only about twenty of the 3,800 unaccompanied minors with whom KIND had been working were reviewed for prosecutorial discretion by ICE attorneys.[40]

REPATRIATION

When an immigration judge determines that a youth entered the country in violation of US immigration law and is deportable, or if the child agrees to voluntary departure, they are returned to their home country. Repatriation practices vary from country to country, and some NGOs have begun pilot projects to assist in the process when children are traveling alone. The largest of these is KIND's program in Guatemala.

Since early 2011, KIND has collaborated with ORR and nongovernmental agencies in Guatemala in a pilot project designed to identify and incorporate best practices for repatriated youth and their families. By March 2013, KIND had assisted 115 repatriated Guatemalan youth.[41] KIND conducts a needs assessment prior to the youth's repatriation and, based on those findings, develops a plan to provide job skills training, health care, education, assistance with family reintegration, and other services as needed. The plan is then transmitted to local partners on the ground in Guatemala for implementation. The hope is that by collaborating with local NGOs that have linguistic and cultural competency, KIND can create options to allow the youth to stay in Guatemala rather than immediately trying to return to the United States (Somers 2012a).

The 2008 TVPRA took steps to ensure that children are safely repatriated, but many advocates say they do not go far enough. As a case in point, KIND and other NGOs request information from DHS so they can arrange for local partners to transport parents or other family members to the airport to meet the child upon arrival, and bring him or her back to the home community. Yet DHS has been unwilling to share this information, especially regarding changes in the child's travel plan, citing security risks. This stance undermines efforts by NGOs to work with families and local community members, and results in parents sometimes making the journey to the airport expecting to meet their child, only to learn after the plane lands that the child will, instead, be on another flight a week later. As Wendy Young of KIND told us:

> We have had some incidents where the consulate and ORR have been told that the child is going back on March 18. We facilitate family to come to Guatemala City, which is quite expensive and difficult for these families because they come from very remote areas usually, and the kid doesn't show up and DHS made a change of plans and just didn't bother to tell us. So this is why we are asking them because they know, let us know. And they say it is the security of their staff, which drives me crazy because we, literally, when we are at the airport, we are on the other side of a closed door. We never see the deportation officer that is traveling with these kids.[42]

When children are repatriated, their return is generally marked by shame and stigma. The difficulties that led to their initial decision to migrate have not gone away. Family finances are even more depleted now, because they have gone to paying a *coyote*. The family may be paying an exorbitant interest rate on the loan of these funds, and they may have lost their land if it was held as collateral, leaving the family with no land to farm or place to live, but debts still due.

STRUCTURAL MECHANISMS THAT EXACERBATE HARM

As we have seen, unaccompanied minors undertake an arduous, perilous journey, leaving conditions that they consider untenable in hopes of reaching safety and security in the United States. Once in the United States, that "treacherous journey" (KIND/Center for Gender and Refugee Status 2014) continues as youth navigate the US immigration system alone. We turn next to a more explicit consideration of the structural mechanisms that exacerbate, or conversely, mitigate, harm for unaccompanied minors.

Lack of Guaranteed Legal Representation

Lack of guaranteed legal representation emerges from our analysis as the primary structural, systemic factor that exacerbates harm for unaccompanied minors. Attorneys, advocates, and government officials all have called for guaranteed legal representation, noting that youth are seriously disadvantaged in its absence. In many areas of law, they note, children are represented by legal counsel and appointed an advocate whose responsibility it is to consider the child's best interests, beyond solely their legal interests. Yet neither an attorney nor an advocate is guaranteed for youth who must confront a complicated adversarial process on their own.

Many attorneys also recommended that legal services provisions be funded through the Department of Justice to reduce ORR's monopoly over funding decisions. Regardless of how the money flows, the reality—that most children appear before an immigration judge without legal representation—is unlikely to change without specific legislation mandating appointment of something equivalent to a public defender for unaccompanied minors.

System Stressors Exacerbated by the Surge in Numbers of Unaccompanied Minors

The staggering growth in the numbers of unaccompanied youth has severely stressed resources, from the point at which the youth is apprehended through conclusion of the child's legal case. As Wendy Young of KIND told us, "The numbers, starting in October 2011, just started to soar. . . . And by spring 2012, it was a full-blown crisis, to the point where the Border Patrol called it a child migration emergency. . . . And then ORR was scrambling for bed space; they ended up opening temporary emergency shelters in places like the air force base in San Antonio. Obviously not good practice, but they had to do something."[43] The number of youth in ORR custody has continued to soar, exceeding 57,000 by the end of fiscal year 2014.

NGOs remind us that this is "not just an ORR influx; it is a humanitarian crisis."[44] Recognizing that once again youth are being housed in Air Force facilities and other sites that are far from ideal and that every governmental agency and service provider organization is stressed to the breaking point, they are asking how services can be injected into the facilities, how sufficient services and monitoring can be established once youth are released to families, and how to help repatriated youth get home safely.

As we have discussed, youth caught near the border are screened by CBP agents to determine whether they are unaccompanied minors. Mexican youth are quickly turned back if they are not thought to be victims of trafficking or eligible for other forms of protection. According to children's advocates and attorneys, this screening has never been adequate, largely because CBP officers have an enforcement, rather than a social services, background and mandate. Even with improved training, they are likely to miss signs of trauma and exploitation under the best of circumstances, and the onslaught of cases makes more than a cursory evaluation unlikely. As a result, what has been called the revolving door for Mexican youth continues to go round and round (KIND /Center for Gender and Refugee Status 2014; Terrio 2015; UNHCR 2014). A more robust screening process, many suggest, would be possible if initial screenings were conducted in ORR shelters rather than at the border.

In many ways, the real challenge begins once the youth is turned over to ORR. Finding a sufficient number of beds in licensed facilities is especially difficult in light of the growing numbers of youth entering the country.[45] Assessing their needs and providing initial legal, health, educational, and social services for the growing numbers of children requires an expanded set of providers and time, neither of which is likely in the present context. In their absence, the children are not being adequately served. And while reuniting youth with family members as quickly as possible is on its face a positive outcome, advocates and social service providers fear that the reunifications are occurring too quickly, that the pendulum has swung too far, and children are being placed without adequately ensuring their safety.

Each of these evaluations requires street-level workers—CBP officers, ORR bureaucrats and caseworkers, and pro bono attorneys—to exercise a high degree of discretionary decision making (Lipsky 1980; see also Brodkin 2011; Harwood 1986; Maynard-Moody and Musheno 2003, 2012). Within the space of a few minutes, they must determine which youth are eligible for—or deserving of—protective status, and evaluate and attend to the child's most immediate and pressing needs. Like the prosecutorial discretion exercised by ICE officials, these street-level bureaucrats make what may well be life-and-death decisions based on very limited information. And, depending upon how they envision their responsibilities and the circumstances, these decisions may not always be guided by or reflect the best interests of the child.

Limited Use of Prosecutorial Discretion

Prosecutorial discretion is rarely mentioned by attorneys working with unaccompanied minors. Because they are recent entrants, ICE attorneys do not regularly consider them for prosecutorial discretion, even though their age should be a positive factor. Rather than counting on ICE for prosecutorial discretion, attorneys are more likely to turn to ICE's sister agency, Citizenship and Immigration Services, for consideration for T and U visas, SIJ status, and asylum.

Youth with Special Vulnerabilities

Some unaccompanied minors are especially vulnerable. Indigenous Guatemalan youth, for example, have unique service needs. Most will require interpreters so that they are able to properly tell their stories and potentially gain legal relief. Most ORR staff members and pro bono attorneys do not speak the Mayan languages, and if the youth is not fluent in Spanish, communication with staff members becomes even more difficult (Heidbrink 2014). Youth are entitled to an interpreter in court, but this is complicated when youth speak indigenous Mayan or other languages for which interpreters are not readily available. As Anne Marie Mulcahy, director of the Vera Institute's Unaccompanied Children Program explained, "Often it has to be done through relay interpretation. The judge will speak English. The Spanish interpreter interprets the English to Spanish for the K'iché interpreter, and then the K'iché interpreter will interpret the Spanish to K'iché for the child. Then the same relay process happens in reverse."[46] The complexities go beyond the youths' legal needs. For an indigenous youth from rural Guatemala who may have attended school only a few hours a day, if at all, to integrate into what are by comparison large and confusing urban and suburban American schools can be quite daunting.

Young children also have special vulnerabilities, and their social service, medical, and legal needs differ from those of older youth. If they are traveling alone, they are at high risk of targeting for abuse. Their ability to deal with the traumas they may have endured, their understandings of the legal proceedings and life circumstances confronting them, and their manner of disclosing information will all differ depending upon their developmental stage, requiring child-appropriate interviewing techniques that meet the needs of youth at every age.

Preadolescent and adolescent girls have unique needs and challenges, especially if they have survived rape and other traumas for which immigration officials, and even service providers, may not have adequate experience. Pregnant girls and teenage mothers with babies also require specialized services. And, with increased numbers of children migrating, it can be assumed that there will be increasing numbers of children who are lesbian/gay/bisexual/transgender and may have been victimized for their sexual orientation along the way. Thus far, the numbers of transgender youth coming across the border are thought to be low, but as one provider told us, "I can only believe that they would be highly targeted and highly vulnerable."

STRUCTURAL MECHANISMS THAT MITIGATE HARM

Many of the changes that have resulted in improved conditions for unaccompanied minors have been procedural in nature. Specialized juvenile dockets, providing legal orientations to family members as well as the youth themselves, delaying scheduling of children's first master calendar hearing until they have reunited with family members, and expanding SIJ status to include youth who are able to reunite with one parent are examples of such incremental procedural improvements in law, policy, and practice. Similarly, the partnership with AmeriCorps to pilot a means of providing youth with legal representation may demonstrate that having counsel makes court processing more efficient, although the salaries are so low that they may draw only inexperienced attorneys.

Wendy Young, who has been at the center of work with unaccompanied minors and refugee women and children for more than twenty years, brought the strategy of promoting procedural, rather than substantive, change to our attention. She recounted the history of advocating on behalf of unaccompanied minors to members of Congress, recalling, "And when we advocated on this, we were going to offices basically saying, 'This is about children and this is about process, and affording new process to these kids.' And I think that helped a lot."[47]

Committed Focus on the Best Interests of the Child

A committed focus on the best interests of the child at all stages of immigration processing would go a long way in mitigating harm. As the KIND/Center for Gender and Refugee Studies report concludes, "The 'best interests of the child' standard is the cornerstone principle of child protection both internationally and in the U.S. child welfare and juvenile justice systems" (2014, iii). The best interests of the child are already identified in the TVPRA of 2008 and are to be considered in determining a child's eligibility for SIJ status.

A Best Interests Subcommittee of the Interagency Working Group on Unaccompanied Children, led by Maria Woltjen and Jennifer Nagda of the University of Chicago Law School's Young Center for Immigrant Children's Rights, has been meeting since late 2012 to identify means of ensuring that the best interests of children are considered at all stages, from apprehension to safe repatriation. The working group has sought to apply the lessons learned in family and juvenile courts to the situation of unaccompanied minors, thereby bringing "our immigration law in line with the child welfare laws of all 50 states, under which the state is required to consider the best interests of the child" (Young Center 2013).

Integrating best interests principles into immigration proceedings would likely require new legislation. The subcommittee has proposed incorporating a best interests standard into the Immigration and Naturalization Act (INA), including creation of a best interests visa when all other forms of relief have been denied, and provision of a child advocate to make best interests recommendations to judges and other decision makers.

Although incorporation of this standard and of a new visa into the INA would require congressional action, best interests mechanisms have been identified that have potential to mitigate harm at all stages of immigration proceedings. By working with government and nongovernmental partners and reporting on their progress at regular meetings of the Interagency Working Group, the subcommittee was able to obtain input and support from senior officials in the Department of Justice, the Department of Homeland Security, the Department of State, and the Department of Health and Human Service's Office of Refugee Resettlement, thereby making incorporation of the standards within their agencies more likely.

Considering Geography: The Mapping Project, "Do Nothing" Pilot, and Placements of Youth Potentially Eligible for SIJ

Youth may miss their court appearance if the Notice to Appear is filed in the jurisdiction where they were picked up rather than where they ultimately settled, especially if they do not have legal counsel. Accordingly, the Departments of Homeland Security and Health and Human Services collaborated on what they call a "mapping project." As the name suggests, they are mapping where youth enter the country, where they are processed, where services are available, and where parents or other sponsors reside. Their hope is that by streamlining provision of services, they can reduce the need for long-term care and custody by ORR and make court processing more efficient.

Consistent with this general plan and with recommendations from NGOs such as the Women's Refugee Commission (2012), the Executive Office for Immigration Review initiated a "Do Nothing" pilot project in Houston, San Antonio, and Harlingen, Texas. Between April 16 and May 29, 2013, these three courts delayed master calendar hearings on 1,800 cases, most of them in Harlingen, for seventy-five days.[48] During this time, children were reunited with family members and the case could be transferred to the closest immigration court. As a government official told us:

> The courts' and judges' times are wasted, not used well, when 80–90 percent of these kids will be released prior to completion of the case. Judges know this, they may have three to four hearings for a kid before the local court, and the kid or the kid's attorney or an NGO asks for more and more time. What's the point of going forward when the kid will be leaving? So kick the can down the road a bit more. . . . By just scheduling cases differently, we can reduce the caseload by 80 percent in a *meaningful* way. . . . They jokingly call this "the pilot to do nothing for seventy-five days." Because just doing nothing for 75 days may solve a lot of problems.

Experts in the field anticipated that this pilot, or something like it, would expand. As immigration attorney Maria Woltjen told us, "It just saves everybody time. It means the kids don't have to go to court while they are in custody unless they want to leave. It means they don't have to start focusing on their legal case until they get to where they are going. . . . I think that's going to happen. The Notice to Appear will get filed in the jurisdiction where the kids are going. I'm sure there will be complications because kids go one place and then they move. I still think it will be a better system for everybody."[49] In June 2014, we were informed that DHS was likely to start delaying service of Notice to Appears on the detained courts, waiting instead until most children are released to sponsors. This is expected to result in far fewer detained children's cases being scheduled for hearings, and renders the pilot unnecessary.

There is a risk, though, that waiting until the child has reunited with family before initiating court proceedings will reduce their access to legal representation. Unlike adults, for whom the likelihood of having legal representation is much higher among those released from detention, the opposite holds for youth. A government official told us:

> ORR has funded and built pro bono programs in areas where they hold kids in custody, so kids in custody have the best chance of representation. . . . It is high if the case is completed while the youth is in custody. . . . Once the kids are released to rural, or small metropolitan areas, they may be hours away from already overwhelmed LOP [Legal Orientation] programs. . . . The government is trying through LOP to expand telephone orientations. There are now LOP for Custodians at fourteen sites, but the program needs to further expand to reach kids in rural areas and small towns.

If, however, the justice AmeriCorps program expands and more youth are provided access to counsel, then this problem would largely be resolved.

As we discussed earlier, geography also matters in SIJ cases, with some jurisdictions far more willing to consider youth for SIJ status than others. We have heard anecdotal evidence that, in some cases, ORR will place youth who are potentially eligible for SIJ into foster care or other placements in counties where judges are favorable—or at least not explicitly unfavorable—toward SIJ determinations. As one source told us, "They won't say this officially, but ORR may identify a child as a likely SIJ and then what they'll do is transfer the child to a long-term foster care facility in SIJ friendly places." To do this, however, requires a viable best interests factor that would legitimately compel such a move. As an attorney explained, "So when a kid is eligible, everybody has to think of a reason that this kid needs to be moved. Should they go to a therapeutic, do they need therapy and they need to move to a therapeutic facility, or can they be stepped down, they don't need to be in a high-security facility anymore. But it is so tricky. I mean, it is really tricky for ORR . . . [and] it is tragic for some kids."

Specialized Juvenile Dockets

Specialized juvenile dockets began about 1996 or 1997 in Arizona. Soon after, a pro bono program began operating in Harlingen, Texas, and the nation's second juvenile docket emerged. All youth in ORR custody come into court on juvenile dockets, but the likelihood of appearing before a juvenile docket decreases as youth move away from detention centers. Terrio reports, "Of the 59 immigration courts nationwide, only 25 had specialized juvenile dockets in 2013. Of that number, 8 courts held hearings for nondetained minors, 8 for detained, and 9 for detained as well as nondetained minors" (2015, 226 n. 18).

Juvenile dockets serve at least two purposes. First, officials in the Department of Justice told us that it is easier for children to gain access to counsel when there are specialized juvenile dockets. Because unaccompanied minors are not guaranteed legal counsel and instead must rely on a network of pro bono attorneys, it is simply more efficient for those attorneys to handle multiple cases at once, in a specialized docket, rather than going from court to court. Second, specialized dockets allow immigration judges to better understand and appreciate the youths' circumstances, and to hold court proceedings in as child-sensitive a format as possible, thus simultaneously reducing trauma and providing the judge with the most complete and contextualized information about the case. For these reasons, as of May 20, 2014, every immigration court nationwide has a juvenile docket, although some were not yet operational on that date.[50]

CONCLUSIONS

The image of tired and scared children crossing thousands of miles alone, subject to unspeakable dangers, is not the typical portrayal of undocumented immigrants in the United States. More typical images are of either hardworking parents trying to support their families as nannies, maids, landscapers, construction workers, or migrant farmers, or, more disreputably, of drug dealers and other nefarious characters. Yet tens of thousands of unaccompanied minors enter the United States each year, leaving behind what are often horrendous conditions, hoping to reunite with parents or older siblings whom they have not seen in years. This chapter reviews how and why they come to the United States and their interactions with the immigration system following apprehension. We have not sought to tell their stories in their own words—others have done so quite effectively. Instead we focus on how immigration policy and practice—the law on the books and in action—respond to these youth, as understood by the attorneys, advocates, and social service providers working with them and by government officials.

Unaccompanied children present a conundrum to the state. They are children in need of protection, and in the absence of their parents the state becomes their protector. Yet they are also being prosecuted by the state for violation of immigration law. In other areas of law, children have legal representation and an independent child advocate, typically a guardian ad litem, speaks to the best interests of the child. But with few exceptions, children in immigration proceedings do not have that independent advocate, and they often do not even have legal counsel. The vulnerability and agency of youth create a series of dilemmas for social service providers, attorneys, and government officials. They are vulnerable children in need of protection from those who would abuse or exploit them and from dangers that they may be too young to fully understand, and they also have agency, as reflected in their having undertaken unbearably dangerous journeys and made life and death decisions for themselves and others.

One of the ways in which these contradictions manifest themselves can be seen in the power that ORR wields over children's lives. Thus Heidbrink concludes, "Rather than reinforcing the distinctions between the moral, ethical, and legal obligations to children, ORR policies and organizational practices blur the bright line between the humanitarian and law enforcement regimes in their treatment of migrant children and youth" (2014, 112). Similarly, Terrio questions whether the conflict of interest has been resolved "between the government's role as a prosecutor arguing for the deportation of undocumented minors and as a protector of their right to humane treatment in custody?" (2015, 54–55). These are important questions for public policy and legal advocacy, as well as for sociolegal scholars, and the growing number of unaccompanied minors brings these dilemmas into even starker relief.

Yet for all the media attention focusing on the surge of unaccompanied minors entering the country in the past few years, we must remember that they are a small fraction of the undocumented youth living in the United States. The traumas many of these youth have endured make their situations unique and compelling, but comprehensive immigration reform is needed to address the full range of issues confronting immigrant youth and their families.

CHAPTER 6

Conclusions and Recommendations

I think this will get done in a bipartisan manner. . . . It's a three-prong strategy calling for action from House Republicans, action from the White House to stop senseless deportations, and action from our community. We need to focus on our community raising their voices. We need to work with the DREAMers in the local communities, and with the faith-based organizations. We need to come together as one community and say, "this has to happen now."

—Jorge Plasencia, chair of National Council of La Raza (Dahlberg 2014)

As President Barack Obama's second term began, there was once again a major push to enact comprehensive immigration reform. Perhaps the Obama administration was correct, that it had to demonstrate a willingness to stand tough on border control and deportations of anyone who might constitute a threat to public safety, including parents of US citizens convicted of minor offenses such as driving while intoxicated. Or perhaps legislators saw that the Deferred Action for Childhood Arrivals (DACA) program proceeded smoothly, demonstrating that a wider legalization plan could as well. A multitude of possibilities might explain why comprehensive reform appeared viable once again. However, like other efforts to enact comprehensive immigration reform over the past decade, these collapsed as well. The fact remains, as of December 2014, we are not any closer toward the establishment of comprehensive immigration reform.

Comprehensive immigration legislation would likely place those who came to the United States as young children (i.e., Dreamers) and agricultural workers on a shortened path to citizenship and allow all those without criminal histories to regularize their status and, eventually, to apply for citizenship. Some of the mechanisms to reduce harm to children, youth, and families discussed in earlier chapters, such as legal assistance for unaccompanied minors, have been incorporated into draft comprehensive immigration reform legislation. Certainly, changing the way in which quotas are calculated so that some of the millions in the waiting line for green cards could receive them more quickly could be included as part of comprehensive immigration reform. Yet any iteration of comprehensive immigration law likely to be enacted in the future will still leave a large number of immigrants and their families in legal limbo, and will have little effect on unaccompanied minors who continue to see no other option than to try to enter the United States.

Dreams and Nightmares: Immigration Policy, Youth, and Families identifies the immigration policies and practices proposed during the Obama presidency in the absence of legislative comprehensive immigration reform. We focused our attention on three areas: (1) young people who came to the United States as children, known as Dreamers, and mixed status families more generally, (2) parental detention and deportation, and (3) unaccompanied children entering the United States without authorization. Our goal was to place relevant policies in historical perspective and to highlight the mechanisms by which policies and practices affect youth and families. In particular, we describe the mechanisms, both large and small, that mitigate the vulnerable state of youth and families, and those that exacerbate their harm.

In chapter 1, we briefly reviewed the history of US immigration policy and organizational changes in immigration enforcement following the attacks of September 11, 2001. We then turned to the conflicts and dilemmas confronting the Obama administration as it sought to enact immigration reform in an antagonistic political climate characterized by congressional gridlock.

The broader context of immigration reform continues to be highly polarized. On the one hand, there is the need to be sensitive to the calls for addressing uncontrolled immigration. On the other, there is a desperate need to grapple with the plight of large numbers of unauthorized immigrants living and raising families in the United States. Different positions on immigration, coupled with competing goals, have made immigration reform extremely difficult. Yet, with more than 11 million unauthorized immigrants in the United States, there has to be a way to manage such tensions. As described throughout our book, prosecutorial discretion can help balance the competing goals of public safety and family unification, within a context of limited resources.

In response to a Congress that refused to act on any reform, prosecutorial discretion became a defining feature of immigration policy and practice under the Obama administration. As we demonstrated in chapter 2, the flexibility of prosecutorial discretion made it useful and practical, but also controversial and not without political challenges. Factors central in the application of prosecutorial discretion guidelines such as a person's immigration status, length of residence in the United States, history of prior immigration violations or criminal offenses, family ties, and US military service reveal the complexities surrounding use of this mechanism to prioritize enforcement goals and strategies. Our focus on this issue is unique in that immigration scholars have overwhelmingly addressed either the law itself or immigrants' experiences of social integration or exclusion, and not how prosecutorial discretion shapes the practice of immigration enforcement (see Hing 2013; Motomura 2012; Olivas 2012a; Rabin 2014; Wadhia 2013, 2010 for exceptions).

In the absence of comprehensive immigration reform, the law in action has taken the form of policy memos outlining guidelines for immigration enforcement and DACA, which specifies how prosecutorial discretion is to be exercised in cases involving eligible young people brought to the United States as children. As we have demonstrated, these efforts led to numerous challenges. From within Immigration and Customs Enforcement (ICE), there were accusations that the Obama administration was using prosecutorial discretion as an unofficial form of amnesty. Immigrants' advocates and the Latino community also challenged the administration, distressed that prosecutorial discretion was not being used more broadly to aid immigrants. The record high number of deportations, especially of parents of US-citizen children, fueled anger and created greater tension when data showed that immigrants deported because of criminal histories are not typically serious violent criminals, but rather drug or DUI offenders. In the end, challenges and dilemmas center on finding the proper balance between the competing goals of public safety and humanitarian concerns.

In chapter 3 we focused our attention on "mixed status" families. These are families in which some members may be citizens, some may have temporary or permanent legal residency, and still others may be undocumented. Some members of these families may be unaccompanied minors, attempting to rejoin a parent or family that includes new siblings born in the United States. Some may be "Dreamers" who came to the United States with their parents as young children and have grown up here, and who may be eligible for DACA. Dreamers and their supporters have put a face to all the young people who lived in the shadows, now attempting to claim rights and privileges. They continue to pressure Congress and the Obama administration to enact some form of relief so their loved ones can live, work, and receive an education without fear of deportation.

In other families, all of the children may be US citizens, but one or both parents may be undocumented or have temporary residency. When parents are undocumented, they may not seek out benefits for which children are eligible for fear of detection. Regardless of their structure, all of these families attempt to navigate, in their own way, immigration law and policy.

In chapter 4 we examined parental detention and deportation processes in light of the 5.5 million children who have at least one parent who is undocumented. Most of these children—4.5 million—are US citizens (Passel and Cohn 2011). We highlighted the trauma and sense of loss experienced by children and family members when undocumented parents are picked up in workplace raids and traffic stops, and detained in centers far from the family. Parents who are legal permanent residents are also at risk of detention and deportation for minor offenses, even those committed well in the past, as a consequence of the expanded bases for removal in the 1996 laws.

We draw on the growing literature on the effects of parental incarceration to explore the similarities and differences between parental incarceration and parental immigration detention. Research has established that the fear of deportation and the uncertainty of family life in light of a parent's deportation compound the trauma experienced by children. There is also evidence of the many difficulties faced by remaining caregivers in providing for the children and family. When a parent is detained and possibly deported, the convergence of the immigration, criminal justice, and child welfare systems can create a cascade of consequences for children and families (e.g., foster care and adoption proceedings, moving to an unknown country with deported parents). In these cases, the lack of or limited discretion afforded immigration judges, along with the disconnect between the immigration and child welfare systems, exacerbate the harm to children and families. This is all taking place in an environment in which the child welfare system is already heavily strained and overburdened.

At the same time, a number of structural mechanisms were developed to mitigate harm. These include ICE's online detainee locator, computerized risk assessment tool, and its transfer and parental interests directives, which are designed to minimize long-distance transfers of detainees and to facilitate detained parents staying in contact with their children and participating in child welfare hearings. Other mechanisms that reduce harm include legal orientations, the detained parent's toolkit developed by the Women's Refugee Commission, and increased engagement with consular officials from the parents' home countries.

Significantly, President Obama announced a set of executive actions on immigration in November 2014. These include an expansion of the deferred action program to parents of US-citizen or legal permanent resident children, expansion of provisional waivers to spouses and children of legal permanent residents, and removal of the age limit for eligibility for deferred action for childhood arrivals. These steps will help bring an estimated 5 million immigrants out of the shadows, protecting families and strengthening communities. Yet because they are executive actions and not legislation, these policies may be overturned by a new administration. They do not carry the weight of law, and do not set immigrants, even those who have lived in the United States for many years, on a path to citizenship. Also, as discussed in chapter 4, some deported parents have minor criminal histories, such as DUIs or possession of small quantities of drugs, and they are excluded from deferred action.

These reforms were thought to be imminent, and then delayed, multiple times throughout the spring, summer and fall of 2014, finally being announced shortly after the mid-term elections. The controversies surrounding whether and when these reforms would be announced typify the contradictions and complexities associated with parental detention and deportation.

In chapter 5 we turn our attention to the rapidly escalating numbers of unaccompanied minors entering the United States since 2011. These youth fled violence and extreme poverty in hopes of safety and the opportunity to reunite with parents or older siblings. Unaccompanied minors present a unique challenge to the state. They are children and deserve its protection when they do not have adult guardians. However, this means the state must protect the child against itself, given its enforcement capacity. Although the care and custody of unaccompanied minors moved to ORR and out of the enforcement arena in 2003, ongoing concerns regarding minors remain, including the length of detention within ORR facilities, children's uncertainty as to what will happen to them, unwarranted levels of security for children, and the capacity of ORR to provide adequate and sufficient legal, educational, medical, and psychological resources for youth. According to our research, attorneys, advocates, immigration scholars, and government officials identified legal representation as a vital need of children. Legal assistance, they contend, should entail far more than the currently mandated brief orientation and screening. There is general agreement that children should be represented by legal counsel in court, because they are entering into adversarial hearings in which the power balance is enormous and they often do not understand what is being said or its importance.

Our analyses highlight the structural mechanisms available to the state that may mitigate or exacerbate harm to unaccompanied minors. We discussed how the lack of guaranteed legal representation, the inability of the system to serve the massive numbers of unaccompanied minors, some with very unique service needs, and the limited use of prosecutorial discretion all intensify harm to unaccompanied minors.

We also identified the structural mechanisms that have improved conditions for unaccompanied minors. These "best interests of the child" initiatives include specialized juvenile dockets, legal orientations for family members and youth, delaying immigration hearings until youth have reunited with family members, and expanding special immigrant juvenile(SIJ) status to include youth who are able to reunite with one parent. Legal representation for unaccompanied minors has been a key recommendation from the advocacy community for decades and was incorporated into the Senate's 2013 immigration bill. The decision by the Obama administration in May 2014 to provide government resources to pay a small number of attorneys to represent youth was a major step forward; even though it will only meet the needs of a few children, it demonstrates adherence to the ideal that children should receive legal representation. Thus although unaccompanied minors present a unique challenge to the state, some procedural improvements in policy and practice are attempting to reduce the harm experienced by such children.

To that end, the larger context remains politically charged, with divisions over how to balance an orderly immigration process and the pursuit of public safety, on the one hand, and humanitarian concerns on the other. Regardless of the nature of future immigration reform, there are a few factors that will be critical in the application of policy and practice.

First, there must be a primary focus on the best interests of children at all stages of immigration processing. Whether they are unaccompanied minors or children of parents who have been detained and deported, these children are extremely vulnerable given their fragmented family systems. It is well documented that the surge of children is driven primarily by conditions in Central America. These children are extremely young, often escaping gang ties and larger structural violence, and risk sexual abuse and assaults. Their vulnerabilities only heighten the importance of addressing their needs and providing them with a safe haven at the end of their dangerous journey to the United States. To this end, the announcement in September 2014 that the United States would establish in-country refugee processing centers for children in El Salvador, Honduras, and Guatemala is a step forward, potentially reducing the number of children undertaking the dangerous journey north (Shear 2014). However, many questions remain, including how long this process will take and whether that waiting time is viable for youth who are fleeing violence and likely death.

The poverty and violence that children are escaping have made the response to the enormous number of unaccompanied minors a humanitarian crisis. Nongovernmental organizations (NGOs) have urged that children who are identified as gang affiliated but who are fleeing gang violence be treated like child soldiers and given refugee status. However, given their perceived threat to public safety, they are almost always denied protection. A review of literature on gangs in the United States shows the frequency at which gang status or affiliation is contested in the courts. Future pursuits to single out children for their alleged ties to criminal networks must be tempered with a clear sense of whether they truly constitute a threat to public safety.

Some media accounts suggest that perhaps Central American youth, and their families in the United States, believe that they might qualify for some form of relief under DACA, other administrative remedies, or comprehensive immigration reform. Such supposition ignores the fact that the exponential growth in the number of unaccompanied minors entering the United States began in 2011, long before DACA or current discussions of other administrative reforms. The NGOs and scholars such as Jacqueline Bhabha (2014), Lauren Heidbrink (2014), and Susan Terrio (2015) have provided abundant evidence of the basis for this growing humanitarian crisis, and there is no solid evidence that youth think they will necessarily obtain legal status in the United States —they just do not feel they have any viable choice *but* to come north.

A second crucial feature of future policy and practice is the degree to which all key players are able to come together to resolve the tensions between their competing goals and objectives. This includes NGOs, Congress, and the criminal justice, immigration, and child welfare systems. Some strides have been made in working collaboratively, as exemplified by the Interagency Working Group on Unaccompanied Minors, which brings together officials from various governmental agencies and NGOs in an effort to share information and strategize as to the best interests of the child. Yet too often the systems collide, with the result that loving, responsible parents lose custody of their children, children must leave the only home they have known to join parents who have been deported, or youth waiting in line for visas age out of opportunities for relief. In these and other situations, children and families continue to get caught in the middle. At the heart of these tensions and conflicts are the competing needs for an orderly immigration process and family unification. The capacity for all parties to enforce existing law *and* assist youth and families is not only difficult to describe in theory but even more difficult to implement in practice, given their distinct, albeit sometimes overlapping, aims and perspectives.

One step in the right direction is the ICE Parental Interests Directive, which includes placement of an ICE point of contact in each detention center who is charged with facilitating parental interests, including coordination with child protective services agencies. How well this will work in practice remains to be seen, but, in combination with ICE's agreement to have a copy of the Women's Refugee Commission toolkit for immigrant parents available in all detention centers, it reflects a willingness, at least at the policy levels, for ICE officials to work together with other agencies and nongovernmental organizations. Similarly, USCIS in spring 2014 published educational materials intended to educate juvenile court officials and child welfare workers about special immigrant juvenile status, because this status requires coordination between the juvenile court and immigration services. The need for coordination also extends to international relations. The capacity of the United States to work with governments in Mexico and Central America to disrupt criminal organizations operating in both the state and non-state arenas, protect youth from violence, abuse, neglect, and exploitation, and provide educational and employment opportunities will play a significant role in immigration reform. It is this web of actors and the contradictions in the missions they pursue that make immigration policy and practice so challenging and difficult to predict.

A third characteristic that will be important in the application of future policy and practice is the extent to which state laws will be enacted to reduce the harm to children and families. California's Reuniting Immigrant Families Act (SB 1064) was signed into law on September 30, 2012, and explicitly addresses family separation as a consequence of immigration enforcement.

Also, in August 2014, California Democrats and Governor Jerry Brown proposed a bill that would provide legal services to unaccompanied minors. Attempts by local and state government to prioritize family unification and provide services to those in need will mitigate harms and has potential to create a culture in which family-centric approaches are aspired to and exercised via policy and practice in realms beyond the federal government. Similarly, state laws that permit undocumented immigrants to obtain in-state college tuition and financial aid so youth may continue their educations, and that provide opportunities for work authorization, driver's licenses, and car insurance will go far, both to mitigate harm to youth and families and to further public safety and the nation's economic goals.

We end our discussion where it began, highlighting the critical role and continuing potential of prosecutorial discretion in immigration policy and practice. Prosecutorial discretion enables the managing of workloads by setting priorities on who can be removed. However, it has its limits. For the youth and families deeply entrenched in immigration processing, prosecutorial discretion has failed to alleviate harm and, in some instances, only served to exacerbate their dire state. The use or absence of discretion in immigration reform will continue to have a profound impact on children's well-being. Shining a light on how such discretion plays out in policy and practice enables a more comprehensive understanding of the circumstances confronting youth and families. For regardless of the nature of future immigration reform, there will be contradictions in how various systems execute policy, and its impact will likely be driven by how discretion is exercised.

As we described in our book, the complications and contradictions that arise when immigration enforcement, child welfare, and the criminal justice system meet can have devastating impacts on children and families. Identifying those circumstances where the systems can meet their respective goals (public safety and humanitarian concerns) without collateral consequences for families will be key. For example, under which circumstances will it be beneficial for unaccompanied minors to be involved with child welfare and the foster care system so that they can obtain post-release services *without* being separated from their parents for extended periods of time and risking adoption proceedings? Our capacity to address questions like this will move us closer toward an effective and humane public policy.

Dreams and Nightmares: Immigration Policy, Youth, and Families bridges various bodies of work in order to conduct an overarching social analysis of policies and practices that affect youth and families in the absence of comprehensive immigration reform. Social scientists have given much empirical attention to immigrant integration and the purported link between crime and immigration, while legal scholars have emphasized immigration law and immigrants' rights. Our analyses connect these literatures through a focus on the structural, systemic mechanisms that reduce or exacerbate harm for youth and families.

We encourage future assessments of immigration reform to incorporate an overarching analysis such as ours. We also hope that any discussion on race, crime, and justice is placed in the broader context of immigration. Our work informs studies on mass incarceration that for the most part focus only on the increasing number of Latinos in state and federal prisons and not those in deportation centers. Our analysis is also important for research on the collateral consequences of incarceration, given that immigration detention and deportation processes significantly alter the lives of children and families. It also speaks to the expansion of prison privatization to meet mass incarceration needs, and consequently, makes beds available for detention. Last, our work informs the literature on crimmigration. This growing area of study examines the interweaving of the criminal justice system and immigration system due in large part to 287(g) programs and new technologies that enhance ICE's enforcement mission, and that have resulted in net-widening as more people are identified as undocumented and deportable. In the end, we hope our book will contribute to sounder immigration policy and practice, and not ignore the dreams and nightmares of children.

NOTES

1. INTRODUCTION AND HISTORICAL CONTEXT

1. Total numbers for each fiscal year were provided by the Office of Refugee Resettlement (2014) and ORR spokesperson Lisa Raffonelli, personal email November 12, 2014. These numbers do not include Mexican youth who were turned around at the border. US Customs and Border Protection reports 68,541 unaccompanied minors were apprehended along the southern border in fiscal year 2014; 15,634 of these youth were from Mexico (US Customs and Border Patrol [USCBP] 2014).

2. PROSECUTORIAL DISCRETION

1. An earlier version of this chapter was published in *Law & Social Inquiry* (39(3):666–689) as "The Limits of Discretion: Challenges and Dilemmas of Prosecutorial Discretion in Immigration Enforcement."

2. We do not explicitly consider the decisions of immigration judges because their discretion has been severely limited since the 1996 laws. Nor do we consider the actions of local and state police or correctional officers; though their discretionary decision making is important, it is beyond the scope of this chapter.

3. Interview with David Martin, August 21, 2012.

4. Interview with Lindsay Marshall, February 2, 2012.

5. The importance of this letter was raised in interviews with David Martin, on August 21, 2012, and Doris Meissner, on December 6, 2012.

6. Interview with Lindsay Marshall, February 2, 2012.

7. Interview with Roxana Bacon, April 25, 2013.

8. Although the memo was unchanged except for addition of the standard disclaimer and thus should for substantive historical purposes be thought of as having been issued in June 2010, it is typical to cite reissued memoranda by the reissue date.

9. Interview with Mary Giovagnoli, October 10, 2012.

10. Comments by Alejandro Mayorkas, director, USCIS, at forum, "The New Deferred Action Program: Strategies for Success," Migration Policy Institute, August 7, 2012.

11. DACA renewals began June 5, 2014. As of June 30, 2014, 10,587 renewal applications had been received. These renewals are not counted in our totals.

12. Email communication to the first author, August 26, 2014.

13. Interview with Mary Giovagnoli, October 10, 2012.

14. Interview with Nina Rabin, February 23, 2012.

15. Interviews with Victoria López, June 22, 2012, and Yali Lincroft, October 3, 2012.

16. Interview with Michelle Brané and Jennifer Podkul, July 8, 2013.

17. Interview with Roxana Bacon, April 25, 2013.

18. Interview with Victoria López, June 22, 2012.

19. Interview with Nina Rabin, February 23, 2012.

20. Interview with Mary Giovagnoli, October 10, 2012.

21. Interview with Emily Butera, February 13, 2012.

22. Secretary Napolitano also described DHS as "a fairly large consumer in the private prison realm" (House Appropriations Subcommittee on Homeland Security 2013, 41). The heavy reliance on private prisons to service immigration detention has led some to question whether the insistence on detaining 34,000 immigrants per day rather than using cheaper alternatives to incarceration is inappropriately tied to the financial interests of the private prison industry (Golash-Boza 2012; Morgenthau 2014; Welch 2002, 2013). This question is reinforced by findings by investigative reporters of close ties between the private prison industry and the American Legislative Exchange Council, which helped write some of the most virulent anti-immigrant legislation, including Arizona's SB 1070 (Sullivan 2010).

23. Interview with Randy Capps, October 23, 2012.

24. Yet while the percentage of deportations involving criminal offenders has increased, TRAC reported in July 2013 that new filings in immigration courts for deportations of persons alleged to be criminal offenders decreased in FY 2013 to 14.7 percent, a slight decline from the 16.1 percent seen in the last year of the Bush administration and a substantial drop from twenty years ago, when 28.5 percent of new filings were for immigrants with alleged criminal activity (TRAC 2013b).

25. It is important to note that these court cases involve legal permanent residents facing deportation. Those persons in the United States without authorization are subject to deportation regardless of whether or not they committed a crime.

26. This figure reflects the total number of removals of parents of US-born children in 2013. The number of individuals who were deported is slightly lower, 69,410, because some parents were removed more than once during the calendar year (Foley 2014; USICE 2014a, 2014b).

3. LEGISLATIVE INACTION AND EXECUTIVE ACTION

1. Interview with Lorella Praeli, May 14, 2014.

2. Interview with Nina Rabin, February 23, 2012.

3. Between 2005 and 2011, more than 8,000 immigration-related laws and resolutions were introduced in state legislatures across the country, and 1,700 of these laws and resolutions were enacted (National Conference of State Legislatures 2012).

4. Interview with Victoria López, June 22, 2012.

5. Interview with Emily Butera, February 13, 2012.

6. Interview with Lorella Praeli, May 14, 2014.

7. Ibid.

8. Others will become eligible as they reach the age of fifteen or return to school, but they are not considered in the immediately eligible population.

9. Interview with Allison Posner, November 19, 2013.

10. Interview with Lorella Praeli, May 14, 2014.

11. Interview with Doris Meissner, December 6, 2012.

4. FAMILIES TORN APART

1. Interview with Wendy Young, March 18, 2013.

2. Interview with M. Aryah Somers, July 2, 2013.

3. This number spirals up if we include state laws, totaling more than a thousand different crimes.

4. Interview with Emily Butera, February 13, 2012.

5. Interview with Lindsay Marshall, February 2, 2012.

6. Ibid.

7. Although it is now easier for caseworkers and family members to find and communicate with detained parents due to improvements discussed later in this chapter, many of the difficulties with visitation and completion of parenting plans remain.

8. Interview with Lindsay Marshall, February 2, 2012.

9. Interview with Nina Rabin, February 23, 2012.

10. Ibid.

11. Ibid.

12. Interview with Emily Butera, February 13, 2012.

13. Interview with Lindsay Marshall, February 2, 2012.

14. Interview with Emily Butera, February 13, 2012.

15. Interview with Beth Rosenberg, February 10, 2012.

16. Interview with Emily Butera, February 13, 2012.

17. Interview with Evelyn Cruz, February 28, 2012.

18. Interview with Emily Butera, February 13, 2012.

19. Interview with Anne Marie Mulcahy, February 24, 2012.

20. On November 20, 2014, President Obama announced an expansion of deferred action to include parents of US citizen or legal permanent resident children who have

lived in the United States for at least five years, pass a criminal background check, and pay taxes, and lifting of the age limit for DACA, among other measures. Recipients of deferred action are eligible for work authorization, and the deferred action will last for three years, instead of two, thus taking recipients a year past the 2016 presidential elections.

21. Interview with Yali Lincroft, October 3, 2012.

22. Interview with Victoria López, June 22, 2012.

23. Interview with Emily Butera, February 13, 2012.

24. Interview with Anne Marie Mulcahy, February 24, 2012.

25. Interview with Emily Butera, February 13, 2012.

26. Interview with Victoria López, June 22, 2012.

27. Interview with Michelle Brané and Jennifer Podkul, July 8, 2013.

28. Interview with Victoria López, June 22, 2012.

29. Statement made in a meeting of the Interagency Working Group on Unaccompanied Minor Children, December 12, 2013, Washington, DC.

30. Women's Refugee Commission, http://womensrefugeecommission.org/programs/migrant-rights/parental-rights/toolkit-and-educational-resources.

31. Personal email communication from Michelle Brané to author, September 1, 2014.

32. Statement by Jennifer Podkul in a meeting of the Interagency Working Group on Unaccompanied Minor Children, December 12, 2013, Washington, DC.

33. Email May 5, 2014, from Cindy Schlosser, Social Services Coordinator for the Florence Immigrant and Refugee Rights Project to the Childimmigration listserv managed by the Lutheran Immigration and Refugee Service (LIRS). This guide is available at www.firrp.org/media/Parental-Rights-Guide-2013.pdf.

34. Interview with M. Aryah Somers, July 2, 2013.

35. Interview with Michelle Brané and Jennifer Podkul, July 8, 2013.

36. See also http://saladeprensa.sre.gob.mx/images/phocagallery/apppromo2.pdf).

37. Interview with Yali Lincroft, August 22, 2013.

5. NO GOOD OPTIONS

1. Personal email communication from ORR spokesperson Lisa Raffonelli to first author, November 12, 2012

2. Statements by DHS and ORR officials at the meeting of the Interagency Working Group on Unaccompanied Minors, May 22, 2014.

3. Interview with Kimberly Haynes, February 12, 2014.

4. Statements by government officials at the meeting of the Interagency Working Group on Unaccompanied Minors, May 22, 2014.

5. Personal email communication from ORR spokesperson Lisa Raffonelli to first author, March 26, 2014.

6. Interview with Lindsay Marshall, February 2, 2012.

7. Comments by USCCB delegation participants at launch of USCCB report, January 9, 2014.

8. Interview with Kristyn Peck, March 3, 2014.

9. Personal communication from Lauren Heidbrink to first author, March 10, 2014.

10. Interview with M. Aryah Somers, July 2, 2013.

11. Interview with Kimberly Haynes, February 12, 2014.

12. Bhabha and Schmidt (2011) find variation in the percentage of youth admitted to secure facilities (including therapeutic and staff-secure) prior to the surge. They report that 8.9 percent of ORR admissions were to secure facilities in FY 2004, dropping to 3.6 percent in FY 2005, and then slowly rising to 4.6 percent in FY 2006, 5.8 percent in FY 2007, 7.6 percent in FY 2008, 10.3 percent in FY 2009, and 10.5 percent in FY 2010.

13. Statement by ORR representative at the meeting of the Interagency Working Group on Unaccompanied Minors, May 29, 2013.

14. Statements by ORR and DHS officials at the meeting of the Interagency Working Group on Unaccompanied Minors, May 22, 2014.

15. Interview with Kimberly Haynes, February 12, 2014.

16. Statement of ORR representative at the meeting of the Interagency Working Group on Unaccompanied Minors, January 15, 2014.

17. Interview with Michelle Brané and Jennifer Podkul, July 8, 2013.

18. Interview with Wendy Young, March 18, 2013.

19. Personal email communication from ORR spokesperson Lisa Raffonelli to first author, March 26, 2014.

20. Interview with Kimberly Haynes, February 12, 2014.

21. A home study shall be conducted for a child who is a victim of a severe form of trafficking in persons, a special needs child with a disability (as defined in section 3 of the Americans with Disabilities Act of 1990 (42 U.S.C. 12102(2))). William Wilberforce Trafficking Victims Protection Reauthorization Act of 2008 § 235(c)(3) (B), 8 U.S.C.A. § 1232(c)(6) (2009).

22. Interview with Maria Woltjen, December 19, 2012.

23. Statement by ORR representative at the meeting of the Interagency Working Group on Unaccompanied Minors, December 12, 2013.

24. Interview with Kimberly Haynes, February 12, 2014.

25. Personal email communication from ORR spokesperson Lisa Raffonelli to first author, March 26, 2014.

26. Ibid.

27. Interview with Kristyn Peck, March 3, 2014.

28. Statement by Department of Justice representative at the meeting of the Interagency Working Group on Unaccompanied Minors, May 22, 2014.

29. Interview with Anne Marie Mulcahy, February 24, 2012.

30. Interview with Maria Woltjen, December 19, 2012.

31. Interview with Ashley Feasley, February 26, 2014.

32. White House press release, emailed to the first author by White House representative Julie Rodriguez in preparation for a stakeholders conference call on unaccompanied minors, July 8, 2014.

33. Interview with Jennifer Podkul, February 23, 2012.

34. Ibid.

35. Personal communication to members of the Interagency Working Group on Unaccompanied Minors, email distribution June 5, 2014.

36. U.S. Committee for Refugees and Immigrants webpage on Gang-Related Asylum Resources www.refugees.org/resources/for-lawyers/asylum-research/gang-related-asylum-resources/gang-related-asylum-articles.html.

37. Interview with Kristyn Peck, March 3, 2014.

38. Interview with Kimberly Haynes, February 12, 2014.

39. Comments by panelist Lisa Frydman at the launch of "A Treacherous Journey: Child Migrants Navigating the U.S. Immigration System." February 27, 2014, Migration Policy Institute, Washington, DC.

40. Comments by Wendy Young at a forum on "Unaccompanied Minors and Their Journey through the US Immigration System," July 30, 2012, Migration Policy Institute, Washington, DC.

41. Interview with Wendy Young, March 18, 2013.

42. Ibid.

43. Ibid.

44. Statement at the meeting of the Interagency Working Group on Unaccompanied Minors, May 22, 2014.

45. By June 2014, large numbers of young mothers with babies and toddlers were also entering the United States. Finding appropriate housing for these families has been a struggle; as of August 2014, more than 600 women and children were warehoused at a detention center in Artesia, New Mexico.

46. Interview with Anne Marie Mulcahy, February 24, 2012.

47. Interview with Wendy Young, March 18, 2013.

48. Statement at the meeting of the Interagency Working Group on Unaccompanied Minors, May 29, 2013.

49. Interview with Maria Woltjen, December 19, 2012.

50. Statement at the meeting of the Interagency Working Group on Unaccompanied Minors, May 22, 2014.

REFERENCES

Abbott, Katherine R. 2013. "The Real American Court: Immigration Courts and the Ecology of Reform." PhD diss., Arizona State University.

Aber, Shaina and Mary Small. 2013. "Citizen or Subordinate: Permutations of Belonging in the United States and the Dominican Republic." *Journal on Migration and Human Security* 1(3):76–96.

Abrams, Kerry. 2005. "Polygamy, Prostitution, and the Federalization of Immigration Law." *Columbia Law Review* 105:641–716.

Abrego, Leisy J. 2006. "'I Can't Go to College Because I Don't Have Papers': Incorporation Patterns of Latino Undocumented Youth." *Latino Studies* 4:212–31.

———. 2008. "Legitimacy, Social Identity, and the Mobilization of Law: The Effects of Assembly Bill 540 on Undocumented Students in California." *Law & Social Inquiry* 33(3):709–34.

———. 2011. "Legal Consciousness of Undocumented Latinos: Fear and Stigma as Barriers to Claims-Making for First- and 1.5-Generation Immigrants," *Law and Society Review* 45(2):337–69.

———. 2014. *Sacrificing Families: Navigating Laws, Labor, and Love across Borders.* Stanford: Stanford University Press.

Abrego, Leisy J. and Roberto G. Gonzales. 2010. "Blocked Paths, Uncertain Futures: The Postsecondary Education and Labor Market Prospects of Undocumented Latino Youth." *Journal of Education for Students Placed at Risk* 15:144–57.

American Immigration Lawyers Association and American Immigration Council. 2011. "Holding DHS Accountable on Prosecutorial Discretion." November. www.aila.org/content/default.aspx?docid = 37615.

Amnesty International. 2010. *Invisible Victims: Migrants on the Move in Mexico.* London: Amnesty International Publications. www.amnesty.org/en/library/asset/AMR41/014/2010/en/8459f0ac-03ce-4302-8bd2-3305bdae9cde/amr410142010eng.pdf.

Annie E. Casey Foundation. 2011. "When a Parent Is Incarcerated: A Primer for Social Workers." Baltimore: Annie E. Casey Foundation. www.aecf.org/~/media/Pubs /Topics/Special%20Interest%20Areas/Children%20with%20Incarcerated%20 Parents/WhenaParentisIncarceratedPrimer/WhenAParentIsIncarceratedPrimer .pdf.

Arditti, Joyce A. 2012. *Parental Incarceration and the Family: Psychological and Social Effects of Imprisonment on Children, Parents and Caregivers.* New York: New York University Press.

Ashcroft, John. 2002. "Prepared Remarks on the National Security Entry-Exit Registration System." June 6. Washington, DC: Office of the Attorney General, US Department of Justice. www.usdoj.gov/archive/ag/speeches/2002/060502agprep aredremarks.htm.

Baker, Bryan and Nancy Rytina. 2013. "Estimates of the Unauthorized Immigrant Population Residing in the United States: January 2012." Washington, DC: Department of Homeland Security Office of Immigration Statistics. www.dhs.gov/sites /default/files/publications/ois_ill_pe_2012_2.pdf.

Banks, Angela M. 2013. "The Normative and Historical Case for Proportional Deportation." *Emory Law Journal* 62:1243–1307.

Batalova, Jeanne, Sarah Hooker, and Randy Capps with James D. Bachmeier and Erin Cox. 2013. *Deferred Action for Childhood Arrivals at the One-Year Mark: A Profile of Currently Eligible Youth and Applicants.* Washington, DC: Migration Policy Institute.

Batalova, Jeanne and Michelle Mittelstadt. 2012. *Relief from Deportation: Demographic Profile of the DREAMers Potentially Eligible under the Deferred Action Policy.* Washington, DC: Migration Policy Institute.

Bernsen, Sam. 1976. "Legal Opinion Regarding Service Exercise of Prosecutorial Discretion." July 15. www.ice.gov/doclib/foia/prosecutorial-discretion/service-exercise-pd.pdf.

Bhabha, Jacqueline. 2014. *Child Migration and Human Rights in a Global Age.* Princeton: Princeton University Press.

Bhabha, Jacqueline and Susan Schmidt. 2006. *Seeking Asylum Alone: Unaccompanied and Separated Children and Refugee Protection in the U.S.* Cambridge, MA: Harvard University Committee on Human Rights.

———. 2011. "From Kafka to Wilberforce: Is the U.S. Government's Approach to Child Migrants Improving?" *Immigration Briefings* 11(2):1–30.

Boehm, Deborah A. 2012. *Intimate Migrations: Gender, Family, and Illegality among Transnational Mexicans.* New York: New York University Press.

Brabeck, Kalina and Quingwen Xu. 2010. "The Impact of Detention and Deportation on Latino Immigrant Children and Families: A Quantitative Explanation." *Hispanic Journal of Behavioral Sciences* 32(3):341–61.

Brané, Michelle. 2011. "Delayed Justice for Guatemalan Mother Encarnación Bail Romero." January 27. www.womensrefugeecommission.org/blog/1098-delayed-justice-for-guatemalan-mother-encarnacion-bail-romero.

Brodkin, Evelyn Z. 2011. "Policy Work: Street-Level Organizations under New Managerialism." *Journal of Public Administration Research and Theory* 21 (Supplement 2):i253–77.

Brotherton, David C. and Luis Barrios. 2011. *Banished to the Homeland: Dominican Deportees and Their Stories of Exile.* New York: Columbia University Press.

Butera, Emily. 2013. "ICE's Parental Interests Directive: Helping Families Caught between the Immigration and Child Welfare System." August 26. http://womensrefugeecommission.org/blog/1713-new-ice-directive-helps-families-caught-between-the-immigration-and-child-welfare-systems?utm_source = Migration+%26+Child+Welfare+National+Network+E-News&utm_campaign = a59112e7fd-MCWNN_E_News_061013&utm_medium = email&utm_term = 0_4a8508bf17-a59112e7fd-66938977.

Butera, Emily and Wendy Cervantes. 2013. "Family Unity in the Face of Immigration Enforcement: Past, Present, and Future." In *Children in Harm's Way: Criminal Justice, Immigration Enforcement, and Child Welfare,* edited by Susan D. Phillips, Wendy Cervantes, Yali Lincroft, Alan J. Dettlaff, and Lara Bruce, 11–21. Washington, DC: Sentencing Project and First Focus.

Bybee, Jay S. 2002. "Memorandum for the Attorney General." April 3. Washington, DC: Office of the Assistant Attorney General, Office of Legal Counsel, US Department of Justice. www.aclu.org/files/FilesPDFs/ACF27DA.pdf (redacted).

Byrne, Olga. 2008. *Unaccompanied Children in the United States: A Literature Review.* New York: Vera Institute of Justice.

Byrne, Olga and Elise Miller. 2012. *The Flow of Unaccompanied Children through the Immigration System: A Resource for Practitioners, Policy Makers, and Researchers.* New York: Vera Institute of Justice.

Calavita, Kitty. 1984. *U.S. Immigration Law and the Control of Labor: 1820–1924.* Orlando, FL: Academic Press.

———. 1989. "The Contradictions of Immigration Lawmaking: The Immigration Reform and Control Act of 1986." *Law & Policy* 11(1):17–47.

———. 1992. *Inside the State: The Bracero Program, Immigration, and the I.N.S.* New York: Routledge.

———. 2007. "Immigration Law, Race, and Identity." *Annual Review of Law and Social Science* 3:1–20.

Capps, Randy, Rosa Maria Castañeda, Ajay Chaudry, and Robert Santos. 2007. *Paying the Price: The Impact of Immigration Raids on America's Children.* Washington, DC: National Council of La Raza and Urban Institute.

Capps, Randy and Michael Fix, eds. 2012. *Young Children of Black Immigrants in America: Changing Flows, Changing Faces.* Washington, DC: Migration Policy Institute.

Carroll, Susan. 2011. "Report: Feds Downplayed ICE Case Dismissals." *Houston Chronicle.* June 27. www.chron.com/news/houston-texas/article/Report-Feds-downplayed-ICE-case-dismissals-2080532.php.

Cavendish, Betsy and Maru Cortazar. 2011. *Children at the Border: The Screening, Protection and Repatriation of Unaccompanied Mexican Minors.* Washington, DC: Appleseed.

Cavendish, Betsy, Steven Schulman, Amjad Mahmood Khan, and Erica Abshez. 2014. *A DREAM Deferred: From DACA to Citizenship: Lessons from DACA for Advocates and Policymakers.* Washington, DC: Appleseed.

Cervantes, Wendy. 2013. "In Deportation Process, Lack of Communication Puts U.S. Kids in Harm's Way." *Chronicle of Social Change,* February 12. file:///Users/atmsz/Documents/Collateral%20Conseq%20of%20Wars%20on%20Crime%20&%20Border%20Book/parental%20det%20&%20dep%20chapter/Deportation%20Process%20Often%20Puts%20Children%20in%20Harm's%20Way%20%20%20The%20Chronicle%20of%20Social%20Change.html.

Chambliss, William J. 1979. "On Law Making." *British Journal of Law and Society* 6:149–71.

Chambliss, William J. and Marjorie S. Zatz, eds. 1993. *Making Law: The State, the Law, and Structural Contradictions.* Bloomington: Indiana University Press.

Champion, Dean, ed. 1989. *The U.S. Sentencing Guidelines: Implications for Criminal Justice.* New York: Praeger.

Chaudry, Ajay, Randy Capps, Juan Manuel Pedroza, Rosa Maria Castañeda, Robert Santos, and Molly M. Scott. 2010. *Facing Our Future: Children in the Aftermath of Immigration Enforcement.* Washington, DC: Urban Institute. February. www.urban.org/uploadedpdf/412020_FacingOurFuture_final.pdf.

Chavez, Leo R. 2008. *The Latino Threat: Constructing Immigrants, Citizens and the Nation.* Stanford: Stanford University Press.

Comfort, Megan. 2008. *Doing Time Together: Love and Family in the Shadow of the Prison.* Chicago: University of Chicago Press.

Congressional Hispanic Caucus. n.d. "Working Draft Memorandum to Secretary Johnson." www.washingtonpost.com/r/2010–2019/WashingtonPost/2014/04/04/Editorial-Opinion/Graphics/CHC_Request%20to%20Jeh%20Johnson.pdf.

Constable, Pamela. 2014. "Young Illegal Immigrants Get Two-Year Ticket to Earn, Learn, and Enjoy Self-Respect." *Washington Post,* April 6. www.washingtonpost.com/local/young-illegal-immigrants-get-two-year-ticket-to-earn-learn-and-gain-self-respect/2014/04/06/7693dbaa-bb5b-11e3–9c3c-311301e2167d_story.html.

Cooper, Bo. 1999. "INS Exercise of Prosecutorial Discretion." October 4. Copy on file with the authors.

Cornyn, John et al. 2010. "Letter to Secretary of Homeland Security Janet Napolitano." October 21. Pages 109–10 of 200 in FOIA request. www.scribd.com/doc/58810530/2011-ICE-Report-FOIA-request.

Corporation for National and Community Service. 2014. "Justice Department and CNCS Announce New Partnership to Enhance Immigration Courts and Provide Critical Legal Assistance to Unaccompanied Minors." Press release, June 6. www.nationalservice.gov/newsroom/press-releases/2014/justice-department-and-cncs-announce-new-partnership-enhance.

Coutin, Susan Bibler. 2000. *Legalizing Moves: Salvadoran Immigrants' Struggle for U.S. Residency.* Ann Arbor: University of Michigan Press.

———. 2003. "Borderlands, Illegality and the Spaces of Non-existence." In *Globalization under Construction: Governmentality, Law, and Identity*, edited by Richard Perry and Bill Maurer, 171–202. Minneapolis: University of Minnesota Press.

———. 2007. *Nations of Emigrants: Shifting Boundaries of Citizenship in El Salvador and the United States*. Ithaca: Cornell University Press.

Cox, Adam B. and Cristina M. Rodríguez. 2009. "The President and Immigration Law." *Yale Law Review* 119:458–547.

Crane, Chris. 2011. "Vote of No Confidence." National Council 118-Immigration and Customs Enforcement, American Federation of Government Employees (AFL-CIO) Press Release, June 25. www.aila.org/content/default.aspx?docid = 32801.

Cruz, Evelyn H. 2012. "Unearthing and Confronting the Social Skeletons of Immigration Status in Our Criminal Justice System." In *Punishing Immigrants: Policy, Politics, and Injustice*, edited by Charis E. Kubrin, Marjorie S. Zatz, and Ramiro Martínez Jr., 91–112. New York: New York University Press.

Dahlberg, Nancy. 2014. "FWD.us Hosts Panel on Immigration Reform." *Miami Herald*, June 4. www.miamiherald.com/2014/06/04/4157865/fwdus-hosts-panel-on-immigration.html.

Davenport, Maria-Teresa. 2006. "Deportation and Driving: Felony DUI and Reckless Driving as Crimes of Violence Following Leocal v. Ashcroft." *Journal of Criminal Law and Criminology* 96(3):849–75.

DeGenova, Nicholas P. 2002. "Migrant 'Illegality' and Deportability in Everyday Life." *Annual Review of Anthropology* 31:419–47.

Dreby, Joanna. 2010. *Divided by Borders: Mexican Migrants and Their Children*. Berkeley: University of California Press.

———. 2012. "How Today's Immigration Enforcement Policies Impact Children, Families, and Communities: A View from the Ground." August. Washington, DC: Center for American Progress. www.americanprogress.org/wp-content/uploads/2012/08/DrebyImmigrationFamiliesFINAL.pdf.

Eagly, Ingrid V. 2013. "Criminal Justice for Noncitizens: An Analysis of Variation in Local Enforcement." *New York University Law Review* 88:1126–1223.

Edelman, Lauren B. 1992. "Legal Ambiguity and Symbolic Structures: Organizational Mediation of Civil Rights Law." *American Journal of Sociology* 97(6):1531–76.

Edelman, Lauren B., Linda H. Krieger, Scott R. Eliason, Catherine R. Albiston, and Virginia Mellema. 2011. "When Organizations Rule: Judicial Deference to Institutionalized Employment Structures. " *American Journal of Sociology* 117(3): 888–954.

Epstein, Reid J. 2014. "National Council of La Raza Calls Barack Obama 'Deporter-in-Chief.'" *Politico*. March 4. www.politico.com/story/2014/03/national-council-of-la-raza-janet-murguia-barack-obama-deporter-in-chief-immigration-104217.html.

Ewing, Walter A. 2014. "The Growth of the U.S. Deportation Machine." March. Washington, DC: Immigration Policy Center. www.immigrationpolicy.org/just-facts/growth-us-deportation-machine.

Federation for American Immigration Reform. 2013. "The Morton Memos: Giving Illegal Aliens Administrative Amnesty." www.fairus.org/morton-memos.

Feere, Jon. 2011. "ICE Agent's Union Blasts Obama Administration, ICE Director." Center for Immigration Studies. http://cis.org/feere/ICE-union-discretion-memo. June 24.

FitzGerald, David S. and David Cook-Martín. 2014. *Culling the Masses: The Democratic Origins of Racist Immigration Policy in the Americas.* Cambridge, MA: Harvard University Press.

Flores, Stella M. 2010. "State Dream Acts: The Effect of In-State Resident Tuition Policies on the College Enrollment of Undocumented Latino Students in the United States." *Review of Higher Education* 33(2): 239–83.

Foley, Elise. 2013. "Obama Confronts Hecklers at Immigration Speech." *Huffington Post,* November 25. www.huffingtonpost.com/2013/11/25/barack-obama-hecklers-immigration_n_4338945.html.

———. 2014. "Deportation Separated Thousands of U.S.-Born Children from Parents in 2013." *Huffington Post,* June 25. www.huffingtonpost.com/2014/06/25/parents-deportation_n_5531552.html.

Frydman, Lisa and Neha Desai. 2012. "Beacon of Hope or Failure of Protection? U.S. Treatment of Asylum Claims Based on Persecution by Organized Gangs." *Immigration Briefings.* 12(10):1–49.

Gamboa, Suzanne. 2011. "Drunken Driving, Traffic Crime Deportations Way Up." Associated Press. July 22. http://news.yahoo.com/drunken-driving-traffic-crime-deportations-way-072604914.html.

Gardner Martha. 2005. *The Qualities of a Citizen: Women, Immigration, and Citizenship: 1870–1965.* Princeton: Princeton University Press.

Gilbert, Lauren. 2013. "Obama's Ruby Slippers: Enforcement Discretion in the Absence of Immigration Reform." *West Virginia Law Review* 116(1):255–312.

Gleeson, Shannon and Roberto G. Gonzales. 2012. "When Do Papers Matter? An Institutional Analysis of Undocumented Life in the United States." *International Migration* 50(4):1–19.

Golash-Boza, Tanya M. 2012. *Immigration Nation: Raids, Detentions and Deportations in Post-9/11 America.* Boulder CO: Paradigm Publishers.

Gonzales, Roberto G. 2010. "On the Wrong Side of the Tracks: The Consequences of School Stratification Systems for Unauthorized Mexican Students." *Peabody Journal of Education* 85(4):469–85.

———. 2011. "Learning to be Illegal: Undocumented Youth and Shifting Legal Contexts in the Transition to Adulthood." *American Sociological Review* 76(4):602–19.

Gonzales, Roberto G. and Leo Chavez. 2012. "'Awakening to a Nightmare': Abjectivity and Illegality in the Lives of Undocumented 1.5-Generation Latino Immigrants in the United States." *Current Anthropology* 53(3):255–268.

Gonzales, Roberto G., Veronica Terriquez, and Stephen Ruszczyk. 2014. "Becoming DACAmented: Assessing the Short-Term Benefits of Deferred Action for Childhood Arrivals (DACA)." *American Behavioral Scientist* 58(14):1852–72.

Gonzalez-Barrera, Ana, Jens Manuel Krogstad, and Mark Hugo Lopez. 2014. *Many Mexican Child Migrants Caught Multiple Times at Border*. August 4. Washington, DC: Pew Research Center. www.pewresearch.org/fact-tank/2014/08/04/many-mexican-child-migrants-caught-multiple-times-at-border/.

González, Daniel. 2012. "Stats Detail Deportation of Parents with U.S.-Born Children." *Arizona Republic*, April 4. www.azcentral.com/news/articles/20120404deportation-stats-detail-parents-american-born-children.html.

Gould, Jon and Scott Barclay. 2012. "Mind the Gap: The Place of Gap Studies in Sociolegal Scholarship." *Annual Review of Law and Social Science* 8:323–35.

Grijalva, Raul M. et al. 2013. "Letter from 29 Members of Congress to President Barack Obama." December 5. 20Letter%20on%20Pausing%20Deportations.pdf.

Grimes, Mark, Elyse Golob, Alexandra Durcikova, and Jay Nunamaker. 2013. *Reasons and Resolve to Cross the Line: A Post-Apprehension Survey of Unauthorized Immigrants along the U.S.-Mexico Border*. Tucson: National Center for Border Security and Immigration, University of Arizona. May 31. www.borders.arizona.edu/cms/sites/default/files/Post-Apprehension-Survey-REPORT%20may31–2013.pdf.

Hagan, Jacqueline, Karl Eschbach, and Nestor Rodríguez. 2008. "U.S. Deportation Policy, Family Separation, and Circular Migration." *International Migration Review* 42(1):64–88.

Hagan, Jacqueline, Nestor Rodríguez, and Brianna Castro. 2011. "Social Effects of Mass Deportations by the United States Government, 2000–2010." *Ethnic and Racial Studies* 34(8):1374–91.

Hagan, John and Ronit Dinovitzer. 1999. "Collateral Consequences of Imprisonment for Children, Communities and Prisoners." *Crime and Justice* 26:121–60.

Harwood, Edwin. 1986. *In Liberty's Shadow: Illegal Aliens and Immigration Law Enforcement*. Stanford, VA: Hoover Institution Press.

Heidbrink, Lauren. 2014. *Migrant Youth, Transnational Families, and the State: Care and Contested Interests*. Philadelphia: University of Pennsylvania Press.

Hidalgo, Rosie. 2013. "Crossroads: The Intersection of Immigrant Enforcement and the Child Welfare System." *Synergy* 16(1):2–8.

Hing, Bill Ong. 1980. "The Ninth Circuit: No Place for Drug Offenders." *Golden Gate University Law Review* 10(1):1–12.

———. 2004. *Defining America through Immigration Policy*. Philadelphia: Temple University Press.

———. 2013. "The Failure of Prosecutorial Discretion and the Deportation of Oscar Martinez." *Scholar: St Mary's Law Review and Social Justice* 15:437–533.

Howard, William J. 2005. "Prosecutorial Discretion." October 24. h/www.scribd.com/doc/22092975/ICE-Guidance-Memo-Prosecutorial-Discretion-William-J-Howard-10–24–05.

Human Rights Watch. 2007. "Forced Apart: Families Separated and Immigrants Harmed by United States Deportation Policy." July 17. www.hrw.org/reports/2007/07/16/forced-apart-0.

———. 2013. "Turning Migrants into Criminals: The Harmful Impact of US Border Prosecutions." May. /www.hrw.org/sites/default/files/reports/us0513_ForUpload_2 .pdf.

Hyde, Rep. Henry et al. 1999. "RE: Guidelines for Use of Prosecutorial Discretion in Removal Proceedings." Letter signed by 28 members of the House of Representatives. November 4. www.ice.gov/doclib/foia/prosecutorial-discretion/991104congress-letter.pdf.

Immigrant Legal Resources Center. 2010. "Practice Advisory: One-Parent Special Immigrant Juvenile Status Claims." On file with the authors.

———. 2013. "Immigration Options for Undocumented Immigrant Children." July. www.ilrc.org/files/documents/ilrc-immig_options_undoc_children-2013–07.pdf.

Immigration Policy Center. 2012. "Falling through the Cracks: The Impact of Immigration Enforcement on Children Caught up in the Child Welfare System." December 12. Washington, DC: American Immigration Council. www.immigrationpolicy .org/just-facts/falling-through-cracks.

———. 2014. "Taking Attendance: New Data Finds Majority of Children Appear in Immigration Court." July 29. Washington, DC: American Immigration Council. www.immigrationpolicy.org/just-facts/taking-attendance-new-data-finds-majority-children-appear-immigration-court.

Johnson, Jeh. 2014. "Exercising Prosecutorial Discretion with Respect to Individuals Who Came to the United States as Children and with Respect to Certain Individuals Who Are the Parents of U.S. Citizens or Permanent Residents." November 20. US Department of Homeland Security. http://www.dhs.gov/sites/default /files/publications/14_1120_memo_deferred_action.pdf.

Johnson, Kevin. 2003. The "Huddled Masses" Myth: Immigration and Civil Rights. Philadelphia: Temple University Press.

Junck, Angie. 2012. "Special Immigrant Juvenile Status: Relief for Neglected, Abused, and Abandoned Undocumented Children." Juvenile and Family Court Journal 63(1):48–62.

Kanstroom, Daniel. 2012. Aftermath: Deportation Law and the New American Diaspora. New York: Oxford University Press.

Kids In Need of Defense (KIND). 2013. The Time Is Now: Understanding and Addressing the Protection of Immigrant Children Who Come Alone to the United States. February. Washington, DC.

Kids In Need of Defense and Center for Gender and Refugee Studies, UC Hastings College of Law. 2014. "A Treacherous Journey: Child Migrants Navigating the U.S. Immigration System." February. Washington, DC and San Francisco, CA.

King, Shani M. 2013. "Alone and Unrepresented: A Call to Congress to Provide Counsel for Unaccompanied Minors." Harvard Journal on Legislation 50:331–84.

Kirkwood, R. Cort. 2012. "Drunk Driving Bolivian Gets Twenty Years for Killing Nun." New American. February 6. www.thenewamerican.com/usnews/immigration /item/2174-drunk-driving-bolivian-gets-20-years-for-killing-nun.

Kmiec, Douglas W. 1989. "Memorandum for Joseph R. Davis Assistant Director— Legal Counsel FBI." April 11. Washington, DC: Office of the Assistant Attorney

General, Office of Legal Counsel, Department of Justice. www.aclu.org/files/images/asset_upload_file438_299070.pdf.

Kobach, Kris W. 2005. "The Quintessential Force Multiplier: The Inherent Authority of Local Police to Make Immigration Arrests." *Albany Law Review* 69:179–235.

Koulish, Robert and Mark Noferi. 2013. "Unlocking Immigrant Detention Reform." *Baltimore Sun*. February 20. www.baltimoresun.com/news/opinion/oped/bs-ed-immigrant-detention-20130220,0,5653483.story.

———. 2015. *Immigration Detention in the Risk Classification Assessment Era*. Washington, DC: Migration Policy Institute.

Krogstad, Jens Manuel, Ana Gonzalez-Barrera, and Mark Hugo Lopez. 2014. *At the Border, A Sharp Rise in Unaccompanied Girls Fleeing Honduras*. July 25. Washington, DC: Pew Research Center. www.pewresearch.org/fact-tank/2014/07/25/at-the-border-a-sharp-rise-in-unaccompanied-girls-fleeing-honduras/.

Kubrin, Charis, Marjorie S. Zatz, and Ramiro Martínez Jr., eds. 2012. *Punishing Immigrants: Policy, Politics and Injustice*. New York: New York University Press.

Kuhnhenn, Jim. 2014. "White House Wants Delay in DOD Immigration Plan." Associated Press. June 2. http://hosted.ap.org/dynamic/stories/U/US_OBAMA_IMMIGRATION?SITE = AP.

Layton, Lyndsey. 2014. "Former Post Owner Hoping to Send Dreamers to College." *Washington Post*. February 3. www.washingtonpost.com/local/education/former-post-owner-launches-scholarship-fund-for-undocumented-students/2014/02/03/f41dea2a-8aaf-11e3-916e-e01534b1e132_story.html.

Legomsky, Stephen H. 2007. "A New Path of Immigration Law: Asymmetric Incorporation of Criminal Justice Norms." *Washington and Lee Law Review* 64:469–528.

Lincroft, Yali. 2013. "'The Reuniting Immigrant Families Act': A Case Study on California's Senate Bill 1064." State Policy Advocacy and Reform Center. May. http://childwelfaresparc.files.wordpress.com/2013/05/reuniting-immigrant-families-act-brief.pdf.

Lipsky, Michael. 1980. *Street-Level Bureaucracy: Dilemmas of the Individual in Public Services*. New York: Russell Sage Foundation.

Longazel, Jamie. 2013. "Moral Panic as Racial Degradation Ceremony: Racial Stratification and the Local-Level Backlash against Latino/a Immigrants." *Punishment and Society* 15(1): 96–119.

Macauley, Stewart. 1984. "Law and the Behavioral Sciences: Is There Any There There?" *Law & Policy* 6:149–87.

Marshall, Lindsay. 2012. *Families on the Front Lines: How Immigration Advocates Can Build a Bridge Between the Immigration and Child Welfare Systems*. Washington, DC: First Focus. www.firstfocus.net/sites/default/files/Families%20on%20the%20Front%20Lines.pdf.

Martin, David A. 2012. "A Defense of Immigration Enforcement Discretion: The Legal and Policy Flaws in Kris Kobach's Latest Crusade." *Yale Law Journal Online* 122: 167–86. http://yalelawjournal.org/2012/12/20/martin.html.

Maynard-Moody, Steven and Michael Musheno. 2003. *Cops, Teachers, Counselors: Stories from the Front Lines of Public Service.* Ann Arbor: University of Michigan Press.

———. 2012. "Social Equities and Inequities in Practice: Street-level Workers as Agents and Pragmatists." *Public Administration Review* 72:S16–23.

McCoy, Candace. 1984. "Determinate Sentencing, Plea Bargaining Bans and Hydraulic Discretion in California." *Justice System Journal* 9:256–75.

Meissner, Doris. 2000. "Exercising Prosecutorial Discretion." November 17. US Department of Justice: Immigration and Naturalization Service. Copy on file with the authors.

Meissner, Doris, Donald M. Kerwin, Muzaffar Chishti, and Claire Bergeron. 2013. *Immigration Enforcement in the United States: The Rise of a Formidable Machinery.* Washington, DC: Migration Policy Institute.

Meithe, Terance D. and Charles A. Moore. 1985. "Socioeconomic Disparities under Determinate Sentencing Systems: A Comparison of Preguideline and Postguideline Practices in Minnesota." *Criminology* 23(2):337–63.

Menjívar, Cecilia. 2006. "Liminal Legality: Salvadoran and Guatemalan Immigrants' Lives in the United States." *American Journal of Sociology* 111:999–1037.

———. 2011. *Enduring Violence: Ladina Women's Lives in Guatemala.* Berkeley: University of California Press.

———. 2012. "Transnational Parenting and Immigration Law: Central Americans in the United States." *Journal of Ethnic and Migration Studies* 38(2):301–22.

Menjívar, Cecilia and Leisy Abrego. 2009. "Parents and Children across Borders: Legal Instability and Intergenerational Relations in Guatemalan and Salvadoran Families." In *Across Generations: Immigrant Families in America,* edited by Nancy Foner, 160–89. New York: New York University Press.

———. 2012. "Legal Violence: Immigration Law and the Lives of Central American Immigrants." *American Journal of Sociology* 117(5):1380–1421.

Menjívar, Cecilia and Dan Kanstroom, eds. 2013. *Constructing Illegality in America: Immigrant Experiences, Critiques, and Resistance.* New York: Cambridge University Press.

Migration and Child Welfare National Network. 2013. "Issue Brief: Implications of Important State Child Welfare/Immigration-Related Appellate Court Opinions." Compiled by Howard Davidson. April 10. On file with the authors.

Migration Policy Institute. 2012. "As Many as 1.76 Million Unauthorized Immigrant Youth Could Gain Relief from Deportation under Deferred Action for Childhood Arrivals Initiative." August 7. www.migrationpolicy.org/news/2012_08_07.php.

———. 2013. "New Smartphone App Launched to Assist Mexican Nationals in U.S." https://mbasic.facebook.com/notes/migration-policy-institute/new-smartphone-app-launched-to-assist-mexican-nationals-in-us/10151950136639430/?refid = 17&ref = stream.

Montgomery, John D. 2014. "Cost of Counsel in Immigration: Economic Analysis of Proposal Providing Public Counsel to Indigent Persons Subject to Immigration Removal Proceedings." May 28. Chicago: National Economic Research Associates. www.nera.com/67_8564.htm.

Morgenthau, Robert M. 2014. "The US Keeps 34,000 Immigrants in Detention Each Day Simply to Meet a Quota." *The Nation.* August 13. www.thenation.com/article/180972/us-keeps-34000-immigrants-detention-each-day-simply-meet-quota.

Morton, John. 2011a. "Civil Immigration Enforcement: Priorities for the Apprehension, Detention, and Removal of Aliens." March 2 (initially released June 30, 2010). US Department of Homeland Security: US Immigration and Customs Enforcement www.ice.gov/doclib/news/releases/2011/110302washingtondc.pdf.

———. 2011b. "Prosecutorial Discretion: Certain Victims, Witnesses, and Plaintiffs." June 17. US Department of Homeland Security: US Immigration and Customs Enforcement. www.ice.gov/doclib/secure-communities/pdf/domestic-violence.pdf.

———. 2011c. "Exercising Prosecutorial Discretion Consistent with the Civil Immigration Enforcement Priorities of the Agency for the Apprehension, Detention, and Removal of Aliens." June 17. US Department of Homeland Security: US Immigration and Customs Enforcement. www.ice.gov/doclib/secure-communities/pdf/prosecutorial-discretion-memo.pdf.

———. 2012. "Civil Immigration Enforcement: Guidance on the Use of Detainers in the Federal, State, Local, and Tribal Criminal Justice Systems." December 21. US Department of Homeland Security: US Immigration and Customs Enforcement. www.ice.gov/doclib/detention-reform/pdf/detainer-policy.pdf.

Motomura, Hiroshi. 2012. *Prosecutorial Discretion in Context: How Discretion Is Exercised throughout our Immigration System.* April. Washington, DC: Immigration Policy Center, American Immigration Council.

———. 2014. *Immigration outside the Law.* New York: Oxford University Press.

Motomura, Hiroshi et al. 2012. "Executive Authority to Grant Administrative Relief for DREAM Act Beneficiaries." Letter to President Barack Obama signed by ninety-five law professors. May 28. Copy on file with the authors.

Murray, Joseph and David P. Farrington. 2008. "The Effects of Parental Imprisonment on Children." In *Crime and Justice: A Review of Research,* edited by Michael Tonry, 133–206. Chicago: University of Chicago Press.

Myers, Julie I. 2007. *Prosecutorial and Custody Discretion.* November 7. Copy on file with the authors.

N., José Ángel. 2014. *Illegal: Reflections of an Undocumented Immigrant.* Urbana: University of Illinois Press.

Nakamura, David. 2014. "Obama Orders Delay of Immigration Deportation Review." *Washington Post.* May 27. www.washingtonpost.com/blogs/post-politics/wp/2014/05/27/obama-orders-delay-of-immigration-deportation-review/

Napolitano, Janet. 2012. "Exercising Prosecutorial Discretion with Respect to Individuals Who Came to the United States as Children." June 15. US Department of Homeland Security. www.dhs.gov/xlibrary/assets/s1-exercising-prosecutorial-discretion-individuals-who-came-to-us-as-children.pdf.

National Conference of State Legislatures. 2012. "2012 Immigration Related Laws and Resolutions in the States (January 1—June 30, 2012)." www.ncsl.org/issues-research/immig/2012-immigration-related-laws-and-resolutions.aspx.

———. 2014a. "Undocumented Student Tuition: Overview." May. www.ncsl.org /research/education/undocumented-student-tuition-overview.aspx.

———. 2014b. "States Offering Driver's Licenses to Immigrants." April 3. www.ncsl. org/research/immigration/states-offering-driver-s-licenses-to-immigrants.aspx.

National Immigrant Justice Center. 2013. "Fact Sheet: Children Detained by the Department of Homeland Security in Adult Detention Facilities." May. www .immigrantjustice.org/sites/immigrantjustice.org/files/NIJC%20Fact%20Sheet%20 Minors%20in%20ICE%20Custody%202013%2005%2030%20FINAL_0.pdf.

———. 2014. "Unaccompanied Immigrant Children." January. https://immigrantjustice.org/sites/immigrantjustice.org/files/NIJC%20Policy%20Brief%20-%20Unaccompanied%20Immigrant%20Children%20FINAL%20Winter%202014.pdf.

Nazario, Sonia. 2006. *Enrique's Journey: The Story of a Boy's Dangerous Odyssey to Reunite with His Mother.* New York: Random House.

Navas, Yoli. 2013. "DREAMer, DACA Recipient Yoli Navas: 'We Live in Fear Every Day.'" *America's Voice.* June 25. http://americasvoiceonline.org/blog /dreamer-daca-recipient-yoli-navas-we-live-in-fear-every-day/.

Newton, Lina. 2008. *Illegal, Alien, or Immigrant: The Politics of Immigration Reform.* New York: New York University Press.

New York Times Editorial Board. 2014. "Yes He Can, on Immigration." *New York Times.* April 5. www.nytimes.com/2014/04/06/opinion/sunday/yes-he-can-on-immigration.html?nlid = 66600761&src = recpb.

Ngai Mae. 2004. *Impossible Subjects: Illegal Aliens and the Making of Modern America.* Princeton: Princeton University Press.

Noferi, Mark and Robert Koulish. 2015. "Assessing Immigration Risk Assessments." *Georgetown Immigration Law Journal* 29(1): forthcoming.

Office of Refugee Resettlement. 2013a. "UAC Fact Sheet." US Department of Health and Human Services. April. www.acf.hhs.gov/sites/default/files/orr/unaccompanied_ childrens_services.pdf.

———. 2013b. "UAC Fact Sheet." December. US Department of Health and Human Services. www.acf.hhs.gov/sites/default/files/orr/unaccompanied_childrens_ services_fact_sheet.pdf.

———. 2014. "About Unaccompanied Children's Services." www.acf.hhs.gov /programs/orr/programs/ucs/about.

Olivas, Michael A. 2012a. "Dreams Deferred: Deferred Action, Prosecutorial Discretion and the Vexing Case(s) of Dream Act Students. " *William and Mary Bill of Rights Journal* 21:463–547.

———. 2012b. *No Undocumented Child Left Behind: Plyler v. Doe and the Education of Undocumented Schoolchildren.* New York: New York University Press.

Passel, Jeffrey and D'Vera Cohn. 2009. "A Portrait of Unauthorized Immigrants in the United States." Pew Hispanic Center. April 14. www.pewhispanic.org/2009 /04/14/a-portrait-of-unauthorized-immigrants-in-the-united-states/.

———. 2011. "Unauthorized Immigrant Population: National and State Trends, 2010." Pew Hispanic Center. www.pewhispanic.org/2011/02/01/iii-births-and-children/.

Passel, Jeffrey, D'Vera Cohn, and Ana Gonzalez-Barrera. 2012. "Net Migration from Mexico Falls to Zero—And Perhaps Less." Pew Hispanic Center. April 23. www .pewhispanic.org/2012/04/23/ii-migration-between-the-u-s-and-mexico/.

———. 2013. "Population Decline of Unauthorized Immigrants Stalls, May Have Reversed." Pew Research Hispanic Trends Project. September 23. www.pewhis-panic.org/2013/09/23/population-decline-of-unauthorized-immigrants-stalls-may-have-reversed/.

Passel, Jeffrey, D'Vera Cohn, Jens Manuel Krogstad, and Ana Gonzalez-Barrera. 2014. "As Growth Stalls, Unauthorized Immigrant Population Becomes More Settled." Pew Research Hispanic Trends Project. September 3. http://www.pewhispanic .org/2014/09/03/as-growth-stalls-unauthorized-immigrant-population-becomes-more-settled/.

Phillips, Susan D., Wendy Cervantes, Yali Lincroft, Alan J. Dettlaff, and Lara Bruce, eds. 2013. *Children in Harm's Way: Criminal Justice, Immigration Enforcement, and Child Welfare.* Washington, DC: Sentencing Project and First Focus. January. http://sentencingproject.org/doc/publications/cc_Children%20in%20Harm's%20 Way-final.pdf.

Praeli, Lorella. 2014. "[Infographic] Five Things Obama Can Do Right Now to Provide Relief to the Undocumented Community. #WeCantWait." Last update May 1, 2014. http://unitedwedream.org/five-things-president-obama-can-do/.

Pratt, Geraldine. 2012. *Families Apart: Migrant Mothers and the Conflicts of Labor and Love.* Minneapolis: University of Minnesota Press.

Preston, Julia. 2011. "State Lawmakers Outline Plans to End Birthright Citizenship, Drawing Outcry." *New York Times.* January 5. www.nytimes.com/2011/01/06 /us/06immig.html?_r = 0.

———. 2013. "Single-Minded Mission to Block an Immigration Bill." *New York Times.* June 1. www.nytimes.com/2013/06/02/us/for-chris-crane-a-quest-to-block-an-immigration-bill.html?pagewanted = all.

———. 2014. "Young Immigrants Turn Focus to President in Struggles over Deportations." *New York Times.* February 23. www.nytimes.com/2014/02/24/us /politics/young-immigrants-turn-focus-to-president-in-struggle-over-deportations .html.

Rabin, Nina. 2011. "Disappearing Parents: A Report on Immigration Enforcement and the Child Welfare System." *Connecticut Law Review* 44(1):99–160.

———. 2014. "Victims or Criminals? Discretion, Sorting, and Bureaucratic Culture in the U.S. Immigration System." *Southern California Review of Law and Social Justice* 23(2):195–247.

Rainey, Libby. 2013. "Napolitano Announces New $5 Million Initiative to Aid Undoc-umented Students." *Daily Californian.* October 31. www.dailycal.org/2013/10/30 /napolitano-announces-new-initiative-undocumented-students-uc/.

Ramakrishnan, Karthick and Pratheepan Gulasekaram. 2013. "Can Obama Unilaterally Ban Deportations?" *Los Angeles Times,* December 5. file://localhost/Users /atmsz/Documents/Collateral%20Conseq%20of%20Wars%20on%20Crime%20&%

20Border%20Book/PD%20chapter/Can%20Obama%20unilaterally%20ban%20 deportations%20%20-%20latimes.com.html.

Rodriguez, Nancy, Hilary Smith, and Marjorie S. Zatz. 2009. "Youth Is Enmeshed in a Highly Dysfunctional Family System: Exploring the Relationship among Dysfunctional Families, Parental Incarceration, and Juvenile Court Decision Making." *Criminology* 47:177–207.

Roseborough, Teresa Wynn. 1996. "Memorandum Opinion for the U.S. Attorney South District of California." February 5. US Department of Justice, Office of the Deputy Assistant Attorney General, Office of Legal Counsel. www.justice.gov/olc /immstop01a.htm.

Rucker, Philip and Peter Wallsten. 2013. "President Obama Exercises a Fluid Grip on the Levers of Power." *Washington Post.* May 18. http://articles.washingtonpost. com/2013–05–18/politics/39353014_1_president-obama-laurence-tribe-executive-power.

Sandweg, John. 2013. "Facilitating Parental Interests in the Course of Civil Immigration Enforcement Activities." April 23. US Department of Homeland Security, US Immigration and Customs Enforcement. www.ice.gov/doclib/detention-reform /pdf/parental_interest_directive_signed.pdf.

Savelsberg, Joachim. 1992. "Law That Does Not Fit Society: Sentencing Guidelines as a Neoclassical Reaction to the Dilemmas of Substantive Law." *American Journal of Sociology* 97(5):1346–81.

Shaina, Aber and Mary Small. 2013. "Citizen or Subordinate: Permutations of Belonging in the United States and the Dominican Republic." *Journal on Migration and Human Security* 1(3):76–96.

Sharry, Frank. 2013. "How Did We Build an Immigrant Movement? We Learned from Gay Rights Advocates." *Washington Post.* March 22. www.washingtonpost .com/opinions/how-did-we-build-an-immigrant-movement-we-learned-from-gay-rights-advocates/2013/03/22/8a0d2b9a-916e-11e2-bdea-e32ad90da239_story.html.

Shear, Michael D. 2014. "Obama Approves Plan to Let Children in Central America Apply for Refugee Status." *New York Times.* September 30. http://www.nytimes .com/2014/10/01/us/obama-approves-plan-to-let-children-apply-for-refugee-status-in-central-america.html?_r=0.

Singer, Audrey and Nicole P. Svejlenka. 2013. "Immigration Facts: Deferred Action for Childhood Arrivals (DACA)." Washington, DC: Brookings Institution. www .brookings.edu/research/reports/2013/08/14-daca-immigration-singer.

Sklansky, David A. 2012. "Crime, Immigration, and Ad Hoc Instrumentalism." *New Criminal Law Review* 15(2):157–223.

Smith, Lamar and Robert B. Aderholt. 2011. "Letter to Homeland Security Secretary Janet Napolitano." July 5. www.ice.gov/doclib/foia/prosecutorial-discretion /110705smith-aderholt.pdf.

Somers, M. Aryah. 2011. "Voice, Agency, and Vulnerability: The Immigration of Children through Systems of Protection and Enforcement." *International Migration* 49(5):3–14.

———. 2012a. "Preliminary Program Highlights: Fulbright Scholar Research in Guatemala." August. On file with the authors.

———. 2012b. "Zealous Advocacy for the Right to be Heard for Children and Youth in Deportation Proceedings." *CUNY Law Review* 15:189–205.

Somers, M. Aryah, Pedro Herrero, Lucia Rodriguez. 2010. "Constructions of Childhood and Unaccompanied Children in the Immigration System in the United States." *UC Davis Journal of Juvenile Law and Policy* 14:311–80.

Starr, Penny. 2013. "Union Leader: 'ICE Crumbling from Within' Because Obama Won't Let Agents Arrest Illegals." *cnsnews.com*. February 13. http://cnsnews.com/news/article/union-leader-ice-crumbling-within-because-obama-wont-let-agents-arrest-illegals.

Stith, Kate and Steve Y. Koh. 1993. "The Politics of Sentencing Reform: The Legislative History of the Federal Sentencing Guidelines." *Wake Forest Law Review* 28:223–90.

Stumpf, Juliet. 2009. "Fitting Punishment." *Washington and Lee Law Review* 66:1683–1741.

Suárez-Orozco, Carola and Marcelo Suárez-Orozco. 2001. *Children of Immigrants*. Cambridge, MA: Harvard University Press.

Suárez-Orozco, Carola, Marcelo Suárez-Orozco, and Irina Todorova. 2008. *Learning a New Land: Immigrant Students in American Society*. Cambridge, MA: Harvard University Press.

Suárez-Orozco, Carola, Irina L.G. Todorova, and Josephine Louie. 2002. "Making Up for Lost Time: The Experience of Separation and Reunification among Immigrant Families." *Family Process* 41(4):625–43.

Suárez-Orozco, Carola, Hirokazu Yoshikawa, Robert T. Teranishi, and Marcelo M. Suárez-Orozco. 2011. "Growing Up in the Shadows: The Developmental Implications of Undocumented Status." *Harvard Educational Review* 81(3):438–72.

Sullivan, Laura. 2010. "Prison Economics Help Drive Ariz. Immigration Law." *National Public Radio*. October 28. www.npr.org/2010/10/28/130833741/prison-economics-help-drive-ariz-immigration-law.

Tasca, Melinda, Nancy Rodriguez, and Marjorie S. Zatz. 2011. "Family and Residential Instability in the Context of Paternal and Maternal Incarceration." *Criminal Justice and Behavior* 38:231–47.

Tasca, Melinda, Jillian Turanovic, Clair Vaughn-Uding, and Nancy Rodriguez. 2014. "Prisoners' Assessments of Mental Health Difficulties among Their Children." *International Journal of Offender Therapy and Comparative Criminology* 58(2):154–73.

Taylor, Paul, Mark Hugo Lopez, Jeffrey Passel, and Seth Motel. 2011. "Unauthorized Immigrants: Length of Residency, Patterns of Parenthood." Pew Research Hispanic Trends Project. December 1. www.pewhispanic.org/2011/12/01/unauthorized-immigrants-length-of-residency-patterns-of-parenthood/.

Terrio, Susan. 2015. *Whose Child Am I? Unaccompanied Undocumented Children in U.S. Immigration Custody*. Berkeley: University of California Press.

Thompson, Amy. 2008. *A Child Alone and Without Papers: A Report on the Return and Repatriation of Unaccompanied Undocumented Children by the United States*. Austin: Center for Public Policy Priorities.

Thompson, Ginger. 2009. "After Losing Freedom, Some Immigrants Face Loss of Custody of Their Children." *New York Times*. April 22. www.nytimes.com/2009/04/23/us/23children.html?pagewanted = 1&_r = 3&sq&st = nyt&scp = 1.

Thompson, Ginger and Sarah Cohen. 2014. "More Deportations Follow Minor Crimes, Records Show." *New York Times*. April 6. www.nytimes.com/2014/04/07/us/more-deportations-follow-minor-crimes-data-shows.html.

Thronson, David B. 2010. "Thinking Small: The Need for Big Changes in Immigration Law's Treatment of Children." *UC Davis Journal of Juvenile Law and Policy* 14(2):239–62.

———. 2013. "Immigration Enforcement and Family Courts." In *Children in Harm's Way: Criminal Justice, Immigration Enforcement, and Child Welfare*, edited by Susan Phillips, Susan, Wendy Cervantes, Yali Lincroft, Alan Dettlaff, and Lara Bruce, 51–65. January. Washington, DC: Sentencing Project and First Focus.

Toch, Hans. 2012. *Cop Watch: Spectators, Social Media, and Police Reform*. Washington, DC: American Psychological Association.

Transactional Records Access Clearinghouse. 2013a. "Immigration Prosecutions Reached All-time High in FY 2013." November 25. http://trac.syr.edu/whatsnew/email.131125.html.

———. 2013b. "Criminal Activity Cited in Smaller Fraction of Deportation Filings." July 8. http://trac.syr.edu/whatsnew/email.130708.html.

———. 2013c. "Who Are the Targets of ICE Detainers?" February 20. http://trac.syr.edu/immigration/reports/310/.

———. 2013d. "Few ICE Detainers Target Serious Criminals." September 17. http://trac.syr.edu/immigration/reports/330/.

———. 2014a. "Immigration Cases Closed Based on Prosecutorial Discretion." June 30. http://trac.syr.edu/immigration/prosdiscretion/.

———. 2014b. "Once Intended to Reduce Immigration Court Backlog, Prosecutorial Discretion Closures Continue Unabated." January 15. http://trac.syr.edu/immigration/reports/339/.

Turanovic, Jillian J., Nancy Rodriguez, and Travis C. Pratt. 2012. "The Collateral Consequences of Incarceration Revisited: A Qualitative Analysis of the Effects on Caregivers of Children of Incarcerated Parents." *Criminology* 50(4):913–59.

Ulmer, Jeffery T. and John H. Kramer. 1996. "Court Communities under Sentencing Guidelines: Dilemmas of Formal Rationality and Sentencing Disparity." *Criminology* 4(3):306–332.

United Nations High Commissioner for Refugees. 2014. *Children on the Run: Unaccompanied Children Leaving Central America and Mexico and the Need for International Protection*. Washington, DC: UNHCR Regional Office for the United States and the Caribbean.

United Nations Office on Drugs and Crime. 2014. *Global Study on Homicide 2013: Trends, Context, Data*. Vienna: United Nations. www.unodc.org/documents/gsh/pdfs/2014_GLOBAL_HOMICIDE_BOOK_web.pdf.

United States Citizenship and Immigration Services. 2013a. "Deferred Action for Childhood Arrivals." September 11. www.uscis.gov/sites/default/files/USCIS /Resources/Reports%20and%20Studies/Immigration%20Forms%20Data/All%20 Form%20Types/DACA/daca-13-9–11.pdf.

———. 2013b. "Frequently Asked Questions." Updated January 18, 2013. www .uscis.gov/humanitarian/consideration-deferred-action-childhood-arrivals-process /frequently-asked-questions.

———. 2014. "Number of I-821D, Consideration of Deferred Action for Childhood Arrivals by Fiscal Year, Quarter, Intake, Biometrics and Case Status: 2012–2014." June. www.uscis.gov/sites/default/files/USCIS/Resources/Reports%20and%20 Studies/Immigration%20Forms%20Data/All%20Form%20Types/DACA/DACA_ fy2014_qtr3.pdf

United States Committee for Refugees and Immigrants. 2013. *A Profile of the Modern Salvadoran Migrant*. December. Washington, DC: USCRI.

United States Conference of Catholic Bishops. 2014. *Mission to Central America: The Flight of Unaccompanied Children to the United States*. Washington, DC: USCCB.

———. n.d. "Post-Release Services: Family Preservation Services for Immigrant Children Released from Federal Custody. Frequently Asked Questions." www.usccb.org/about /children-and-migration/upload/LIRS-and-USCCB-Post-Release-Services-FAWs- Final.pdf.

United States Customs and Border Patrol. 2014. "Southwest Border Unaccompanied Alien Children." www.cbp.gov/newsroom/stats/southwest-border-unaccompa- nied-children.

United States Department of Homeland Security, Office of Inspector General. 2009. "Removals Involving Illegal Alien Parents of United States Citizen Children." January. www.oig.dhs.gov/assets/Mgmt/OIG_09–15_Jan09.pdf.

———. 2010. "CBP's Handling of Unaccompanied Alien Children." September. www. oig.dhs.gov/assets/Mgmt/OIG_10–117_Sep10.pdf.

United States House of Representatives. 2013. *Transcript of House Appropriations Sub- committee on Homeland Security Hearing on President Obama's Fiscal 2014 Budget Pro- posal for the Homeland Security Department*. April 11. www.micevhill.com/attachments /immigration_documents/hosted_documents/113th_congress/TranscriptOfHouse AppropriationsSubcommitteeHearingOnFY14DHSAppropriations.pdf.

United States Immigration and Customs Enforcement, Department of Homeland Security. 2011. "FY 2011: ICE Announces Year-End Removal Numbers, Highlights Focus on Key Priorities Including Threats to Public Safety and National Security." October 18. www.ice.gov/news/releases/1110/111018washingtondc.htm.

———— 2012a. "Removal Statistics." Updated December 21, 2012. www.ice.gov/removal- statistics/.

———. 2012b. "Deportation of Parents of U.S.-Born Citizens: Fiscal Year 2011 Report to Congress, Second Semi-Annual Report." March 26. www.scribd.com /doc/87388663/ICE-Deport-of-Parents-of-US-Cit-FY-2011–2nd-Half.

———. 2012c. "FY 2012: ICE Announces Year-End Removal Numbers, Highlights Focus on Key Priorities and Issues New National Detainer Guidance to Further Focus Resources." December 24. www.ice.gov/news/releases/1212/121221washingt ondc2.htm.

———. 2012d. "ICE Total Removals Through August 25th, 2012." www.ice.gov /doclib/about/offices/ero/pdf/ero-removals1.pdf.

———. 2013. "FY 2013 ICE Immigration Removals." www.ice.gov/removal-statistics /index.htm.

———.2014a. "Deportation of Aliens Claiming U.S.-Born Children, First Semi-Annual, Calendar Year 2013: Report to Congress." April 28. http://big.assets. huffingtonpost.com/2013report1.pdf.

———. 2014b. "Deportation of Aliens Claiming U.S.-Born Children, Second Half, Calendar Year 2013: Report to Congress." April 28. http://big.assets.huffingtonpost .com/2013report2.pdf.

University of California-Berkeley School of Law and University of California-Davis School of Law. 2010. *In the Child's Best Interest? The Consequences of Losing a Lawful Immigrant Parent to Deportation.* March. Berkeley: International Human Rights Law Clinic and Chief Justice Earl Warren Institute on Race, Ethnicity and Diversity, University of California, Berkeley, School of Law and Immigration law Clinic, University of California, Davis, School of Law.

Van Hook, Jennifer, Nancy S. Landale, and Marianne M. Hillemeier. 2013. *Is the United States Bad for Children's Health? Risk and Resilience among Young Children of Immigrants.* Washington, DC: Migration Policy Institute.

Vanison, Denise A., Roxana Bacon, Debra A. Rogers, and Donald Neufeld. n.d. "Administrative Alternatives to Comprehensive Immigration Reform." http:// abcnews.go.com/images/Politics/memo-on-alternatives-to-comprehensive-immi-gration-reform.pdf.

Varsanyi, Monica W., ed. 2010. *Taking Local Control: Immigration Policy Activism in U.S. Cities and States.* Stanford: Stanford University Press.

Wadhia, Shoba S. 2010. "The Role of Prosecutorial Discretion in Immigration Law." *Connecticut Public Interest Law Journal* 9:243–99.

———. 2013. "My Great FOIA Adventure and Discoveries of Deferred Action Cases at ICE." *Georgetown Immigration Law Journal* 27(2):345–85.

Wadhia, Shoba S. et al. 2014. "Executive Authority to Protect Individuals or Groups from Deportation." Letter from 136 law professors to President Barack Obama. On file with the authors.

Wakefield, Sara and Christopher Wildeman 2013. *Children of the Prison Boom: Mass Incarceration and the Future of American Inequality.* New York: Oxford University Press.

Ward, T. W. 2013. *Gangsters without Borders: An Ethnography of a Salvadoran Street Gang.* New York: Oxford.

Weber, Leanne and Sharon Pickering. 2011. *Globalization and Borders: Death at the Global Frontier.* New York: Palgrave Macmillan.

Weiner, Rachel. 2013. "How Immigration Reform Failed, Over and Over." *Washington Post.* January 30. www.washingtonpost.com/blogs/the-fix/wp/2013/01/30/how-immigration-reform-failed-over-and-over/.

Welch, Michael. 2002. *Detained: Immigration Laws and the Expanding I.N.S. Jail Complex.* Philadelphia: Temple University Press.

———. 2013. "Panic, Risk, Control: Conceptualizing Threats in a Post-9/11 Society." In *Punishing Immigrants: Policy, Politics, and Injustice,* edited by Charis E. Kubrin, Marjorie S. Zatz, and Ramiro Martínez Jr., 17–41. New York: New York University Press.

Wessler, Seth Freed. 2011a. "U.S. Deports 46K Parents with Citizen Kids in Just Six Months." *Colorlines.* November 3. http://colorlines.com/archives/2011/11/shocking_data_on_parents_deported_with_citizen_children.html.

———. 2011b. *Shattered Families: The Perilous Intersection of Immigration Enforcement and the Child Welfare System.* November. Applied Research Center.

———. 2012a. "Nearly 205K Deportations of Parents of U.S. Citizens in Just Over Two Years." *Colorlines.* December 17. http://colorlines.com/archives/2012/12/us_deports_more_than_200k_parents.html.

———. 2012b. "A Deported Father Wins a Long, Painful Fight to Keep His Kids." *Colorlines.* November 28. http://colorlines.com/archives/2012/11/nc_judge_reunites_deported_father_with_three_us_citizen_children.html.

———. 2013a. "Deported Father Who Returned to U.S. Makes Final Plea to Remain." *Colorlines.* March 21. http://colorlines.com/archives/2013/03/felipe_montes_a_deported_father_who_returned_makes_final_plea_to_remain_in_us.html.

———. 2013b. "Felipe Montes Departs the United States for Mexico, with his Children." *Colorlines.* March 22. http://colorlines.com/archives/2013/03/felipe_montes_departs_the_united_states_for_mexico_with_his_children.html.

———. 2013c. "'I'm Here, My Children Are Over There': Immigration and its Impact on Families." *Elle* August 27. www.elle.com/life-love/society-career/immigration-families.

Western, Bruce and Christopher Muller. 2013. "Mass Incarceration, Macrosociology, and the Poor." *ANNALS of the American Academy of Political and Social Science* 647:166–89.

Wildeman, Christopher. 2010. "Paternal Incarceration and Children's Physically Aggressive Behaviors: Evidence from the Fragile Families and Child Wellbeing Study." *Social Forces* 89: 285–310.

Winograd, Ben. 2012. "Supreme Court Case Highlights Cruel Intersection of Immigration and Drug Laws." *Immigration Impact.* October 9. Washington, DC: American Immigration Council. http://immigrationimpact.com/2012/10/09/supreme-court-case-highlights-cruel-intersection-of-immigration-and-drug-laws/.

Willen, Sarah S. 2007. "Toward a Critical Phenomenology of 'Illegality': State Power, Criminality and Abjectivity among Undocumented Migrant Workers in Tel Aviv, Israel." *International Migration* 45(3):8–38.

Wishnie, Michael J. 2012. "Immigration Law and the Proportionality Requirement." *UC Irvine Law Review* 2:415–452.

Women's Refugee Commission. 2009. *Halfway Home: Unaccompanied Children in Immigration Custody.* February. Washington, DC.

———. 2010. *Torn Apart by Immigration Enforcement: Parental Rights and Immigration Detention.* December. Washington, DC.

———. 2012. *Forced from Home: The Lost Boys and Girls of Central America.* October. Washington, DC.

Wong, Tom K., Angela S. García, Marisa Abrajano, David FitzGerald, Karthick Ramakrishnan, and Sally Le. 2013. "Undocumented No More: A Nationwide Analysis of Deferred Action for Childhood Arrivals, or DACA." September. Washington, DC: Center for American Progress. www.americanprogress.org /wp-content/uploads/2013/09/DACAReportCC-2-1.pdf.

Yoshikawa, Hirokazu. 2011. *Immigrants Raising Citizens: Undocumented Parents and Their Young Children.* New York: Russell Sage Foundation.

Yoshikawa, Hirokazu and Jenya Kholoptseva. 2012. *Unauthorized Immigrant Parents and Their Children's Development: A Summary of the Evidence.* Washington, DC: Migration Policy Institute. March.

Young Center. 2013. "Best Interests Policy Advocacy." University of Chicago Law School. http://theyoungcenter.org/learn/best-interests-policy-advocacy/.

Zatz, Marjorie S. 1987. "The Changing Forms of Racial/Ethnic Biases in Sentencing." *Journal of Research in Crime and Delinquency* 24(1):69–92.

———. 1984. "Race, Ethnicity, and Determinate Sentencing: A New Dimension to an Old Controversy." *Criminology* 22:147–171.

Zatz, Marjorie S. and Hilary Smith. 2012. "Immigration, Crime and Victimization: Rhetoric and Reality." *Annual Review of Law and Social Science* 8:141–59.

CASES CITED

Bowe v. INS, 597 F.2d 1158 (9th Cir. Feb., 1979).

Crane v. Napolitano, 3:12-cv-03247-O (N.D. Tex., filed Aug. 23, 2012).

Franco-Gonzalez v. Holder. U.S. District Court for the Central District of California Decided April 23, 2013.

In re Adoption of C.M.B.R. (Supreme Court of Missouri, 332 S.W.3d 793, January 25, 2011). Filed July 21, 2010 in Missouri Court of Appeals, Southern District.

In re Interest of Angelica L. and Daniel L., 277 Neb. 984, 767 N.W.2d 74 (2009).

In re John Doe (Supreme Court of Idaho, 281 P.3d 95, June 20, 2012).

INS v. St. Cyr, 533 U.S. 289 (2001) 229 F. 3d 406.

J.E.F.M. v. Holder. U.S. District Court for the Western District of Washington at Seattle. Filed July 9, 2014.

Leocal v. Ashcroft, 543 U.S. 1 (2004).

Moncrieffe v. Holder, 133 S. Ct. 1678 (2013).

Nicholas v. INS, 590 F.2d 802 (9th Cir. Feb., 1979).

Padilla v. Kentucky 559 U.S. (2010), 130 S. Ct. 1473.

Plyler v. Doe 457 U.S. 2002 (1982).

Reno v. American-Arab Anti-Discrimination Committee, 525 U.S. 471 (1999) 119 F. 3d 1367.

STATUTES CITED

Antiterrorism and Effective Death Penalty Act of 1996 (AEDPA), Pub. L. No. 104–132, 110 Stat. 1214.

Homeland Security Act of 2002, Pub. L. No. 107–296, 116 Stat. 2135.

Illegal Immigration Reform and Immigrant Responsibility Act of 1996 (IIRIRA), Pub. L. No. 104–208, 110 Stat. 3009–546.

Immigration Reform and Control Act of 1986 (IRCA), Pub. L. No. 99–603, 100 Stat. 3359.

William Wilberforce Trafficking Victims Protection Reauthorization Act of 2008, Pub. L. No. 110–457, 122 Stat. 5044.

INDEX

abjectivity, 57

Abrego, Leisy J., 57, 58

abuse, 7, 13, 114, 164. *See also* sexual abuse and violence; child welfare system and allegations against parents of, 87, 93, 96; parental detention and deportation leading to vulnerability to, 82, 86; unaccompanied minors as victims of, 117–20, 123–25, 129–31, 142–44, 150, 155

Aderholt, Robert, 35, 42

"Administrative Alternatives for Comprehensive Immigration Reform" (Bacon, Rogers, and Neufeld), 28

administrative relief, 63–64, 70–72, 75, 163. *See also* executive action

adoption proceedings, 79, 87, 89, 94–99, 108–10, 160, 165

Adoption and Safe Families Act (ASFA; 1997), 94, 95, 97

Affordable Care Act (2010), 73

African immigrants, 67

aggravated felonies, 24, 44–45, 82–83

Air Force facilities, 127, 128, 148

Alabama, 60

Albright, Madeleine, 77

Alien Law (1918), 21

Alien and Sedition Acts (1798), 21

American Bar Association, 103, 139

American Civil Liberties Union (ACLU), 38, 40, 55–56, 98, 100, 103, 104

American Immigration Council, 65

American Immigration Lawyers Association, 66

American Legislative Exchange Council, 168n22

AmeriCorps, 139, 151, 153

amnesty, 5, 6, 34–35, 40, 159

Amnesty International, 122

Annie E. Casey Foundation, 91

Anti-Drug Abuse Act (1988), 82

anti-immigration legislation, 4, 33, 36, 55, 60, 168n22

Antiterrorism and Effective Death Penalty Act (AEDPA; 1996), 3, 19, 23, 82

Appleseed Foundation, 115

Arizona, 59, 85, 91, 108, 128; ACLU in, 38–40, 55–56, 104; adoption in, 87; anti-immigrant legislation in, 36, 54–55, 60, 168n22; border crossings in, 62; juvenile dockets in, 154; U visas in, 141–42

Arizona, University of: Immigration Law Clinic, 40; National Center for Border Security and Immigration, 81

Artesia (New Mexico), 172n45

Ashcroft, John, 36

Asian immigrants, 67

asylum, 8, 78, 135, 140–42, 144–45, 149

Bacon, Roxana, 27, 37, 39, 70

Barclay, Scott, 16

Barrio 18 gang, 118

Batalova, Jeanne, 66, 67

benefits, access to, 55, 73, 75, 95, 143, 160
Bernsen, Sam, 18, 22
best interests of the child, 77–78, 80, 113, 80,
    129, 140, 145, 148, 155; child welfare system
    and, 94, 98–99, 164; focus on, to mitigate
    harm, 151–52; prosecutorial discretion
    and, 8–10, 149; special immigrant juvenile
    status and, 142, 154, 162
Bhabha, Jacqueline, 8, 77, 90, 143, 144, 163,
    171n12
Bill and Melinda Gates Foundation, 69
Bloomberg Philanthropies, 69
Boehner, John, 6
Bolivia, 45
Bowe v. INS (1979), 44
Bracero Period, 22
Brané, Michelle, 38–39, 97, 103, 108, 129
Brennan, William J., 56
Brodkin, Evelyn, 17
Brown, Jerry, 165
Bush, George W., 4, 26, 27, 45, 168n24
Butera, Emily, 40, 50, 77, 84, 93–94, 96, 101–3,
    106–7
Bybee, Jay, 36

Calavita, Kitty, 21
California, 57, 66, 68, 93, 110–11, 128, 164–65.
    See also specific cities; University of, 69, 80,
    106
Canada, 13, 115
Capps, Randy, 4, 42, 54, 56, 80
Catholic Legal Immigration Network Inc.
    (CLINIC), 67–68, 134
Center for Gender and Refugee Studies, 135, 151
Central America, 11, 124, 131, 164. See also
    specific nations; child welfare assistance
    agencies in, 107; DACA applicants from,
    67; gang violence in, 118–19, 162–63; US
    citizen children in, 79
Central America Free Trade Agreement
    (CAFTA), 7
Central Intelligence Agency (CIA), 26
Cervantes, Wendy, 91
Charlotte, 41
Chaudry, Ajay, 4, 54, 56, 80, 85
Chavez, Leo, 49, 57
Chicago, 117, 143
Chicago, University of: Immigrant Child
    Advocacy Project, 98; Law School, Young
    Center for Immigrant Children's Rights,
    138, 151

Chicano movement, 62
child development, 13, 50, 53–55, 86, 135
Child Protective Services (CPS), 87–95, 103,
    104, 109, 134, 141
child soldiers, 145, 163
child welfare systems, 111–12, 125, 143–44,
    151–52, 160–65. See also Child Protective
    Services
China, immigrants from, 21, 53–54, 67,
    116, 131
"Civil Immigration Enforcement: Guidance
    on the Use of Detainers in the Federal,
    State, Local, and Tribal Criminal Justice
    Systems" (Morton), 30
"Civil Immigration Enforcement: Priorities
    for the Apprehension, Detention, and
    Removal of Aliens" (Morton), 28
Civil Rights movement, 61
Clinton, Bill, 24
Coast Guard, US, 26
Cohn, D'Vera, 59
comprehensive immigration reform (CIR),
    4–6, 10, 12, 15, 17, 41–43, 106, 156; alterna-
    tives to, 15, 27–28. (See also Deferred
    Action for Childhood Arrivals (DACA);
    executive action; prosecutorial discre-
    tion); failure to enact legislation for, 23,
    30, 63, 47, 71, 73, 99, 157–59, 166
Congress, US, 83, 111, 151, 158, 160, 163. See also
    House of Representatives; Senate; His-
    panic Caucus, 70; immigration enforce-
    ment appropriations of, 5, 39, 41; and
    prosecutorial discretion and, 12, 15, 22–24,
    28, 35–37; ratification of UN conventions
    and covenants by, 77
Constable, Pamela, 69
Constitution, US, Fourteenth Amendment,
    60
constitutional law, 3, 37
Controlled Substances Act (1970), 45
Cooper, Bo, 24
Cornyn, John, 34, 42
corruption, 7, 119
Coutin, Susan, 57, 114
Coven, Phyllis, 34, 35
Crane, Chris, 15, 34, 35, 37, 106
Criminal Alien Program, 79
criminal justice system, 25, 40; intersection of
    child welfare and immigration systems
    and, 13, 42, 76, 78, 91, 112, 160, 163, 165, 166
criminal law, 17, 18, 43, 83

Cruz, Evelyn, 96–97
Cuba, 113
Customs and Border Control (CBP), 3, 26, 34, 132; annual spending for, 79; Interagency Working Group on Unaccompanied Minors representative of, 11; unaccompanied minors apprehended by, 13–14, 115, 124–27, 148, 149, 167n1

Davenport, Maria Teresa, 45
Defense Department, US, 61
Deferred Action for Childhood Arrivals (DACA), 22, 46, 49–50, 62, 64–71, 159; challenges to, 33–37; Dreamer movement role in development of, 12–13; eligibility for, 31–33, 47, 65–66, 170n20; families impacted by, 47–48, 86–87, 106–7, 112; harm mitigated by structural mechanisms of, 73–75; implementation of, 5–6, 31, 66–69, 157; renewal of, 69–71
Democrats, 5, 27, 71, 165
deportation, 1, 59, 63; crime-related, 43–46, 82–84; government agencies responsible for. See specific agencies; Obama administration policies on, 6–7, 15–16, 42, 47, 63, 71–72, 75–76, 157; of parents. See parental detention and deportation; prosecutorial discretion in, See prosecutorial discretion; of unaccompanied minors, 114, 116, 132, 136, 139, 156
determinate sentencing statutes, 18, 19
Development, Relief, and Education for Alien Minors Act. See DREAM Act
Dodd, Chris, 61
domestic violence, 29, 30, 46, 85, 91–92, 107, 134, 141
Dominicans, 53
DREAM Act, 10, 12, 30, 38, 48, 50, 60–63, 72–74
Dreamers, 4, 30–31, 50–52, 61–64, 72, 157–59; college and university resource centers for, 66; prosecutorial discretion for deferred action on. See Deferred Action for Childhood Arrivals (DACA)
Dreby, Joanna, 87
driving under the influence (DUI) offenses, 43–46, 83–84, 159, 161
drug cartels, 7, 118, 123
drug offenses, 19, 44–46, 64, 96, 155, 161; deportation for, 84–86, 89, 159
due process, 3, 37, 89, 98, 109, 111, 139

early education, 13, 50, 52–54
economic opportunity, lack of, 7, 119
Edelman, Lauren, 16
education, 50, 52–54, 56, 72–75, 134. See also schools; access to, 138, 144, 160; DACA requirements for, 31–32, 65, 69, 73–74; higher, 57, 59, 60, 68–69, 73, 74; opportunities for, 13, 79, 118–20, 164–75. See also Development, Relief, Education for Alien Minors (DREAM) Act; in ORR facilities, 125–26, 149, 161; for repatriated youth, 146
Education Not Deportation (END) campaign, 63
El Salvador, 2, 67, 112, 116–18, 120, 122–23, 142, 163
equal protection requirements, 3, 37
executive action, 15, 47, 75–76, 81, 99, 134, 139, 161, 162, 169n20
Executive Office for Immigration Review, 140, 152
"Exercising Prosecutorial Discretion Consistent with the Civil Enforcement Priorities of the Agency of Apprehension, Detention, and Removal of Aliens" (Morton), 29
"Exercising Prosecutorial Discretion with Respect to Individuals Who Came to the United States as Children" (Napolitano), 31

Facebook, 66
"Facilitating Parental Interests in the Course of Civil Immigration Enforcement Activities" (Sandweg), 46–47, 105
Facing our Future: Children in the Aftermath of Immigration Enforcement (Chaudry et al.), 80
Families on the Front Lines: How Immigration Advocates can Build a Bridge between the Immigration and Child Welfare Systems (Marshall), 91
family dynamics, strained, 13, 51–52
Feasley, Ashley, 138
Federal Bureau of Investigation (FBI), 26, 46
Federal Emergency Management Agency, 26
Federal Law Enforcement Officers Association, 35
Federal Law Enforcement Training Center, 26
Federal Poverty Level, 69
Federal Sentencing Guidelines, 18–19
felonies, 24, 31, 44–45; reckless driving. See driving under the influence

First Focus Campaign for Children, 91, 111

Florence Immigrant and Refugee Rights Project, 23, 85, 91, 108, 121

Flores Settlement Agreement (1997), 125, 127

Florida, 61

foster care, 70, 143, 165; adoption of children in, 87, 94–98, 109, 160; children of detained or deported parents in, 5, 79, 89, 91–93, 97, 111; ORR placement of unaccompanied minors in, 126–28, 154

Franco-Gonzalez v. Holder (2013), 139

Freedom of Information Act (FOIA; 1966) 41, 67, 102, 103

Frydman, Lisa, 145

gangs, 7, 30, 117–22, 124, 125, 144–45, 162–63

Georgia, 44–45, 60

Giovagnoli, Mary, 1, 30, 38, 40

GLBT movement, 61–62

Gleeson, Shannon, 56–57

Gonzales, Roberto G., 49, 56–58, 68

González, Elián, 113, 115

Gould, Jon, 16

Graham, Donald, 69

Guatemala, 2, 67, 98, 112, 116–17, 119, 123, 145–47, 150, 163

Guide for Detained and Removed Parents with Child Custody Concerns (Women's Refugee Commission), 107–8

Gulasekaram, Pratheepan, 15

Gutiérrez, Luis, 60

Haiti, 142

Harlingen (Texas), 152, 154

Harwood, Edwin, 17, 18

Haynes, Kimberly, 126, 128, 133

health care, 4, 55, 68, 72, 146

Health and Human Services, Department of, 11, 14, 117. *See also* Office of Refugee Resettlement

Heidbrink, Lauren, 114, 121, 125, 126, 131, 135–36, 144, 155–56, 163

Help Separated Families Act, 111

Herrera, Pedro, 114

Hidalgo, Rose, 91

Hing, Bill Ong, 44

Homeland Security, Department of, (DHS), 6–7, 20–22, 27, 55, 69, 153, 168n22; annual spending for, 79; and challenges to prosecutorial discretion, 34–37, 39; congressional appropriation to, 40–42; and DUI

deportations, 46, 83, 84; Freedom of Information Act requests to, 67; immigration agencies in, 3, 11, 26. *See also specific agencies*); Interagency Working Group on Unaccompanied Minors representative of, 11, 117, 152; Office of the Inspector General of, 124; parental deportation concerns of, 80, 90, 164

Homeland Security Act (2002), 3, 26, 115, 124

homicide, 7, 43, 118, 120

Honduras, 2, 7, 67, 112, 116, 117, 119, 123, 142, 145, 163

House of Representatives, US, 4–6, 18, 27, 42–43, 47, 50, 71, 157; Appropriations Committee, Subcommittee on Homeland Security, 42

Houston, 152

Howard, William J., 27, 29

humanitarian concerns, 84, 159, 162, 165; in parole decisions, 70, 89, 105; in prosecutorial discretion, 20, 22, 25, 29, 139; for unaccompanied minors, 2, 14, 126, 145, 148, 156, 163

Human Rights Watch, 81–82

human trafficking, 130–31, 140–41, 145, 148, 171n21. *See also* Trafficking Victims Protection Reauthorization Act

Illegal Immigration Reform and Immigrant Responsibility Act (IIRIRA; 1996), 3, 19, 23, 82

Illinois, 68

Immigrant Legal Resources Center, 144

Immigration Advocates Network, 65

Immigration and Customs Enforcement (ICE), 3, 26, 136, 146, 160, 166; parental detention and deportation by, 52, 55, 83–84, 86, 88–93, 95, 97, 99–109, 103, 132, 146; Parental Interests Directive of, 164; prosecutorial discretion and enforcement practices of, 5, 9, 15, 16, 20–21, 23, 27–30, 32–44, 70, 82, 88, 159; Secure Communities program of, 46; and unaccompanied minors, 115, 125, 131, 135, 146–47

Immigration and Naturalization Act (INA), 152

Immigration and Naturalization Service (INS), 30, 36, 49, 124, 132; DHS agencies replacing. *See specific agencies*; prosecutorial discretion in, 18, 21–22, 24–26, 35; spending by, 79

Immigration Policy Center, 1, 38
Immigration Reform and Control Act
    (IRCA; 1986), 3, 21, 23, 43, 79
Immigration Reform Law Institute, 36
impeachment proceedings, 15, 71
In the Child's Best Interest? (University of
    California report), 80
India, immigrants from, 116, 131
Indiana, 60
indigenous peoples, 119, 121, 150
In the Matter of the TPR of John Doe (2012),
    110
INS v. St. Cyr (2001), 26
Interagency Working Group on Unaccompa-
    nied Minors, 11, 115, 124, 127, 163–64; Best
    Interests Subcommittee of, 151–52
Inter-American Development Bank, 69
International Covenant on Civil and Political
    Rights, 77

Jamaica, 44
Johnson, Jeh, 70–71
judicial discretion, 16, 18, 20, 23, 88
Ju Hong, 15, 47
Justice Department, 3, 11, 18, 37, 99, 108, 117,
    148, 152, 154; Office of Legal Counsel, 36
juvenile court system, 88, 94–95, 114, 140, 151;
    special immigrant juvenile status in,
    142–44, 164

Kansas, 36
Kanstroom, Daniel, 20, 22, 37, 45
Kennedy, Edward M. (Ted), 18, 61
K'iché language, 150
Kids in Need of Defense (KIND), 78, 113,
    117–18, 130, 134–135, 138, 146–48, 151
Kobach, Kris, 36, 37
Koh, Steven, 18
Koreans, 67
Koulish, Robert, 102

Lackland Air Force Base (Texas), 127, 128
Las Cruces (New Mexico), 81
Latinos, 4–5, 38, 43, 63, 67, 159, 166. *See also
    specific nationalities and countries of origin*
Legal Orientation Programs (LOP), 108, 140,
    153
legal permanent residents (LPRs), 13, 23–25,
    29, 100, 112; children as, 9, 70, 75, 161,
    169n20; deportation for criminal offenses
    of, 44, 80, 83, 88, 160, 168n25

legal representation, 9, 40; for unaccompa-
    nied minors, 14, 132, 134, 136–40, 147–48,
    151, 153, 155, 161–62
Legal residents: permanent. *See* legal perma-
    nent residents; temporary, 109
Lennon, John, 64
Leocal v. Ashcroft (2004), 45
liminal legality, 2, 51, 58
Lincroft, Yali, 38, 100
Lipsky, Michael, 17, 129
López, Victoria, 38, 40, 55–56, 100, 103, 104
Los Angeles, 41, 81, 108
Lutheran Immigration and Refugee Service
    (LIRS), 117, 126, 128, 133, 145

Majorkas, Alejandro, 33, 34, 64
Mara Salvatrucha (MS-13) gang, 118
Marshall, Lindsay, 23, 26, 85, 90, 91, 121
Martin, David, 6–7, 23, 36
Mayan languages, 150
Maynard-Moody, Steven, 17, 129
Meissner, Doris, 24–27, 29, 36, 49, 73, 79
Menjívar, Cecilia, 2, 51, 57, 58
mental health issues, 55, 56, 84, 89, 133, 139
Mexico, 13, 110, 117, 121, 141; DACA applicants
    from, 66, 67; drug cartels in, 118; parents
    detained or deported to, 52, 81, 87, 89–90,
    107, 111; unaccompanied minors from, 8,
    115, 120, 124, 131, 148–49, 167n1; US-born
    children in, 79, 95; US-citizen children of
    undocumented parents from, 53
Miami, 61
"MiConsulMex" app, 66, 110
Migration and Child Welfare National Net-
    work, 109–10
Migration Policy Institute, 42, 67
military interventions, US government's his-
    tory of, 7, 119
misdemeanors, 31, 45, 46, 70, 83
Missouri, 97–99
mixed status families, 13, 51–56, 69, 75, 78, 158;
    access to benefits in, 55–56; child develop-
    ment and early education in, 53–55;
    Dreamers in, 71–72, 159; strained family
    dynamics in, 51–52
Moncrieffe v. Holder (2013), 44–45
Montes, Felipe, 89, 97
Montes, Marie, 89
Montinelly Montano, Carlos, 45
Morton, John, 12, 28–30, 34–40, 42, 46, 102,
    106, 146

Mosier, Denise, 45, 83–84
Mulcahy, Anne Marie, 97, 101, 136, 140, 150
murder. *See* homicide
Murguía, Janet, 1
Musheno, Michael, 17, 129
Myers, Julie, 27, 29

Nagda, Jennifer, 151
Napolitano, Janet, 27, 31, 34, 36, 37, 42, 64, 68, 106, 168n22
National Council of La Raza, 1, 157
National Economic Research Council, 139
National Fugitive Operations Program, 79
National Immigrant Justice Center, 117–19, 125
National Immigration and Customs Enforcement Council, 15, 34
National Security Agency (NSA), 26
National Security Entry-Exit Registration System, 26
National Undacamented Research Project, 68
neglect, victims of, 13, 87, 92–93, 110, 164; unaccompanied minors as, 114, 121, 142–44
Neufeld, Donald, 28, 70
New American, 45
New Jersey, 68, 87, 138
New Mexico, 81, 172n45
New York City, 53, 136–38; Bar Association, 139
New York State, 68, 138
Nicaragua, 142
Nicholas v. INS (1979), 44
Noferi, Mark, 102
Nogales (Arizona), 128
nongovernmental organizations (NGOs), 9, 96, 108, 133, 146, 163. *See also specific organizations;* Interagency Working Group on Unaccompanied Minors representatives of, 11–12, 117, 152
North Carolina, 89

Obama, Barack, 4–7, 30–32, 61, 70–73, 157–62; election of, 4, 78; enforcement priorities of, 6–7, 15–16, 42, 47, 157; executive actions of, 75–76, 81, 99, 134, 139, 161, 162, 169n20; and failure to pass DREAM Act, 10, 30, 73; impeachment proceedings threatened against, 15, 71; Napolitano appointed by, 27; prosecutorial discretion advocated by, 5–6, 9, 12, 22, 34, 158–59. *See*
also Deferred Action for Childhood Arrivals; reelection of, 6, 32, 63; Republican antagonism toward, 6, 37
Office of Homeland Security, 26
Office of Refugee Resettlement (ORR), 59, 121, 124–35, 146–50, 152–56; aging out of custody of, 134–35; Division of Children's Services, 115, 116; home studies conducted by, 130–31; Legal Access Project, 138; mitigation of harm by, 152–54; placement in facilities of, 125–30, 171n12; post-release service provided by, 132–34; repatriation efforts of, 146–47; structural mechanisms exacerbating harm by, 148–50; unaccompanied minors transferred to custody of, 13–14, 124–25, 161
Ohio, 87
Olivas, Michael, 61, 74
Omaha, 41
Ono, Yoko, 64
"Own the Dream" campaign, 65
Oxnard (California), 128

Page Act (1875), 21
paper raids, 81
parental detention and deportation, 4, 5, 10, 51–56, 76–112; child welfare system and, 90–94; engaging consular officials with, 108–10; fear of, 51–56, 85–87; improving access to, 100–101; interests directive and point of contact for, 104–6; location of centers for, 102; and loss of parental rights. *See* parental rights, termination of; at point of apprehension, 103–4; prosecutorial discretion in, 38, 40, 46–47, 82–83, 88–90, 99, 104–6; risk classification assessment tool for, 101–2; state laws on, 110–11; toolkit and guide for, 106–8; of US-citizen children, 9, 13, 16, 34, 43, 46
parental rights, termination of, 7, 87, 89, 93. *See also* adoption proceedings; interventions for averting, 105, 107–8, 110–11
Passel, Jeffrey, 59
Paying the Price: The Impact of Immigration Raids on America's Children (Capps et al.), 80
Peck, Kristyn, 122–23, 134, 145
Plasencia, Jorge, 157
Plyler v. Doe (1982), 56, 74, 134
"Pocket DACA" app, 66
Podkul, Jennifer, 38–39, 103, 108, 129, 140–41

Posner, Allison, 67–68
poverty, 53, 54, 72, 109, 161; in Central America, 2, 7, 112, 117, 163
Praeli, Lorella, 49, 51–52, 62–63
Principles of Federal Prosecution, 25
prosecutorial discretion, 5, 12, 15–48, 112, 158–59, 165. See also Deferred Action for Childhood Arrivals; and best interests of the child, 8–10; constitutional basis for, 71; in crime-related deportations, 43–46, 82–84; in criminal law and immigration law, 18–21; historical examples of, 21–22; legal understanding in policy and practiced of, 22–30; limits of, 33–40, 88, 162; need for, 16–17; for parents. See parental detention and deportation, prosecutorial discretion in; risk classification assessment and, 101–2; for unaccompanied minors, 9, 139, 146, 149
"Prosecutorial Discretion: Certain Victims, Witnesses, and Plaintiffs" (Morton), 29
Pulitzer Prize, 62

Rabin, Nina, 38, 40, 53, 88–93
Ramakrishnan, Karthick, 15
Rahmeyer, Nancy, 98–99
Reagan, Ronald, 18
refugees, unaccompanied minor, 18, 128, 142, 144–45, 151, 163
Reno, Janet, 24
Reno v. American-Arab Anti-Discrimination Committee (1999), 25
repatriation, 14–17, 122–23, 144–48, 151
Republicans, 4–6, 15, 27, 34, 37, 64, 71, 157
Reuniting Immigrant Families Act (California, 2012), 111, 164
Ridge, Tom, 26
"Right to Dream" campaign, 63
risk classification assessment, 101–2
Rodriguez, Lucia, 114
Rogers, Debra, 28, 70
Romero, Carlos, 98
Romero, Encarnación Bail, 97–99
Romney, Mitt, 6, 64
Rosenberg, Beth, 96
Roybal-Allard, Lucille, 111
Rucker, Phillip, 6
Rusczyk, Stephen, 68

Salvadorans. See El Salvador
San Antonio, 148, 152

San Diego, 81
Sandweg, John, 46–47, 105–7
Schmidt, Susan, 143, 171n12
schools, 16, 62, 80. See also education; in Central America, 7, 118, 120; DACA eligibility and enrollment in, 31, 65, 66, 68, 74, 87, 169n8; impact of parental detention and deportation on children in, 80, 81, 85, 94, 103; unaccompanied minors in, 133–34, 150; undocumented children and teens in, 50, 52–60, 73, 75
Seattle, 41
Secret Service, 26
Secure Communities program, 43, 46, 70, 79, 83
self-deportation, 6
Senate, US, 6, 18, 47, 50, 70, 71, 139, 162; Judiciary Committee, 15, 34
Sentencing Guidelines Act (1984), 19
September 11, 2001, terrorist attacks (9/11), 3, 26, 158
sexual abuse and violence, 46, 116, 130, 133, 141, 163
Shattered Families (Wessler), 92
Singer, Audrey, 66, 67
smartphone apps, 66, 110
Smith, Lamar, 35, 42
Social Security cards, 57, 58, 69
Somalia, 142
Somers, Aryah, 82, 108, 114, 123, 136, 138–39
South America, 67
South Carolina, 60
South Koreans, 67
Special Immigrant Juvenile (SIJ) status, 65, 142–44, 149, 151, 154, 162
Specter, Arlen, 61
State Department, 11, 117, 152
Stith, Kate, 18
street-level bureaucrats, 10, 17, 33, 129, 149
Suárez-Orozco, Carola and Marcelo, 53, 58–59
substance abuse, 84, 86, 96. See also drug offenses
Sudan, 142
Supreme Court, US, 23, 25, 26, 44–45, 56, 134
Svejlenka, Nicole P., 66, 67
Syracuse University, Transactional Records Access Clearinghouse (TRAC), 41, 44, 85, 139, 168n24

temporary protective status (TPS), 142
Tennessee, 63

Terrio, Susan, 123, 124, 126, 132, 134–36, 143, 145, 154, 163
Terriquez, Veronica, 68
Texas, 62, 127, 128. *See also specific cities*; US District Court for the Northern District of, 35
"TheDream.US," 69
Thronson, David, 55, 78
Toch, Hans, 27
trafficking. *See* human trafficking
Trafficking Victims Protection Reauthorization Act (TVPRA; 2008), 124, 128, 130, 131, 133, 135, 144, 146, 151
Trail of Dreams, 61
Transportation Security Administration, 26
Treacherous Journey, A: Child Migrants Navigating the U.S. Immigration System (KIND/Center for Gender and Refugee Studies), 135, 151
Tucson, 41, 81, 88
T visa, 140–41, 143, 149
Twitter, 66

unaccompanied minors, 7–8, 112–59, 161–65, 167n1; apprehension and transfer to ORR custody of, 124–25; dangerous journey of, 121–24; deportation of, 114, 116, 132, 136, 139, 156; eligibility for protective status of, 140–46, 152–54; family reunification for, 131–35; focus on best interests of, 151–52; humanitarian crisis of, 2, 14, 112, 145, 148, 163; immigration court proceedings for, 135–40, 147–48, 154–55; left behind after parental deportation, 82; parents of, 7–8; placement of, 225–31; prosecutorial discretion for, 9, 139, 146, 149; repatriation of, 8, 14–17, 122–23, 144–48; root causes of surge in, 117–21; with special vulnerabilities, 150
United Kingdom, 64
United Nations, 78; Convention on the Rights of Children, 77; High Commissioner for Refugees, 117–20; Human Rights Commission (UNHRC), 117
United States Citizenship and Immigration Services (USCIS), 3, 26–28, 30, 37, 39; DACA administered by, 32, 46, 64–66; Interagency Working Group on Unaccompanied Minors representative of, 11; unaccompanied minors and, 143, 149

United States Committee for Refugees and Immigrants, 122, 144
United States Conference of Catholic Bishops (USCCB), 8, 117, 118, 122–24, 128, 133, 134, 138
United States District Court: for Central District of California, 139; for the Northern District of Texas, 35
United States Sentencing Commission, 18
United We Dream, 49, 62–63, 65, 69
Urban Institute, 80
U visa, 141–44, 149

Vanison, Denise A., 22, 28, 70
Vargas, Jose Antonio, 62
Vera Institute of Justice, 97, 101, 132, 140; Unaccompanied Children Program, 136–38, 150
violence, 117. *See also* abuse; in Central America, 2, 7, 112, 116, 118–21, 133, 161, 163–64; crimes involving, 19, 43, 45, 159; domestic. *See* domestic violence

Wadhia, Shoba, 20
Wallsten, Peter, 6
Washington, DC, 61, 74
Wessler, Seth, 87, 91–93, 109
When a Parent Is Incarcerated: A Primer for Social Workers (Annie E. Casey Foundation), 91
Willen, Sarah, 57
Woltjen, Maria, 131, 138, 151, 153
Women's Refugee Commission, 38–40, 77, 129, 140, 152, 164; Interagency Working Group on Unaccompanied Minors representative of, 117; Migrant Rights and Justice Program, 109; parental detention and deportation concerns of, 84, 93, 96, 97, 101–3, 106–8, 161; unaccompanied minors interviewed by members of, 59, 113, 121; on violence in Honduras, 119–20
Wong, Tom, 64, 66, 67
workplace raids, 81, 160

Yoshikawa, Hirokazu, 53
Young, Wendy, 78, 113, 130, 146–48, 151

Zetas cartel, 118